The British Imperial Century, 1815–1914

A World History Perspective

SECOND EDITION

Timothy H. Parsons
Washington University

ROWMAN & LITTLEFIELD
Lanham • Boulder • New York • London

Executive Editor: Susan McEachern
Editorial Assistant: Katelyn Turner
Senior Marketing Manager: Kim Lyons

Credits and acknowledgments for material borrowed from other sources, and reproduced with permission, appear on the appropriate page within the text.

Published by Rowman & Littlefield
An imprint of The Rowman & Littlefield Publishing Group, Inc.
4501 Forbes Boulevard, Suite 200, Lanham, Maryland 20706
www.rowman.com

6 Tinworth Street, London SE11 5AL, United Kingdom

British Library Cataloguing in Publication Information Available

Library of Congress Cataloging-in-Publication Data

Names: Parsons, Timothy, 1962– author.
Title: The British imperial century, 1815–1914 : a world history perspective / Timothy H. Parsons.
Description: Second edition. | Lanham : Rowman & Littlefield, [2019] | Series: Critical issues in world and international history | Includes bibliographical references and index.
Identifiers: LCCN 2018039886 (print) | LCCN 2018050721 (ebook) | ISBN 9781442250932 (electronic) | ISBN 9781442250918 (cloth : alk. paper) | ISBN 9781442250925 (pbk. : alk. paper)
Subjects: LCSH: Imperialism—History—19th century. | Imperialism—History—20th century. | World politics—19th century. | Great Britain—Colonies—History—19th century. | Great Britain—Foreign relations—19th century. | Great Britain—Colonies—History—20th century.
Classification: LCC DA16 (ebook) | LCC DA16 .P3176 2019 (print) | DDC 909/.0971241081—dc21
LC record available at https://lccn.loc.gov/2018039886

♾️™ The paper used in this publication meets the minimum requirements of American National Standard for Information Sciences—Permanence of Paper for Printed Library Materials, ANSI/NISO Z39.48-1992.

Printed in the United States of America

Contents

Maps

Once again, for the S.B.

Preface to the Second Edition

The first edition of this book was the product of a different era. It was written in the late 1990s when the United States appeared uncontested in its military power and global economic and social influence and when the era of formal empires appeared to be over. In turning down an invitation to become a Dame of the British Empire, novelist Doris Lessing famously remarked: "But where is this British Empire? Surely, there isn't one."[1] At this point, empires appeared to belong to the swiftly receding past. Yet they still attracted scholarly interest as highly influential global institutions.

This was why Donald Critchlow and Stephen Wrinn approached my senior colleague Richard Davis to write about the British Empire in the nineteenth century. Their newly launched Critical Issues in History series for Rowman & Littlefield Publishers aimed to give readers short, easily accessible histories of key events and movements in world history. Richard always cheerfully described himself as "an old-fashioned British political historian," but he was also interested in the wider British Empire and the histories of its various subject peoples. He was also unflaggingly supportive of his younger colleagues, which is how we came to coteach an advanced seminar entitled "Britain in Africa." So when Richard had to decline the invitation, he suggested to Steve and Don that I write the book for them instead.

British Empire history was definitely a reach for me at that point as I was then a very junior visiting assistant professor specializing in the social history of twentieth-century East Africa. Most Africanists look askance on conventional imperial history because it tends to privilege the perspectives of empire builders over those of subject peoples. In writing the first edition of *The British Imperial Century*, I therefore sought to give equal weight to both the British metropole and the colonial periphery by focusing on how all sorts of people, elites and commoners, rulers and the ruled, experienced empire building. Having also been trained in world history, I viewed the British Empire as a network of exchanges that brought these diverse peoples into closer, if not intimate, contact with each other. My aim was to make the case that while Doris Lessing was correct in saying that Britain's empire no longer existed, empires were still relevant and worthy of study from a world history perspective as powerful engines of globalization.

In the years that followed the publication of *The British Imperial Century*, the Western empires of the nineteenth and twentieth centuries unexpectedly became relevant again. Following the terrorist attacks of 11 September 2001 some historians and strategists argued that formal imperial rule over the Middle East and other turbulent parts of the world was the surest way to restore global order. Implicit in the "neoimperial" position was the depiction of the Western empires as forces for stability and humanitarian good. In turn, the use of imperial precedents to justify hard power as a foreign policy, particularly after the American and British invasion of Iraq in 2003, contributed to a larger ongoing reconsideration of the British Empire by a wide range of scholars. This was at a time when Britons from non-Western backgrounds, many of whom had roots in the former colonies, were beginning to have a significant influence on contemporary British politics and culture.

These two trends helped give rise to what became known as the "new imperial history," a historical field that entailed a more global and holistic view of the British Empire that included the perspectives of its subjects. One of the new imperial historians' central arguments was that the history of metropolitan Britain could not be separated from the history of its empire. They viewed the British Empire as a web of multidirectional threads that connected the British metropole with peripheral territories and the various dominions, colonies, and protectorates with each other. Implicit in this approach were the central contentions that former imperial subjects have a rightful place in modern Britain and that the British Empire was not as civilizing, "modern," or coherent as the neoimperialists claimed it to be.

The original edition of *The British Imperial Century* was not consciously informed by the new imperial history as it preceded it, but the book anticipated the new imperial historians' focus on webs of cross-cultural contact by virtue of its grounding in world and Africanist social history. Credit for this new edition goes primarily to my current Rowman & Littlefield editor, Susan McEachern. Having overseen the production of my *The Second British Empire in the Crucible of the Twentieth Century*, which is essentially a sequel to this book, Susan convinced me that it was time to revisit the central arguments of *The British Imperial Century* in light of the popular and scholarly reconsideration of empire over the last two decades. Initially, the books in the Critical Issues in History series were intended to be short and easily accessible. This is why the first edition of this book had no citations and a strict word limit. In revising it for this new edition I have expanded the coverage of the dominions and Ireland, the West Indies, Central Asia, and Latin America. I also now have the space to consider some of the most recent influential work on the imperial dimensions of race, class, and gender.

But my aim has also been to preserve the accessibility of the first edition, which is why its relatively limited citations are mainly intended to alert the reader to key primary sources and influential secondary works. For those desiring a more thorough treatment of the literature on British Empire in the nineteenth century this edition closes with a new historiographical chapter. My hope is that *The British Imperial Century* and *The Second British Empire in the Crucible of the Twentieth Century* can now be read consecutively as an accessible world history narrative of how the British Empire came to be such a powerful engine of globalization.

Note

1. www.lettersofnote.com/2013/11/dame-of-what.html.

CHAPTER ONE

~

Introduction

Suppose you are embarking on a tour of the world. Of the hundreds of languages spoken today, in most countries you stand the best chance of making yourself understood if you speak English. Although the widespread use of English is partly due to contemporary U.S. cultural dominance, it is also a legacy of the global empire that Britain created during what Ronald Hyam termed the "imperial century." From the end of the Napoleonic Wars and the Congress of Vienna in 1815, to the beginning of the First World War in 1914, British empire builders spread their political, economic, and cultural institutions to the furthest reaches of the world. In addition to the global prevalence of English, the British Empire was also partially responsible for the ubiquity of the parliamentary system, the standard of driving on the left side of the road, the use of bagpipes in national armies, the near universal embrace of football (soccer), and even the popularity of tea time.

Historians have tended to attribute these developments to the "modernization" of the non-Western world through the introduction of Western culture and technology. More accurately, British imperial rule created a medium of cultural exchange that mixed and diffused the various cultures of the empire around the globe, including to metropolitan Britain itself. Britain was indeed the dominant political force during the imperial century, but its administrators had to govern non-Western subjects by co-opting and adapting their social institutions. This process produced new imperial cultures and practices that were never entirely British. Thus, although many Africans and South Asians may drink tea around the same time of day that most

Britons do, they often prepare it in the Indian style by boiling the tea along with milk, sugar, and spices. Football is now even more ubiquitous than tea. British teachers, missionaries, merchants, sailors, and soldiers introduced the world to their game as the British Empire expanded.[1] Today most football players still abide by an updated version of the original English rules, but they have developed playing styles that reflect their own cultural and world views.

Similarly, this book is more than just the story of how Britain acquired a worldwide empire. It takes a broader world history view to examine the political, economic, social, and even biological consequences of the interaction of Western and non-Western peoples through the British Empire's formal and informal networks. The English language, tea, and football are largely British ideas, but they now belong to the world as a result of these imperially driven cross-cultural exchanges. The "second" British Empire of the nineteenth century was surprisingly short-lived, but its influence as driving force of globalization has been profound and enduring.

Terminology

An empire was a political unit that controlled, by authoritarian means, an extensive amount of territory and a heterogeneous mix of subject peoples. The word "empire" dates from Roman times when an "imperium" was the territory ruled by an "imperator" (general). Empires were therefore most always built by conquest. The first imperial territories located overseas consisted of colonies, which were usually settled by migrants from the dominant group in the empire. The word "colony" comes from the Latin *colonia*, which referred to a Roman settlement in a conquered territory. The Europeans who conquered and settled North America and Australia in the seventeenth and eighteenth centuries founded colonies after most of the original inhabitants died out as a result of abuse and contagious disease. The people living in the territories of what could be called the "first" British Empire largely considered themselves to be overseas Britons. The population of the sugar-growing colonies in the West Indies, by comparison, consisted largely of a few British planters and a majority of African slaves.

The Western expansion into the tropical regions of Africa and Asia in the nineteenth century, on the other hand, produced few of these sorts of colonies. These areas were unattractive to European settlers, and it was difficult (if not impossible) to stretch Western political institutions to incorporate their largely unwilling African and Asian populations. In the British Empire, such territories became "protectorates" where local rulers were under the protection of the British Crown, which in practice meant that they had to answer to British administrators. And, unlike the settler colonies of the earlier imperial era, "protected persons" were not British citizens.

Interestingly, the word "imperialism" is relatively new. British political commentators coined the term to portray Louis-Napoleon Bonaparte as a tyrant for having the temerity to claim his uncle's throne by crowning himself Emperor Napoleon III.[2] Nineteenth-century Britons rarely called themselves "imperialists" because of the word's association with absolutism. Indeed, critics worried that Prime Minister Benjamin Disraeli's decision to crown Queen Victoria Empress of India after the collapse of the British East India Company in 1858 was a threat to the democratic traditions of metropolitan Britain. These tensions reflected the reality that nineteenth-century Britain was a parliamentary democracy at home that ruled an overseas empire by largely authoritarian methods.

In time, imperialism also came to describe the process by which a state acquired substantial informal influence over another peoples' political, economic, and social affairs. The main difference between formal and informal empire was the degree of sovereignty surrendered by the subject population. Informal empire was a form of "soft power" whereby a state exercised coercive influence through its status, wealth, and cultural preeminence. Britain was so economically and military dominant in the mid-nineteenth century that it could bend less powerful states and peoples to its will without resorting to hard power and the resulting expense of military conquest and formal direct imperial rule. The result was a highly lucrative but largely inexpensive global financial and commercial network that stretched far beyond the formal political boundaries of the British Empire. From this perspective, Britain's acquisition of vast new territories in Africa and Asia in the late nineteenth century that resulted in what was essentially a second British Empire was inspired more by fear and insecurity than a conscious decision to expand its formal empire.

Empire and Globalization

The standard interpretations of Britain's participation in this imperial scramble have focused on the rise of militaristic nationalism, intense economic competition, and the linkage of new areas to the capitalist economies of Europe.[3] The common factor in these older causative explanations is that they framed this "new imperialism" as a largely Western phenomenon. To be sure, Britons, Frenchmen, Germans, Italians, Portuguese, Belgians, and to a lesser extent Americans and Japanese, were instigators of the new imperial enterprise, but defining imperialism simply as the extension of Western influence fails to consider its impact on the peoples that it subjugated.

Focusing solely on the military and political aspects of empire building obscures key realities of the imperial century. The late nineteenth-century empires were more than authoritarian regimes that imposed foreign rule on conquered peoples. They were also networks of cross-cultural exchange that diffused people, wealth, technology, and culture between the imperial heartland, known as the metropole, and the subject African, Asian, West Indian, and Latin American periphery.

In this sense, the British Empire and its contemporaries were engines of globalization, an ongoing historical process that breaks down barriers of distance and communication that had limited peoples, goods, ideas, plants, animals, and disease-causing pathogens to fixed points on the globe. While globalization became a topic of considerable study and discussion after the end of the Cold War in the 1990s, it is worth noting that the Roman Empire was also an instrument of globalization. However, the scope of these exchanges was not constant, and advances in transportation and communication, particularly after the maritime revolution of the late fifteenth century, accelerated and expanded globalization.

Built on the technical advances of the industrial revolution, the nineteenth-century empires bound the world much more closely together. Railways and steamships compressed time and space by moving people and goods further, faster, and in greater numbers. Undersea telegraph cables made communication between distant corners of the world nearly instantaneous. Yet the consequences of these tighter links were never predetermined. In fact, empire building could be seen as an attempt by the newly industrialized powers to direct and control globalization to ensure that they would be the primary beneficiaries of greater global integration. Nevertheless, the imperial interface worked both ways, and non-Western peoples, in turn, had a degree of influence on the domestic institutions and cultures of Britain and the other imperial nations. Imperial rule was a form of cross-cultural contact, and although Western empire builders might have wished to deny it, such exchanges were never one-sided or unidirectional. While Britain was the dominant influence on the empire, the global culture resulting from these exchanges also reflected the values and institutions of subject peoples.

Britain's Imperial Century

During the nineteenth century, Great Britain added approximately ten million square miles of territory and roughly four hundred million people to its overseas empire. Although these figures include the older British possessions in Australia, North America, and the West Indies, most of the new holdings were in the tropical regions of Africa and Asia. In addition to these formal acquisitions, the British also acquired extensive informal influence in the new nation-states of South America and the much older Chinese, Persian, and Ottoman Empires. Britain was not the only European power to expand its imperial influence during this period. By the end of the nineteenth century its rivals included France, Belgium, Russia, Germany, Italy, the United States, and, in the case of Asia, an unexpectedly powerful Japan. Britain, however, was the pioneering imperial power and, as such, acquired more territory and influence than any of its competitors.

This is rather ironic, for the first British Empire seemed to be in decline at the beginning of the nineteenth century. The thirteen American colonies had already been lost to revolution, and Britain's abolition of the slave trade in 1807 decreased the value of its sugar-producing colonies in the West Indies. Ireland, which was in effect Britain's first subject territory, had become part of the United Kingdom by a joint act of the Irish and British parliaments. Consequently, many British politicians and advocates of free trade questioned whether the returns of the remaining formal empire justified the considerable cost of its administration and defense. India appeared to be the only exception to this trend as the British East India Company continued to consolidate its hold over the subcontinent. Nonetheless, a casual observer in the early decades of the imperial century might well have concluded that the British were losing their taste for empire. In 1815, the formal overseas British Empire consisted of the remaining North American colonies (which would eventually become Canada), the West Indian sugar colonies, India, the Cape Colony in southern Africa, the New South Wales territory in Australia, and a handful of naval bases scattered throughout the globe.

Earlier histories of the British Empire portrayed the temperate territories in North America and Australia as empty or underpopulated before the arrival of Europeans. In reality, the creation of settlement colonies invariably required the subjugation of the non-Western populations already living there. Unlike most of the Africans and Asians that Britain encountered during the course of the imperial century, these aboriginal peoples were in a particularly vulnerable position because of their isolation and their limited political development. Australian Aborigines still relied on stone tools and had no governing institutions beyond loosely structured clans. As a result, the Aborigines and the Amerindians of the New World were virtually exterminated by epidemic disease and wars of conquest in the first wave of European overseas migration in the seventeenth and eighteenth centuries. The survivors were reduced to tiny minorities as successive waves of settlers transplanted British culture and institutions to the New World. These settlement colonies followed a separate path of development during the imperial century as successive metropolitan governments gradually extended the privilege of self-rule to their overseas "kith and kin."

As for Britain's remaining holdings in Africa, Asia, and the Caribbean, by midcentury many Britons had become so confident in the prosperity generated by their industrial strength and commitment to free trade that some influential politicians suggested that colonies were an unnecessary expense. Yet even during this period of official indifference to formal empire, Britain continued to acquire useful territories. These included strategic and economic outposts in Singapore (1819), the Falkland Islands (1833), Aden (1839), Hong Kong (1842), and Lagos (1861), and new settler colonies in New Zealand (1830s) and Natal (1843). Nevertheless, at midcentury imperial strategists preferred informal influence to formal rule.

Few in Britain foresaw that their empire would expand so rapidly and suddenly in the latter part of the nineteenth century. Beginning with the occupation of Egypt in 1882, Britain found itself with a new African empire through its cooperation and competition with rival European powers in partitioning the continent. In Asia, new territories included Malaya, Baluchistan, Upper Burma, and a host of islands in the South Pacific. In addition to these formal annexations, Britain also became more deeply enmeshed in the internal affairs of the Ottoman, Persian, and Chinese Empires as these great Asian powers struggled to cope with Europe's new industrial might. Thus, instead of divesting themselves of supposedly unnecessary overseas colonies, the British found themselves in possession of a truly global empire on the eve of the First World War. Although the ruling culture of this second empire was British, it was, in fact, a hybrid institution encompassing a vast array of peoples, languages, and customs.

Empire and World History

Historians have struggled to explain the apparent ease and rapidity with which Britain acquired such an extensive empire. Imperial subjects were largely an afterthought in these narratives, and, for the most part, historians focused on explaining British motives for imperial expansion. As Thomas Metcalf has noted, conventional imperial history was usually just another version of the history of Western civilization with empire "added in." From the perspective of British history, the assumption was that colonies only existed in relation to the metropole and had no contact with each other.[4] Some historians took the scramble for territory in Africa and Asia after the 1880s as a substantial break with Britain's imperial policies earlier in the century. Others, however, countered that British policy remained largely constant throughout the imperial century and that it was increased political and economic competition from European rivals that forced Britain to establish formal control over regions in which it previously had relied on informal influence to protect its interests.[5]

British imperial motives may have varied, but Western observers assumed that military superiority made it easy for Britons to conquer African and Asian territories once they resolved to do so. Similarly, economic influence backed by the threat of military force allowed Britain to intimidate and coerce Asian empires and Latin American republics. Although this interpretation was largely developed within the framework of conventional British history, it has also been used by historians of Africa and Asia to condemn Britain's subjugation of non-Western peoples and cultures.

But the problem with focusing the history of the new imperialism on European motives and causes is that it assigns an unwarranted degree of cultural superiority to Westerners. At best, this interpretation portrays societies on the imperial periphery as helpless victims in their inability to resist British empire building. At worst, it suggests that the cause of this weakness was some sort of political or cultural failing. Moreover, although explanations of European motives are important, they offer little insight as to why the new imperialism in Africa and Asia was even possible.

To be sure, Britain had the industrial and military might to vanquish most non-European foes on the battlefield by the end of the nineteenth century. Yet the conquest and rule of an unwilling populace was prohibitively expensive. With a population of approximately forty-two million people at the beginning of the twentieth century, Britain had little chance of holding together an overseas empire of four hundred million solely by force of arms. Since it lacked the inclination, resources, and manpower to retain its imperial possessions by military means alone, turning battlefield victories into stable colonial states depended on the ability to win the cooperation of at least a segment of the subject population.

British empire builders usually secured this cooperation by exploiting social and economic divisions within subject societies. To those groups and individuals willing to participate in the imperial enterprise, British rule and influence offered useful political alliances, new products, access to wider markets, employment, Western education, and social mobility. But direct imperial rule also entailed the forceful loss of sovereignty, the destruction or transformation of existing economic systems, institutionalized underdevelopment, racial degradation, and the delegitimization of existing codes of morality and social order. Empire building brought change, and change was never value neutral. Some people in subject societies benefited from the advent of British imperial rule, while others most definitely did not.

Reinterpreting British imperial history from a world history perspective calls into question conventional assumptions about the impact of imperial rule on subject peoples, metropolitan Britain, and indeed the wider world. World history is not the total history of everything that has happened in the world; rather, it compares and contrasts how ordinary people from different cultures experienced common events and processes.[6] In the context of the British Empire, world history analyzes how local subject communities and metropolitan Britain were changed by the shared experience of imperial conquest and governance. Implicit in this new form of historical inquiry is the assumption that imperial subjects have the capacity to influence the form, character, and longevity of empires.

Although the British Empire appeared coherent and well-ordered on maps in London, it was made up of many smaller subempires and networks of influence. British-ruled India, an imperial power in its own right, was so prominent in terms of its size and economic importance that its influence on the wider empire rivaled that of Britain. These imperial linkages provided new ways for a wide variety of people from different cultures to interact with each other, and the resulting cross-cultural exchanges were transformative for both Britons and their subjects. The shared imperial experience shaped national and collective identity and inspired new understandings of religion, class, race, and gender throughout the empire and beyond.[7]

At home, the British Empire gave the peoples of the British Isles a reference point in determining who was British and who was not. Most Irishmen, who elites like Sydney and Beatrice Webb compared to "Hottentots" (an unflattering term for southern African foragers and pastoralists), definitely were not.[8] Conversely, the empire helped weld the United Kingdom together by giving the Welsh, Scots, and English a reason to put aside potential national differences and cooperate in the larger imperial project. Moreover, the primitive stereotypes that Britons bestowed on their non-Western subjects provided comforting confirmation that their prosperity and imperial greatness stemmed from Divine Providence and cultural superiority.

In the wider empire, British rule similarly inspired subject peoples to rework their own collective identities. Having once identified themselves primarily as residents of a particular locality, people now noticed mutual ties of language, religion, and culture to fellow imperial subjects whom they previously might have viewed as strangers. This process of identity building was also taking place in the West in the nineteenth century, particularly on a national scale, but in the British Empire the common reference point was most often the experience of conquest and alien rule. Moreover, the imperial regime's fixation on quantifying and classifying subjects by gender, race, and religion, coupled with its absolute need to recruit local allies, were powerful inducements for imperial subjects to frame these new identities in terms of tribe, caste, clan, and other categories of identity that made sense to Westerners. In the British imagination, subject peoples were tribal people, and all tribes had chiefs. Practically speaking, it was much better to be a chief under British rule than a simple tribesman.

On the other hand, the new imperially influenced identities were often oppressive and confining, particularly when used as an excuse to justify imperial conquests. At home, Britain was a liberal democracy, and liberal democracies were not supposed to fight aggressive wars of conquest. Consequently, the powerful influence of evangelical Christians and secular humanitarians on metropolitan society meant that British empire builders had to justify their authoritarian rule of Africans and Asians by casting them as backward, if not biologically inferior, "races" in need of guidance and moral uplift. In the British imagination, imperial subjects were primitive childlike people unable to cope with the rigors of "modernity." Unlike the subjects of imperial Rome, late nineteenth-century conceptions of race meant that there was little opportunity for these conquered peoples to rise above their subjecthood, much less to become the social equals of their rulers. Frustrated by their stigmatization as permanently backward, Africans and Asians sought social mobility and eventually political liberation by challenging the British Empire's formal categories of identity.

New and conflicting interpretations of gender further reinforced and complicated British imperial rule. Nineteenth-century Britons assumed that the social and sexual roles associated with men and women were fundamental and fixed. But, as was the case with race, the various interpretations of masculinity and femininity were constructions shaped by specific political, economic, and social circumstances. By the turn of the nineteenth century, the British middle and upper classes had begun to assume that "proper" women were mothers and moral guardians of the household who remained apart from the workplace, which was a male sphere. This gender segregation did not entirely apply to the lower classes, where both men and women had to pursue wage labor to survive. But by the end of the nineteenth century, most Britons accepted that gender distinctions were as organic and "natural" as racial ones.

These conceptions of masculinity and femininity played a central role in both legitimizing and facilitating empire building. In the British imagination, subject men were either effeminate weaklings who could not defend themselves and their women, or savages who could not control their sexual urges. Subject women were alternately victims of repressive African and Asian societies that needed the protection of British rule or promiscuous primitives who were sexually available to Western men. These stereotypes reinforced racial distinctions between "whiteness" and "nativeness," particularly in settler colonies where there were significant numbers of European women who supposedly had to be segregated from the subject population for their own protection.[9]

British rule was also inherently patriarchal. Missionaries tried to teach their converts to embrace Western conceptions of masculinity and femininity, and imperial administrators privileged the interests and perspectives of subject men when codifying colonial law and governance. Yet, as was the case with race and collective identity, the new gender norms introduced by British rule were also disruptive and potentially liberating. While colonial governments sought to bolster the authority of African "chiefs," who were most always older men, by codifying their control over younger women, British rule gave these same young women a means of escape through conversion to Christianity and the introduction of Western-style divorce.

Thus, imperial rule did not entirely recast subject societies in the British image. Rather it produced new hybrid cultures that were largely British in style but not entirely British in substance. The British Empire did more than simply impose foreign rule on Asians and Africans. In spreading peoples, identities, technologies, products, languages, religions, and gender norms through its various imperial networks, it was a powerful engine of global change. Additionally, British imperial networks also spread plants, animals, and microbes that transformed the ecology and environment of host colonies and often sparked virulent epidemics. Yet imperial rule did not wipe the slate clean. Subject populations never entirely gave up their precolonial values and practices, and their capacity to adapt British imperial culture to suit local circumstances meant that they too exercised a transformative globalizing influence on Britain and its empire.

Notes

1. David Goldblatt, *The Ball Is Round: A Global History of Soccer* (New York: Riverhead Books, 2014), 76.

2. Richard Koebner and Helmut Dan Schmidt, *Imperialism: The Story and Significance of a Political Word, 1840–1960* (Cambridge: Cambridge University Press, 1964), 1–2.

3. Harrison M. Wright, ed., *The "New Imperialism": Analysis of Late Nineteenth-Century Expansion* (Lexington, MA: D.C. Heath & Co, 1976).

4. Thomas Metcalf, *Imperial Connections: India in the Indian Ocean Arena, 1860–1920* (Berkeley: University of California Press, 2008), 6–7.

5. Ronald Robinson and John Gallagher, *Africa and the Victorians* (New York: St. Martin's Press, 1961), 8.

6. Jerry Bentley, *Shapes of World History in Twentieth-Century Scholarship* (Washington, DC: American Historical Association, 1996), 3.

7. Tony Ballantyne and Antoinette Burton, "Introduction: Bodies, Empires, and World Histories," in *Bodies in Contact: Rethinking Colonial Encounters in World History*, ed. Tony Ballantyne and Antoinette Burton (Durham, NC: Duke University Press, 2005), 11–13.

8. David Fitzpatrick, "Ireland and the Empire," in *The Oxford History of the British Empire*, volume 3: *The Nineteenth Century*, ed. Andrew Porter (Oxford: Oxford University Press, 2004), 499.

9. Ann Stoler, "Making Empire Respectable: The Politics of Race and Sexual Morality in Twentieth-Century Colonial Cultures," in *Situated Lives: Gender and Culture in Everyday Life*, ed. Louise Lamphere, Helena Ragone, and Patricia Zavella (New York: Routledge, 1997), 374; Philippa Levine, "Sexuality, Gender, and Empire," in *Gender and Empire*, ed. Philippa Levine (New York: Oxford University Press, 2004), 135–36.

CHAPTER TWO

~

The Imperial Century

British empire builders' motives for seeking greater global control and influence changed considerably during the course of the nineteenth century. In the wake of thirty years of warfare that left its continental rivals in disarray, Britain emerged from the Napoleonic Wars in 1815 as the world's premier industrial and commercial power. This economic success sent Britons to the far corners of the globe in search of markets and raw materials, but at this point there was little need to add to Britain's formal empire. Facing few serious competitors, British merchants and investors could rely on wealth, free trade, and the might of the Royal Navy to protect their interests. Influence, which was the capacity to induce friends and rivals around the globe to bend to Britain's will, was cheaper and usually more effective than direct imperial rule.

Britain's global economic supremacy lasted from the turn of the nineteenth century until the 1870s, when newly industrialized rivals turned their attention overseas. Faced with increased (and largely unexpected) pressure from this competition, successive British governments moved, often reluctantly, to acquire formal control over regions of the world that they deemed economically or strategically important. Most British strategists and investors still preferred the economy of informal influence to the expense of direct administration. But in cases where there was no alternative to formal rule, Britain faced the difficult task of governing millions of non-European subjects with whom they had little in common. British policy in the imperial century thus shifted from the older mercantilistic style of imperialism that survived until

the end of the Napoleonic Wars, to a secure era of informal imperial influence at midcentury, and then to the grudging embrace of formal empire in
the early 1880s.

The Transformation of the Old Empire

At the core of Britain's first empire was the United Kingdom itself, which
comprised the territories of England, Wales, Scotland, and Ireland. This
was an entity built by the English Crown's conquest of the principality of
Wales and the kingdoms of Scotland and Ireland. The Welsh and Scots
were relatively equal partners in the first British Empire, but the ruling elite
in London viewed the Irish as a barbarous primitive people whose land was
suitable for colonization. Ireland was not officially a colony in the technical
sense, but several waves of English and Scottish settlers produced a ruling minority of Protestant landowners, professionals, and clergymen that
dominated the Catholic majority. Ireland was thus a subordinate territory
within Britain that became a site of imperial experimentation where empire
builders first worked out the practices and ideologies they used to govern
the first British Empire.

In 1800, fears that disgruntled Irish subjects might provide Napoleon with
a backdoor to invade England led to the creation of the United Kingdom
through the merger of the parliaments of Great Britain and Ireland. These
Acts of Union gave one hundred Irish representatives roughly one-seventh
of the seats in the Westminster parliament. However, the union did not
make most Irish Catholics equal subjects of the British Crown. Ireland remained a subordinate territory under the governance of a lord lieutenant,
who was the equivalent of an imperial viceroy. With no systematic economic
and administrative integration into the United Kingdom, the Acts of Union
did not alter Ireland's quasi-colonial status substantially. Nevertheless, Irishmen still played a significant role in the wider empire during the imperial
century, particularly as migrants, missionaries, policemen, and soldiers. In
the 1830s, more than 40 percent of noncommissioned officers in the regular
British army were Irish.[1]

Globally, the formal territories of the first British Empire included India,
parts of southern and western Africa, the West Indies, and North America.
In most cases, chartered companies were the primary agents of British empire
building in the early modern era. Operating under a royal charter from the
British Crown, these private enterprises undertook the expense of forcing
open markets in Asia and establishing settlements in the Western hemisphere. In return, they earned a monopoly on trade in a particular region. In

1757, armed forces of the British East India Company paved the way for the British conquest of India by defeating a Mughal army at the Battle of Plassey. In the short term, the Company's victory gave it the right to collect taxes in Bengal in the name of the Mughal emperor, thereby enriching its employees and shareholders. The chartered companies in North America and the West Indies were not as profitable, because the indigenous populations of the New World were not as wealthy as the Mughals. Instead, the chartered-company era in the Western hemisphere laid the foundations for colonies based on plantation slavery in the Caribbean and settlement in North America.

From an economic standpoint, this first British Empire was organized along mercantilistic principles, which assumed that colonies existed primarily for the economic benefit of the imperial metropole. Mercantilists measured a nation's wealth by its holdings of gold and silver. They sought to conserve precious metal reserves through regulated trade in which colonies supplied raw materials in return for finished products manufactured in the home country. In the eighteenth century, Britain enforced this closed system through exclusive tariffs and legal preferences like the Navigation Acts, which required that exports of important American colonial products (cotton, sugar, tobacco, indigo, and other staple raw materials) travel to British ports on British ships. Most of Britain's overseas commerce during this first imperial era was carried out by the chartered companies, which shared their profits with the Crown. These restrictive and unequal systems of exchange engendered considerable hostility among the North American colonists and were a primary cause of the American Revolution.

Opposition to mercantilism also mounted in metropolitan Britain at the beginning of the imperial century where the development of the steam engine brought about revolutionary economic and social change by reducing reliance on manual labor. The mechanization of textile and hardware production allowed British manufacturers to turn out large quantities of goods much more cheaply than their competitors. Generally speaking, the French, Belgians, Germans, and Americans did not begin to industrialize until the 1830s and 1840s. Although this head start expanded and enriched the great industrial cities of Manchester, Sheffield, and Birmingham in central and northern England, it also made the British economy increasingly dependent on international trade. Since British consumers could not absorb their country's expanded industrial output, manufacturers looked to foreign markets. Furthermore, the British textile industry, which accounted for almost half of Britain's total exports in the 1840s, was almost entirely reliant on imports of raw cotton.[2] Britain's economic health in the early to middle nineteenth century thus became increasingly dependent on unfettered international commerce.

Mercantilism's restrictive system of tariffs and monopolies was incompatible with this new emphasis on free markets. Reformers like Richard Cobden, a radical Member of Parliament, worked to repeal the Corn Laws, which protected the interests of privileged landed elites. These large landowners, who enjoyed disproportional political influence in parliament, profited from inflated food prices that resulted from restrictions on imports of inexpensive foreign grain. Cobden and his supporters allied themselves with industrialists and merchants who were equally frustrated with government interference in the free flow of commerce. In the 1840s, this coalition helped reformers in parliament repeal the Navigation Acts and the Corn Laws. These measures played a role in nearly tripling the volume and value of British trade by 1860. On the other hand, the influx of cheap grain severely damaged Britain's farm sector, and by the late nineteenth century Britain was heavily dependent on agricultural imports.

When the volume of imported food and raw materials surpassed exports of manufactured goods, Britain relied on its globally influential service industries to balance its accounts. These "invisible exports" included shipping, insurance, engineering, communications, and, most important, international banking. Britain also depended heavily on returns from investments in the developing economies of Europe and North America. These factors transformed London into the world's premier center of banking and finance over the course of the imperial century and helped forge an alliance between landed gentlemanly elites and the rising professional and business classes. But this wealth was precarious for Britain's economic health came to depend even more on the free flow of commerce and capital.

In addition to their commitment to free trade, the reformers also attacked formal empire as inherently corrupt. In their eyes the elimination of mercantilistic controls on the flow of trade and investment would prevent private interests from profiting at the public expense. It is thus important to keep in mind that a small but influential segment of the metropolitan public never supported Britain's imperial projects. Arguing that the empire enriched a few administrators and soldiers at the expense of "the many," the Scottish utilitarian philosopher James Mill observed that "the colonies are a grand source of wars."[3]

On the other hand, free trade could also have a darker side in a semi-imperial context. When a fungus destroyed almost half of the Irish potato crop in the late 1840s, Prime Minister Lord John Russell resisted Irish calls for food assistance on the grounds that it was not the place of governments to provide such aid. While the Catholic Church, Choctaw Amerindians, and even the Ottoman sultan contributed to the relief fund, the British government's aid was late and inadequate. This inaction allowed the resulting famine to go largely unchecked. Estimates vary, but it appears that approximately one million Irishmen died of starvation and disease by the early 1850s, with one million more emigrating to the United States and British settler colonies.

More positively, free traders attacked institutionalized slavery as corrupting and contrary to laissez-faire market principles. Their campaign to stamp out the practice in the West Indies found useful allies in Christian evangelicals, who insisted slavery was immoral, and a faction of conservatives who considered it dishonorable. Thomas Fowell Buxton's Society for the Extinction of the Slave Trade played the leading role in the metropolitan abolitionist campaign, which was centered largely in the northern industrial cities. Here, almost half a million people signed petitions calling for an end to the slave trade, which helped bring about a ban on the transport of slaves on British ships in 1807. Plantation owners bitterly protested this threat to their property and prosperity and accused the abolitionists of inciting revolts by raising the slaves' expectations for emancipation. Yet they were powerless to block legislation requiring the total abolition of slavery on British territory in 1833 because the political reforms of the early nineteenth century diluted their influence in London.

These changes also undermined the profitability of Britain's sugar-producing colonies. Slave owners in the West Indies and on the Indian Ocean island of Mauritius received over £20 million in compensation from the British government for the loss of their human "property." However, the continued production of sugar, coffee, and other key exports depended on convincing the former slaves to accept wage labor. In the West Indies, some continued to work on large estates in order to survive, but, quite understandably, most of the newly freed population, which numbered approximately seven hundred and fifty thousand people, sought the security of small farms where they could grow their own food. A plan to force them to continue to work on the plantations for a fixed period of time as "apprentices" failed so badly that the West Indian governments abandoned it prematurely.[4]

These political and economic changes transformed Britain's first overseas empire. The loss of the thirteen North American colonies demonstrated the political danger of trying to force British settlers to remain within the mercantile system, and the abolition of slavery and the adoption of free trade raised serious questions about the overall value of empire. In 1801, a bureaucratic reorganization merged the Colonial Department with the War Department, and in the early decades of the nineteenth century the authorities in London exercised little direct control over the remaining colonies. With the exception of India, which still generated considerable revenue from land taxes, the old empire appeared to cost more than it was worth.

This was particularly true in West Africa where the robust disease environment in Sierra Leone, the Gambia, Lagos, and the Gold Coast made extensive European settlement a virtual impossibility. Long known as the "white man's grave," the West African coast was home to a host of endemic diseases, including dysentery, typhoid, yellow fever, and malaria. More than three-quarters of the soldiers of the Royal Africa Corps stationed at British bases in the Gambia and the Gold Coast between 1819 and 1836 died of disease, and only a handful of the survivors were sufficiently fit for further duty.[5] This is why most European visitors avoided extended stays on the West African coast until medical advances in the mid-nineteenth century made the region more habitable for Europeans.

In the remaining colonies in North America, Britain's growing industrial and commercial supremacy so diminished the threat of foreign competition that successive metropolitan governments found it easy to shift the expense of local administration to settler populations. Most colonists willingly embraced the right of representative government because a short-term economic depression brought about by the end of the Navigation Laws led them to conclude that they needed to look out for their own interests. In 1867, the Westminster parliament passed the British North America Act, which federated the colonies of Upper Canada (Ontario), Lower Canada (Quebec), New Brunswick, and Nova Scotia. By encouraging increased immigration from Britain, the architects of modern Canada hoped to assimilate the population of the former French colony of Quebec by giving both French- and English-speakers greater incentive to remain within the British imperial sphere.

There was some talk of designating the new federation the "Kingdom of Canada," but instead the prominent New Brunswick politician S. L. Tilley invoked a line from Psalm 72:8—"He shall have dominion also from sea to sea, and from the river unto the ends of the earth"—to call it a "dominion."[6] This became the term for federations of self-governing settler colonies in the second British Empire, and the British North America Act was the model for creating similarly efficient administrative units in Australia, New Zealand, and South Africa.

Dominionhood made the subordinate status of the settlers, who were both colonial subjects of the Crown and themselves colonizers in their relationship to indigenous peoples, more palatable by giving transplanted Britons a greater measure of autonomy in dealing with the original inhabitants of the lands they now claimed as their own. This privilege of self-government within the wider empire made the dominions appealing places for the roughly twenty-two million people who embarked from ports in the United Kingdom (a figure that included continental Europeans) between 1815 and 1914. While the United States was the most favored destination, approximately 33 percent of these emigrants settled in the wider British Empire.[7]

Consequently, the population of British North America rose from 250,000 people in 1791 to more than 1.5 million just six decades later. The resulting population pressure in the eastern colonies drove Western expansion and the settlement of the Northwest Territories. These were the preserve of the Hudson's Bay Company, a chartered company that held a royal monopoly on the region's lucrative fur trade. As in the American west, this settlement also entailed the conquest and subjugation of the indigenous "First Nations" living in the region. In the Pacific Northwest, Vancouver Island was the first territory to shift from Company to Crown control in the 1840s, and twenty years later the occupation of the Canadian prairie was well under way after survey parties of scientists and geographers deemed it suitable for settlement and intense cultivation.

In the South Pacific, a similar pattern of expansion and settlement took place in Australia. The initial colonization of the territories of New South Wales and Tasmania in the late eighteenth century was driven primarily by an effort to empty Britain's crowded jails by deporting criminals overseas. The metropolitan authorities favored transportation (as the practice came to be known) because it offered a "humane" alternative to capital punishment, which was a common penalty for a host of minor crimes in eighteenth-century Britain. It also provided cheap labor for the handful of free settlers who followed the deportees to Australia. On the whole, approximately one hundred sixty thousand men, women, and children arrived in Australia as convicts by the 1860s.[8]

Transportation fell out of favor in the nineteenth century as humanitarians and abolitionists attacked the practice as a form of slavery. Nevertheless, the settlement of the Australian continent continued steadily as almost one hundred thousand free immigrants took advantage of sponsored colonization programs beginning in the 1830s. They were joined by a following wave of prospectors drawn by the gold rush of 1851. Successive governments in London had little interest in subsidizing settlers, but individual colonial governments in Australia offered cash bounties to attract a "better type" of settler. Hoping to create a class of self-reliant yeoman farmers, they offered bounties of as much as £30 to entice young, "respectable" married couples to emigrate. On the other end of the class spectrum, the imperial propagandist Edward Gibbon Wakefield sought to transplant the rural English gentry to the colonies to create a class of wealthy landholders whose estates would be worked by tenants. Neither plan came to full fruition, but together they accelerated the rate of free settlement substantially by diminishing Australia's reputation as a land of convicts.

As in the Canadian west, the colonial enthusiasts paid little heed to Australia's Aborigines, and by the mid-nineteenth century disease, warfare, and land seizures had virtually wiped out the original population of the southern island of Tasmania. British settlers reassured themselves, and the metropolitan critics of colonization, that North American Amerindian peoples, Australian Aborigines, and the southern African Khoisan were "dying races" whose inability to cope with the "modern" innovations of the imperial century would open the way for more "advanced races" to repopulate the globe.

New Zealand, however, was another matter. It was the only significant new settlement colony that Britain acquired over the course of the imperial century. British explorers, whalers, and merchants had regular contacts with New Zealand dating back to the mid-eighteenth century. However, the presence of the Maori, a numerous and well-organized people who arrived from Polynesia five centuries earlier, complicated colonization and settlement. Subsisting primarily on sweet potatoes, the Maori developed a highly militaristic culture as rival communities, or *imi*, competed to control the more temperate regions of the islands in which the potatoes could be grown. In 1642, Dutch explorer Abel Tasman found the Maori living in fortified strategic villages known as *pas*, but he was unable to land because they were openly hostile to foreigners. Although the Maori acquired a reputation for savagery by attacking subsequent parties of European explorers, they were willing to trade food for iron products and other manufactured goods. Maori men also served as sailors on European whaling and merchant ships and were a common sight in Australian port cities by the beginning of the nineteenth century. Consequently, the few traders and missionaries who settled in New Zealand in the eighteenth century did so under the protection of Maori chiefs rather than the British Crown. By the 1830s, many Maori spoke English and wore Western-style clothing.

The British government did very little to directly encourage the formal settlement and colonization of New Zealand. In fact, it stood by while the initial efforts of private companies to settle the territory failed in the face of Maori hostility and opposition from the metropolitan humanitarian lobby. It was not until 1839 that Edward Gibbon Wakefield's New Zealand Colonization Company finally established a permanent settlement on the North Island. The rate of immigration increased dramatically once this foothold became firmly established, and by 1850 the British population of New Zealand numbered approximately twenty-five thousand people.[9]

The mere presence of large numbers of British settlers was not enough to force the metropolitan British government to overcome its unwillingness to incur the cost of adding territory to the formal empire. New Zealand became a British protectorate because missionaries and the local British Resident (who had no official authority) convinced the Colonial Office to take responsibility for the growing community of merchants, whalers, seal hunters, military deserters, and land speculators that threatened to plunge the islands into anarchy. In 1840, local officials persuaded Maori leaders to become British subjects in return for vague guarantees that they would retain title to their land. The Maori text of the Treaty of Waitangi, as the agreement came to be known, differed from the English language version, which meant that the Maori land claims had no actual legal protection. This allowed land speculators to exploit local institutions of communal land tenure by buying or seizing large sections of the North Island. The Maori revolted in the 1860s in an attempt to stem the rising tide of settlers, and their defeat gave the settler leaders an excuse to seize an additional three million acres of land from the "treasonous" rebels.

Colonial officials in London had no specific interest in dispossessing the Maori. The settlers and land speculators succeeded in transforming New Zealand into a Crown Colony by compelling the metropolitan government to protect the lives and property of British citizens. In doing so, they maneuvered Britain into acquiring a new settlement colony at a time when most imperial strategists had little desire to add remote overseas regions to the formal empire.

Faced with the expense of administering and defending the growing settlement colonies in North America, Australia, and New Zealand, successive British governments began to explore ways to shift more of the costs of empire onto the settlers. Under self-government, which became known as "responsible government," administrators of colonies with sufficient economic maturity and financial stability now answered to a locally elected assembly, not London. This was particularly important in North America where there were widespread fears that the slow pace of political progress might inspire the colonists to seek annexation by the United States. The British North America Act, which federated the Canadian colonies, facilitated westward expansion and provided an added measure of security from a hostile America angered by British support for the South during the U.S. Civil War. With the success of the Canadian experiment, the metropolitan authorities extended the same privilege of self-government to New Zealand and the Australian colonies (although the appointed governor of New Zealand retained responsibility for the Maori).

The Australian territories did not join together until 1901, when the threat of German and French expansion in the South Pacific and a commitment to limiting further immigration to Europeans convinced the individual colonies to surrender their autonomy. New Zealand declined the opportunity to join the new federation on the grounds that their origins were substantially different from the Australian penal colonies. As with all of the dominions, the authorities in London retained control of the federation's international relations and had the prerogative of vetoing discriminatory tariffs on British imports. But both Australia and New Zealand developed their own expansionist "subimperial" policies, which were instrumental in adding numerous islands in the South Pacific to the British Empire during the last decades of the nineteenth century.

Self-government was more complicated in territories with large non-European majorities, and imperial planners were less willing to extend the privilege to its small African territories and the West Indian sugar colonies. In 1853, humanitarian concerns about the Cape Colony's treatment of its African population meant that the territory received a "representative" rather than "responsible" government. Under this system, a British governor retained greater authority over the locally elected assembly. Natal, which became a Crown Colony in 1856, achieved similar status three decades later. Conversely, the Caribbean planters gave up the right to govern themselves because they were afraid of being swamped by a non-European electorate composed largely of freed slaves. Alarmed by the violence of the 1865 Morant Bay rebellion, the Jamaican Assembly set a precedent for the rest of the West Indies one year later by voting to end nearly two centuries of self-rule to become a Crown Colony with an appointed governor and legislative council.

The Era of Informal Empire

Britain's imperial policy in the mid-nineteenth century was shaped largely by confidence in its industrial and commercial might. The final defeat of Napoleon virtually eliminated the French naval threat to overseas trade, and timely domestic political reforms helped Britain avoid the wave of revolutions that swept across Europe in the 1830s and 1840s. This security led free trade advocates to assume that the mutual benefits of unfettered commerce would usher in an era of world peace under the benevolent umbrella of Britain's global economic dominance. Unthreatened by serious foreign rivals, British governments made up for the budget deficits resulting from the end of protectionist legislation and high tariffs by cutting defense spending. Even though Britain was the world's only global military power during the imperial century, its prosperity was largely dependent on world peace.

When confronted with uncooperative foreign rulers and trading partners, British diplomats and strategists had to weigh the cost of military action against the forced economy brought on by their commitment to low tariffs and free trade. These stringent economic realities sparked an intense debate in British imperial and political circles over the worth of formal empire in relation to the cost of its defense. Although few questioned the value of British India, Richard Cobden, John Bright, and other free trade proponents in what became known as the Manchester school argued that Britain's remaining dependent colonies were an unnecessary expense. In their eyes, influence was cheaper than direct rule, and military force should only be used to compel non-European states and societies to open their markets to British trade.

A few of the most extreme opponents of formal empire argued that Britain should abandon its most expensive and unproductive overseas holdings entirely. In 1865, Sir Charles Adderley stood in Parliament to attack Britain's small West African coastal possessions for their inability to contribute to the cost of imperial defense. He charged that the value of British trade in these territories did not offset the cost of their administration and complained that tensions with African rulers drew Britain into unnecessary and expensive conflicts. In response to Adderley's criticisms, Parliament convened a special committee, which recommended withdrawal from all West African territories except the colony of liberated slaves in Sierra Leone.[10]

At first glance, this indifference (if not outright hostility) of many influential politicians, intellectuals, and humanitarians to formal empire suggested that Britain had no further imperial ambitions. But the committee's proposals never came to pass. Informal empire was never an official government policy, and in spite of this widespread resistance to acquiring new dependencies, the British Empire grew at a rate of nearly one hundred square miles per year during the middle decades of the nineteenth century. With the exception of the relatively insignificant Greek Ionian Islands, Britain did not surrender a single acre of overseas territory during this period. Although imperial strategists resisted taking on the financial burden of new settlement colonies, they were not opposed to acquiring small strategically or economically important islands and bases like the Falklands off the coast of Argentina, Aden on the tip of Arabia, and the port of Hong Kong in China. Similarly, the economic and strategic value of the southern tip of the Malay Peninsula led British strategists to develop Singapore as a base after the Napoleonic Wars. In 1824, they formalized British control of the Straits of Malacca by incorporating Singapore into the Straits Settlements under the jurisdiction of the British East

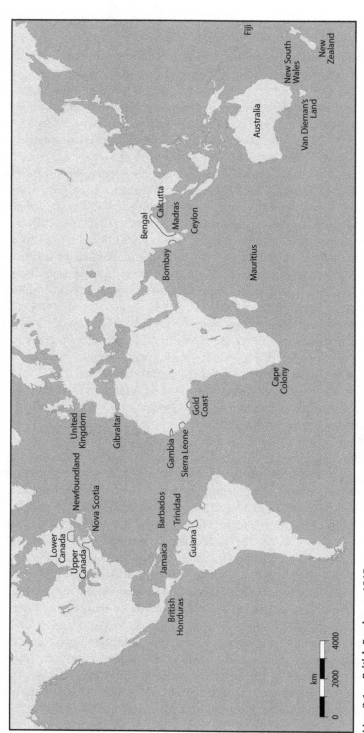

Map 2.1. British Empire, c. 1815

India Company. This network of bases and forts would later provide points of entry into Africa, South America, Asia, and the Middle East.

Moreover, informal empire still required the threat of "hard power" to be effective, and British commercial and political leaders were usually willing to use military means to expand their economic influence overseas. Britain's Opium Wars with China in 1839 and 1856 aimed primarily to force the Chinese to end their restrictions on British commerce. Lord Palmerston, the British prime minister, justified these wars as the defense of free trade and downplayed the fact that the most lucrative British export to China was Indian opium. In 1845, the Royal Navy similarly defeated Argentinean attempts to monopolize trade on the River Plate by blockading the river with gunboats.

Britain was also willing to use violence simply to make an example of those who dared challenge its power. In 1868, the British government sent an expedition of over thirteen thousand British and Indian soldiers into Ethiopia to punish Emperor Tewodros for taking two of its minor diplomats hostage. While British sources depicted the Ethiopian emperor as insane, the hostage taking was actually a futile effort by Tewodros to force Queen Victoria to acknowledge him as an equal sovereign. Costing over £8 million, the operation had few lasting material consequences, apart from forcing Tewodros to commit suicide, because the British imperial forces simply withdrew from the Horn of Africa after inflicting a decisive defeat upon the Ethiopians.

For the most part, however, imperial strategists preferred to avoid expensive military campaigns and assert British influence through existing political institutions. In South America, Prime Minister Robert Peel's government abandoned plans to annex the estuary of the River Plate as unrealistically expensive and concentrated instead on using influence to induce the Latin Americans to restructure their economies to favor British trade and investment. British commercial concerns dominated South American markets, and British investors were the main creditors of the debt-ridden Argentine and Brazilian governments. In the latter half of the imperial century, they accounted for roughly two-thirds of all foreign investment in Latin America.[11] These factors gave Britain such a considerable degree of influence in the region that formal imperial control was an unnecessary expense.

Similarly, Britain's goal in its relations with the Ottoman, Persian, and Chinese Empires was to achieve a maximum degree of influence without incurring the cost and responsibility of direct administration. The Ottoman Empire was an important buffer state that hindered Russia, Britain's main Central Asian rival, from threatening the routes to India. China, on the other hand, had little strategic value, but influential British industrialists and free traders fantasized about the millions of potential customers waiting to buy their products if only the Chinese government could be persuaded to open its markets.

The British aim was to erode the sovereignty of these venerable empires just enough to force their political and economic institutions to become more open. Too much interference threatened to produce political disintegration, economic instability, and a potentially dangerous power vacuum that might open the way for rival powers or force Britain to resort to costly formal annexation. British diplomats therefore hoped to strengthen these "rotten empires" by convincing them to adopt constitutions, free trade, industrial technology, and Western-style education. Few realized that in many ways their cure was worse than the disease. The loss of sovereignty inherent in informal influence, plus the imposition of disruptive foreign cultures and institutions, exacerbated simmering social and political tensions within many non-Western societies.

While informal empire did not entail much political expansion, it definitely facilitated the global spread of British culture. This was particularly the case with Protestant evangelicals, whose propagation of Christianity and Western values further expanded Britain's informal influence. Under the first British Empire groups like the Society for the Promotion of Christian Knowledge and the Society for the Propagation of the Gospel focused primarily on tending to the spiritual needs of settlers and overseas military garrisons. The emergence of explicitly evangelical movements in the late eighteenth century, which were more focused on religious conversion, was part of a religious revival inspired by capitalist change at home and the French Revolution abroad. This revitalized popular Protestantism cut across class lines and affirmed salvation was open to both elites and ordinary people. Believing that capitalism, industrialization, and urbanization had produced a moral crisis in the country, they worked to transform Britain into a sufficiently Christian nation. Their highest priority was spreading the knowledge of God and saving the emerging working classes from the evils of atheism, drink, and sexual license. In the eyes of the religious reformers the metropolitan urban poor were as savage and in need of salvation as primitive tribesmen. Making no allowances for the cultural origins of the sinner, they blurred the distinction between empire and metropole.

Some evangelicals were also not opposed to empire building and viewed Britain's power and overseas influence, particularly after the victory over Napoleon, as evidence of its divine mission in the world. As already noted, one of their main priorities was working with free trade reformers to abolish slavery. As Britain acquired greater global influence at midcentury, they came to feel a profound sense of obligation to share Christianity and British civilization. The evangelicals who became missionaries tended to equate difference with backwardness and viewed cultures different from their own as representative of an earlier, almost childlike stage of development. Although these judgments now seem unacceptably biased, most evangelicals believed they had a moral duty to protect and nurture "backward" societies. Consequently, the mission societies opposed the immoral trade in guns, alcohol, and opium that earned substantial profits for British merchant houses.

To this end, the evangelicals also supported the efforts of Thomas Buxton, who emphasized the humane economic development of Africa as part of his campaign to abolish slavery. In the 1830s, Buxton was active in the Aborigines Protection Society and chaired a parliamentary committee that concluded that free labor brought the same benefits as free trade. But there was a fair degree of hypocrisy in this position. Overlooking Britain's central role in more than three centuries of trans-Atlantic slave trading, Buxton placed most of the blame for slavery on the Africans who supplied captives to foreign merchants. In his view, the emancipation of slaves in British territories had to be accompanied by the total elimination of the institution of slavery in Africa. It was therefore necessary to provide West Africans with sufficiently lucrative alternatives to trafficking in human captives. Buxton and his allies therefore popularized the concept of "legitimate commerce," whereby Africans would turn their energies to the production of the tropical commodities required by industrial Britain. Formal British rule would not be needed to coerce Africans into taking part in this enterprise because both sides would reap the mutual benefits of increased trade.

Many coastal African rulers, however, had a better understanding of the economic realities of slavery and slave trading. In 1848, King Ghezo of Dahomey firmly, but politely, rejected a £2,000 annual subsidy from the British government as an inducement to sign an abolitionist treaty because his kingdom earned a staggering £300,000 per year from the capture and sale of slaves. While Ghezo agreed with the British emissary Brodie Cruickshank that palm oil, coffee, and cotton had value, the king asked how he would run his state and pay his armies while he waited for the crops to mature.[12] Moreover, the evangelicals and abolitionists also tended to excuse the reality that the tropical raw materials that fetched high prices in the West were still produced by enslaved laborers. By this view African systems of slavery somehow became more benign than plantation slavery in the West Indies.

Legitimate commerce thus became part of the missions' central message of salvation. Organizations like the London Missionary Society, the Church Missionary Society, the British Bible Society, and the Church of Scotland Mission linked Christianity, industry, and trade in their preaching. Their primary aim was to establish self-supporting and self-governing "native churches" that would help achieve the larger goal of converting the entire world to their interpretation of Christianity within a single generation. Many politicians supported these goals, but this did not mean that British diplomats and colonial administrators granted the missions special treatment. The mid-nineteenth century was also an era of "religious free trade" where the followers of all faiths, whether Muslim, Christian, or Hindu, competed for believers and converts. In fact, British missionary societies were as likely to operate under foreign powers, both European and non-Western, as they were in the formal British Empire. Moreover, they also freely employed Scandinavian, German, Swiss, and American clergymen when sufficient numbers of British evangelists did not answer their call.

The missionaries often differed with the proponents of informal influence and free trade when they encountered cultural practices or political institutions that they deemed barbarous or antithetical to Christian teaching. In these cases, the churchmen were quite willing to argue for British intervention and even formal annexation on humanitarian grounds. The missionary societies sometimes also painted overly lurid pictures of non-Western "barbarisms" to raise funds and attract followers. This ability to mobilize widespread support among the newly literate middle classes for overseas humanitarian causes helped defeat Adderley's calls for withdrawal from West Africa and provided the cover of legitimacy for territorial annexations during the new imperial era later in the nineteenth century.

Britain and the "New" Imperialism

Britain's rapid acquisition of extensive territories in Africa and Asia in the late nineteenth century appeared to be a sudden and radical departure from its preference for informal influence. For the most part, this renewed embrace of formal empire was a response, and a somewhat panicked response at that, to increased economic and military competition from European rivals. Britain's prosperity and economic strength was built on its industrial head start and isolation from the turbulent affairs of the continent. Yet these advantages came at a price. Without serious competition, British industrialists had little incentive to modernize their factories. They did not take advantage of innovations in production, and many remained heavily dependent on simple manufactures like textiles, iron, and hardware goods. Britain's profitable exports of technology and capital helped its European and American rivals launch a second industrial revolution in the manufacture of chemicals, electrical goods, and steel. In 1870, Britain accounted for roughly one-third of the world's industrial output, but by 1914 this figure had fallen to only one-seventh.[13]

Furthermore, as was the case with most industrial powers, the British economy's reliance on manufacturing made it vulnerable to cycles of high economic prosperity and depression. Generally speaking, Britain experienced an economic downturn every seven to ten years during the nineteenth century. Although most of these crises were followed by periods of profitable recovery, the Great Depression of 1873 was so severe that many feared it would never end. The factors that produced the depression were complex, but its primary cause was the increased industrial capacity of continental Europe and the United States. In other words, there simply were not enough consumers to purchase the resulting manufactured goods. This surplus production drove down prices, diminished opportunities for profitable investment, and created widespread unemployment.

Many in Britain blamed the depression on the high protective tariffs that rival powers threw up to defend their developing industrial bases from British competition. In 1885, the Royal Commission on the Depression of Trade Industry concluded that foreigners had abused the principles of open commerce by using state support to secure an unfair advantage over British manufacturers and traders, who were still playing by the rules. Although the British economy largely recovered by the beginning of the twentieth century, the depression of 1873 led some imperial strategists to question whether informal influence could still protect Britain's overseas interests.

These economic anxieties were compounded by a growing sense of military insecurity. After the Crimean War, Russia's army of over half a million men appeared to threaten British India at a time when the Indian Mutiny of 1857 raised serious doubts about the reliability of the Indian army. In 1906, the commander in chief of British forces in India estimated that he would need one hundred sixty thousand troops to counter a Russian invasion, with an additional three to four hundred thousand reinforcements in the following year.[14] When France and Germany reemerged as major continental powers in the 1870s, British generals began to fear that they were stretched too thinly around the globe. To further complicate matters, Britain was already devoting over a third of its budget to the military and had the highest defense spending per capita of any European nation in the late nineteenth century.[15]

Britain therefore reorganized its armed forces in an effort to simultaneously reduce defense spending and counter new imperial rivals. In 1870, Edward T. Cardwell, secretary of state for war, concentrated the regular British army in India and Britain by withdrawing troops from the dominions and self-governing colonies. Cardwell also ordered an overall force reduction of twenty-five thousand men, so that in 1881 the British army numbered only seventy thousand regular soldiers. By necessity, Britain relied on the Royal Navy and locally recruited colonial forces (many of whom were non-European) to defend its overseas empire.

These mounting economic and military concerns produced a profound crisis of confidence in British economic and political circles. Imperial enthusiasts understood that their empire depended on world peace and the unrestricted flow of commerce and investment. As tensions with continental rivals mounted, they began to worry that they were entering into an era of imperial decline. Fearful that they might suffer the same fate as the Romans, British imperialists adopted a siege mentality focused on defending their global interests.

This change of thinking was particularly apparent in British politics. Apart from a commitment to protecting global free trade, British Liberals and Conservatives were not particularly focused on imperial issues before the Great Depression of the 1870s. Both parties lamented the unfortunate circumstances that compelled Britain to annex new overseas territories and disagreed only over the timing and methods of these acquisitions. Empire became a topic for popular discussion when the Reform Bills of 1867 and 1884 broadened the British electorate and tempted politicians to use the empire to shape public opinion and win votes. The Liberal leader William Gladstone framed imperial issues in high moral terms, while his Conservative counterpart, Benjamin Disraeli, used the empire to attract working-class voters by promoting national pride. Disraeli's successor, the Earl of Salisbury, was a strong advocate of defensive imperialism who worked actively to expand the empire. Joseph Chamberlain, Salisbury's colonial secretary from 1895 to 1902, believed that popular imperialism was the best cure for Britain's growing social and class tensions. In a sharp break with the official commitment to free trade, he argued for an imperial customs union that would promote greater prosperity by using tariffs and preferences to deny Britain's rivals access to its colonial markets.

Although Chamberlain's proposal never came to pass, particularly because the self-governing colonies and dominions refused to accept a subordinate economic role, the Great Depression transformed many of Britain's manufacturing and commercial leaders into unabashed protectionists who hoped to solve the problem of overproduction by expanding and defending their markets. Angered that their competitors were flaunting the natural laws of free trade, they pressed their leaders to intervene forcefully to defend existing markets and open new ones. These industrialists naturally focused on Britain's captive economy in India, but they also called for the acquisition of the hinterlands of Africa to prevent potential rivals from capturing heretofore unmapped areas of economic opportunity. While British manufacturers did not have a great deal of influence in the gentlemanly circles of power in London, these calls for the defensive annexation of potentially valuable overseas territories struck a popular chord.

Over the course of the nineteenth century, Britain's governing class of landed elites became increasingly allied with London financiers and investors. As the decline of British agriculture and the demise of the West Indian sugar plantation complex forced many aristocrats to seek new sources of wealth, London's financiers and merchant bankers became the logical partners for the gentry because they too were products of the public school system and had sufficient leisure and wealth to support an aristocratic lifestyle. These "gentlemanly capitalists" directed a London-based international trading and financial system that raised profitable loans for foreign governments, invested heavily in the infrastructure of developing economies, and provided credit to British merchants.[16] The returns on these foreign investments were not much higher than domestic ones, but the gentlemanly capitalists came to embrace formal empire in the final decades of the nineteenth century because Britain's internal economy could no longer provide enough profitable outlets for its excess capital. As a result, from 1865 to 1914, Britain's foreign investments amounted to about two-thirds of its approximately £5 billion in total savings.[17]

British gentlemanly capitalists thus depended on an integrated global economy that allowed for the free flow of international commerce and investment. Unlike British industrialists, they did not see the need to extend Britain's formal empire to protect its markets. Territorial control was usually unimportant as long as their investments were safe. Nevertheless, they did not oppose the growth of the British Empire in the late nineteenth century, particularly if it forced non-Western societies into their sphere of influence. British investors profited from expansion, and even though less than 10 percent of Britain's total savings went to its protectorates and non-self-governing colonies, the acquisition of new territory in Africa and Asia broadened the scope of the global British economic system.

The main difference between this new imperialism of formal empire and the midcentury empire of informal influence was that it took force to adapt African and Asian economies to the requirements of British commerce and investment. There were few significant opportunities for profitable capitalist investment in these underdeveloped economies. Indeed, a 1912 imperial geographer had to make the following grudging admission about the economic value of the new imperial territories: "Imperial theory suggests that Great

Britain is the densely-peopled Workshop, which the Colonies should supply with raw material and food, but at present, the majority of our supplies comes from foreign lands, and Colonies [and dominions] are developing manufactures."[18] Nonetheless, even though the new subject populations proved to be disappointing customers, substantial profits could be made from the guaranteed loans and subsidies that the British government used to convince well-connected investors to risk their money in the new, less lucrative corners of the empire.

In addition to these economic factors, Britain's embrace of formal empire in the late nineteenth century was driven by shifting social attitudes that made it more politically acceptable to conquer and rule non-European populations. In imperial circles, Social Darwinism and pseudoscientific racism tempered the evangelical zeal of the missionary movement. Although Charles Darwin did not explicitly apply his theory of natural selection and evolution to human societies in his 1859 *The Origin of Species*, in 1902 he declared: "When civilised nations come into contact with barbarians the struggle is short, except where a deadly climate gives its aid to the native race. . . . The grade of [native peoples'] civilisation seems to be a most important element in the success of competing nations."[19] Social Darwinists concluded that "less fit" non-European peoples were incapable of coping with the advances of the Western world and were unable to recognize the merits of Britain's superior culture because they were at a lower stage of evolutionary development. By this line of reasoning, "blackness" equaled backwardness. The Social Darwinists developed new academic disciplines that used the pseudoscientific study of craniology (heads) and comparative anatomy to "prove" the inferiority of Africans and Asians.

On the basis of these specious arguments, the proponents of formal empire declared that they had a paternalistic duty to rule non-European peoples who were incapable of governing themselves. Although some missionaries remained committed to culturally transforming Africans and Asians along European lines, the public mood in Britain shifted after the 1857 Indian Mutiny. The 1865 revolt of ex-slaves in Jamaica further confirmed the assumption that non-Europeans were incapable of civilization, particularly as Governor Edward Eyre explicitly compared the Jamaican rebels to Indian mutineers.[20] While some metropolitan humanitarians condemned the four hundred deaths resulting from Eyre's imposition of martial law, noted British artists and intellectuals like Thomas Carlyle, Charles Kingsley, and Charles Dickens contributed money to the Jamaican colonial governor's defense fund.

The proponents of formal empire linked cultural superiority to the technical advances of the late nineteenth-century industrial revolution that now made it relatively easy for them to extend their influence to the tropical regions of the world. The discovery that microbes caused disease and that quinine, which came from the bark of the South American cinchona tree, offered some protection from malaria made the tropics far less threatening (and deadly) to Westerners. Whereas death rates among Europeans in their first year of residency in West Africa were 250 to 750 per thousand before 1840, by the end of the century, they were just 50 to 100 per thousand.[21] The steamship and the railway opened African and Asian hinterlands to conquest and commerce, and a global network of undersea telegraph cables allowed London to exercise greater administrative control over the far corners of the empire. Before 1850, officials in India needed two to three months to send and receive messages via ship and train from Britain; by the 1870s it took only a day to exchange telegrams on the submarine cable system.[22]

As impressive as these advances in medicine and communication were, no innovation did more to shift the balance of power between Europe and the non-Western world than the development of industrial military technology. Armored British gunboats blockaded Chinese ports during the Opium Wars and forced African merchants and rulers to tolerate open trade on the Niger River. The repeating rifle, the rapid-fire maxim gun, and the explosive field artillery shell all made it relatively inexpensive for a handful of soldiers to defeat a non-European enemy that greatly outnumbered them. Although this arms gap was less pronounced in Asia, it was devastating in Africa. In 1898, British forces at the Battle of Omdurman killed approximately eleven thousand Sudanese in five hours at a cost of a small handful of British and Egyptian soldiers.[23]

The ease with which British forces, many of which were actually the private armies of chartered companies, won these appallingly lopsided battles seemed to validate Social Darwinist thinking. Yet it was all too easy to mistake military dominance for cultural superiority. British imperial enthusiasts failed to realize that although it may have been easy to defeat a poorly equipped non-European foe, it was quite another thing to rule them without resorting to a protracted and expensive period of military occupation.

If British empire builders were blind to this fact, it was because they acquired enormous tracts of territory in Africa and Asia with very little effort in the late nineteenth century. Britain was an active participant in the European conquest and partition of Africa in the 1880s. In addition to expanded coastal holdings in West Africa, Britain's share of the spoils included Egypt, the Sudan, and British Somaliland in Northeast Africa; Zanzibar, Uganda, and what came to be known as Kenya in East Africa; Nyasaland (Malawi),

Northern Rhodesia (Zambia), and Southern Rhodesia (Zimbabwe) in central Africa; and Swaziland, Basutoland (Lesotho), and Bechuanaland (Botswana) in southern Africa. It took a protracted war with the Afrikaners (1899–1902) to consolidate British rule over South Africa.

In Asia, the government of India secured and expanded its frontiers by occupying Burma and what is now Pakistan. Fears that rival European powers might threaten British economic interests in the tin mines on the Malay Peninsula by taking sides in succession squabbles in the local sultanates and feuds between Chinese miners led the government in London to grudgingly accept the "forward" policy of expansionist administrators in the Straits Settlements. British residents posted to the courts of the various Malay sultans were supposed to act as simple advisors, but they used their influence, backed by the threat of force, to assume greater and greater control of local affairs. In 1896, the Colonial Office organized the Perak, Selangor, Pahang, and Negeri Sembilan sultanates into the Federated Malay States under a British resident-general, who in turn reported to the governor of the Straits Settlements. In the next decade, the remaining Malay sultanates also accepted British advisors, although they remained technically autonomous from the Malay federation. To the north, the British and French tacitly agreed to allow Siam to retain its sovereignty as a buffer between the two rival imperial powers.

Although Britain did not acquire formal rule over extensive Ottoman, Persian, and Chinese territory during this period, its relations with these non-European empires changed dramatically under the new imperialism. The occupation of Egypt in 1882 and incorporation of the southern Persia and the Persian Gulf states into the British sphere of influence diminished the strategic importance of the Ottoman Empire as a buffer again Russian expansionism. British financiers came to consider the Ottomans a bad risk, and politicians like Prime Minister Lord Salisbury openly discussed the need to abandon the older "dying nations."

China, on the other hand, was still attractive to British merchants and investors at the end of the nineteenth century. However, the potential dismemberment of the Chinese Empire by European and Japanese rivals forced Britain to abandon its earlier reliance on informal influence to protect its economic interests. Lord Salisbury's government therefore took part in the European "scramble for concessions" in China and pegged out the Yangtze River valley as a specifically British sphere of influence. In addition, Britain leased the port of Weihaiwei for twenty-five years and added the Kowloon New Territories to Hong Kong under a ninety-nine-year lease.

Consolidation of the Second British Empire

By the beginning of the twentieth century, the British Empire had largely reached its full territorial extent. Although imperial partisans often compared themselves to the classical Romans, the former organized their empire along substantially different lines. The British Empire was never a single administrative entity, and it lacked a uniform language, religion, and code of laws. The currency of metropolitan Britain, the West Indian colonies, and the Australasian settlement colonies was gold-based sterling. The Canadian dollar, however, was pegged to the value of the American dollar. India and British East Africa used silver rupees, whereas the Malayan states had silver dollars. Britain's colonies did not adopt a uniform sterling exchange standard until the eve of the First World War. In reality, the second British Empire born of the new imperial era was a decentralized and overlapping conglomeration of diverse territories and cultures whose only common point of reference was interaction with British imperial authority. In fact, one might argue that there were multiple British Empires by the turn of the twentieth century.

The administration of such a heterogeneous mix of peoples and territories was no easy matter. There was never an "Imperial Department" of the British government with jurisdiction over the entire empire. The Foreign Office, India Office, War Office, Colonial Office, Admiralty, and Board of Trade shared responsibility for running the overseas possessions. Colonial matters were largely an afterthought to the Foreign Office, and the Colonial Office was weak and understaffed during the imperial century. In 1907, its London office employed slightly more than one hundred people.[24]

Britain's colonies, protectorates, and other territories were governed through a bewildering array of administrative systems, which were more the result of local improvisation than any coherent philosophy of imperial rule. As already noted, Ireland had a semicolonial status within the larger United Kingdom, and the British East India Company did not give way to an Indian council presided over by a member of the British cabinet (the secretary of state for India) until 1858. The other territories that had non-European majorities were usually Crown Colonies under the autocratic authority of a royal governor, who was the personal representative of the Crown. Canada became the first self-governing dominion in 1867. Most of the colonies acquired during the partition of Africa became protectorates under the initial authority of the Foreign Office. Under this system, local rulers technically retained their sovereignty under the "protection" of the Crown, but most eventually became Crown Colonies upon transfer to Colonial Office control.

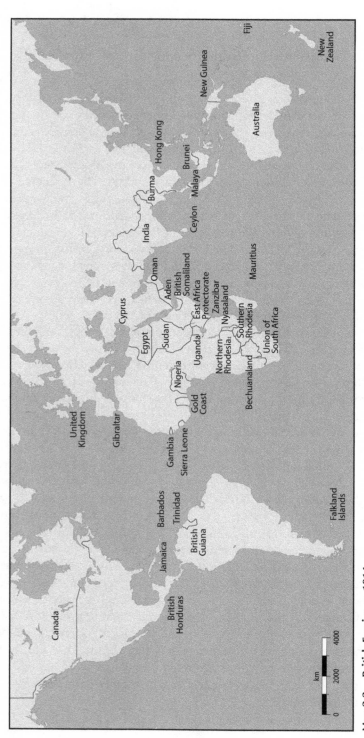

Map 2.2.   British Empire, c. 1914

Many British possessions in the new empire fell outside these relatively straightforward administrative categories. Egypt retained nominal sovereignty but was run by a British consul general, who was theoretically an advisor to the Egyptian cabinet. On the Malay Peninsula, the sultanates that remained outside the Federated Malay States were integrated into the empire by a British official who held the title of "advisor." A hereditary British raja ruled the Sarawak protectorate in northern Borneo, British Somaliland had a commissioner responsible to the Indian government, and a Royal Navy captain ran Ascension Island. In terms of British administrative personnel, the Colonial Office's entire field staff was slightly less than six thousand strong, and all of India was governed by the Indian Civil Service (ICS), which numbered just three thousand men (including a handful of Indians) at the turn of the twentieth century.

Although Britain had a strong domestic tradition of decentralized rule, its diverse imperial administrative policies arose from pragmatic adaptations to the strict financial limitations that the metropolitan Treasury placed on imperial spending. Britain's commitment to free trade precluded revenue-generating tariffs and shifted the financial burden of government to the British taxpayer. The cost of protecting a global empire forced Britain to spend more per capita on defense than any other European power. This meant the Treasury was absolutely adamant that the colonies assume the cost of their own administration and defense. The Chancellor of the Exchequer had absolute authority over foreign and domestic spending, and any colonial government needing metropolitan financial assistance had to submit to the Treasury's ruthless insistence on economy and financial restraint.

These fiscal limitations had a profound influence on the character and scope of British imperial administration. Although Britain could, if it chose, defeat virtually any non-European foe on the battlefield, it could not afford the high cost of prolonged wars of attrition or widespread civil insurrection. For example, the colonial government of Sierra Leone faced severe criticism in London for spending £45,000 to suppress the Hut Tax Rebellion of 1898. On a larger scale, punitive operations in the East Africa Protectorate (Kenya) between 1895 and 1905 cost roughly one-third of the protectorate's total public spending for that period. Furthermore, the regular British army, which only totaled seventy thousand men, was not large enough to provide occupation forces for every territory in the empire with a non-European majority. This meant that empire builders relied heavily on troops borrowed from the Indian army or private chartered company armies, comprised largely of non-Western soldiers, during the new imperial era. Most of the resulting territorial governments had no choice but to continue to raise local military units drawn from poorly paid subject populations. The tremendous amount of coercive force Britain had at its disposal was of little value when it came to the messy problem of imperial governance for the colonial authorities could not afford to provoke widespread discontent and unrest.

The image of an omnipotent colonial state with the power to arbitrarily reorder indigenous economic and social institutions is a myth. British imperial administrators could govern non-European colonies only with the tacit assent of at least a small segment of the subject population. Britain lacked the resources and personnel to govern its global empire exclusively with European officials, which forced it to recruit West Indians, Africans, and Asians as lower-level clerks, translators, artisans, police officers, and soldiers to run the colonies.

Imperial administrators also endeavored to co-opt indigenous elites into the lower levels of the colonial bureaucracy. This system, known as indirect rule, came from India, where the British East India Company governed much of the subcontinent through Indian princes and rajas. At midcentury, Theophilus Shepstone similarly co-opted Zulu elites into the lower levels of the Natal colonial bureaucracy as "chiefs." But indirect rule was much harder to implement in the African territories acquired during the new imperial era because a great many of Britain's new subject populations lived in stateless societies that did not have suitably useful centralized institutions of authority. Consequently, British administrators tended to raise any sufficiently strong or autocratic figure who could demonstrate a measure of local influence to the status of chief (or "headman"). This indirect rule lowered the cost of colonial administration by shrinking the British administrative staff and reducing the possibility that foreign rule might provoke unrest. As Nigerian governor Frederick Lugard put it, "It is one thing to excite an ignorant peasantry against an alien usurper, but quite another thing to challenge a native ruler."[25]

Theoretically, these "native rulers" derived their legitimacy from their "traditional" status in preconquest society. In reality, however, their positions of authority reflected their willingness to participate in the colonial system. Although these British clients often incurred the animosity of their fellow subjects, cooperation had its rewards. Colonial officials relied on their allies to interpret African and Asian society, and these elites consequently had a substantial amount of influence in defining the customs and traditions that became the basis of colonial laws. Consequently, subordinate indirect rulers in the British Empire enjoyed a measure of political power, economic security, and social status that was not readily apparent from the perspective of the Colonial Office in London.

Similarly, British diplomats and traders relied on translators, managers, commercial agents, and, in some cases, Christian converts to exert informal influence in the Ottoman and Chinese Empires. These intermediaries often grew wealthy through their partnership in the British imperial enterprise. In the eighteenth century, the British East India Company's Indian agents helped take over and then dismantle the Mughal Empire. In the nineteenth century, the metropolitan British government did not have the same designs on the Chinese and Ottoman Empires, but in both cases local allies helped penetrate closed domestic markets by weakening the social consensus that had previously excluded foreigners. Although these activities destabilized both empires, the Chinese and the Ottomans escaped the fate of the Mughals. The Westernized Chinese and Ottoman intermediary classes, wealthy as they were, were not powerful enough to undermine the religious and cultural bonds that held these powerful and long-lived empires together.

Ultimately, the expansion of Britain's formal empire and informal influence in the late nineteenth century was shaped by the ability of British empire builders to find partners among the local population. The remaining chapters of this book show that, for the most part, the loss of sovereignty inherent in British imperial rule restructured indigenous political, economic, and social institutions in a manner that created considerable hardship for most of Britain's non-European subjects. Yet the imperial enterprise also offered opportunity to at least a small segment of the colonial populace. Chinese commercial agents, Ottoman translators, Indian princes, Fijian policemen, West Indian clerks, and African soldiers were neither loyal British subjects nor calculating self-interested traitors. Most pragmatically based their decision to participate in the imperial system on the new realities of British rule or, in the case of the Ottoman and Chinese Empires, indirect British influence. Furthermore, the economic austerity of the new imperialism, which led Britain to seek allies among its subjects, tempered some of the worst abuses of the imperial system and created a medium for the diffusion of ideas between metropolitan Britain and its subject populations.

Notes

1. Peter Karsten, "Irish Soldiers in the British Army, 1792–1922: Suborned or Subordinate?," *Journal of Social History* 17 (1983): 31–41; David Fitzpatrick, "Ireland and the Empire," in *The Oxford History of the British Empire*, volume 3: *The Nineteenth Century*, ed. Andrew Porter (Oxford: Oxford University Press, 2004), 500–510.

2. Kenneth Fielden, "The Rise and Fall of Free Trade," in *Britain Pre-Eminent: Studies of British World Influence in the Nineteenth Century*, ed. C. J. Bartlett (London: Macmillan, 1969), 77.

3. James Mill, "Colony: Reprinted from the Supplement to the Encyclopedia Britannica," in *Essays* (London: J. Innes, 1829), 31–33.

4. Kathleen Monteith, "Emancipation and Labour on Jamaican Coffee Plantations, 1838–48," *Slavery & Abolition* 21 (2000): 131.

5. Daniel Headrick, *The Tools of Empire: Technology and European Imperialism in the Nineteenth Century* (New York: Oxford University Press, 1981), 63.

6. Nicholas Mansergh, *The Commonwealth Experience* (New York: Frederick Praeger, 1969), 58.

7. A. N. Porter, ed., *Atlas of British Overseas Expansion* (New York: Simon & Schuster, 1991), 85–86.

8. Robert Hughes, *The Fatal Shore: The Epic of Australia's Founding* (New York: Vintage Books, 1988), 144.

9. Brian Fagan, *Clash of Cultures*, 2nd ed. (Walnut Creek, CA: AltaMira Press, 1998), 284.

10. Great Britain, House of Commons, *Report from the Select Committee on Africa (Western Coast)* (London, 1865), iii.

11. Thomas Skidmore and Peter Smith, *Modern Latin America*, 3rd ed. (New York: Oxford University Press, 1992), 44.

12. "King of Dahomey and the Slave Trade," in *In the Hands of Strangers: Readings on Foreign and Domestic Slave Trading and the Crisis of the Union*, ed. Robert E. Conrad (University Park: Pennsylvania State University Press, 2001), 105.

13. P. J. Cain and A. G. Hopkins, *British Imperialism: Innovation and Expansion, 1688–1914* (London: Longman, 1993), 112.

14. B. R. Tomlinson, "India and the British Empire, 1880–1935," *Indian Economic and Social History Review* 12 (1975): 347.

15. Mansergh, *The Commonwealth Experience*, 122.

16. Peter Cain and Anthony Hopkins developed the highly influential theory of "gentlemanly capitalism" as an inspiration for British empire building. Cain and Hopkins, *British Imperialism*, 12, 28.

17. Lance Davis and Robert Huttenback, *Mammon and the Pursuit of Empire: The Political Economy of British Imperialism, 1860–1912* (Cambridge: Cambridge University Press, 1986), 71–75.

18. J. C. Chute, *Geography Notes: British Empire* (London: J. M. Dent & Sons, 1912), 90.

19. Charles Darwin, *The Descent of Man*, part 1 (New York: American Home Library Company, 1902), 243.

20. Jill Bender, *The 1857 Indian Uprising and the British Empire* (Cambridge: Cambridge University Press, 2016), 115.

21. Headrick, *The Tools of Empire*, 66–70.

22. P. M. Kennedy, "Imperial Communications and Strategy, 1870–1914," *English Historical Review* 86 (1971); John MacKenzie, "Cultural, Intellectual and Religious Networks: Britain's Maritime Exchanges in the Nineteenth and Twentieth Centuries," in *The Victorian Empire and Britain's Maritime World, 1837–1901*, ed. Miles Taylor (New York: Palgrave Macmillan, 2013), 66–68.

23. Winston Churchill, *The River War: An Historical Account of the Reconquest of the Soudan*, volume 2 (New York: Longmans, Green, and Co, 1899), 164.

24. Davis and Huttenback, *Mammon and the Pursuit of Empire*, 12–13.

25. Frederick Lugard, *The Dual Mandate in Tropical Africa* (London: Archon Books, 1965), 196.

CHAPTER THREE

~

India

India was, without question, the most important and influential of Britain's imperial possessions. As such, it does not fall neatly into the categories of the "old" or "new" imperialism. Having been conquered by the British East India Company (BEIC) in the early modern era, India could be considered part of the original British Empire that ended with the independence of the North American colonies in the late eighteenth century. But India was so valuable that not even the harshest critics of empire ever suggested abandoning it during the mid-nineteenth-century enthusiasm for informal empire. Indians paid considerable taxes, were captive consumers of British products, and *sepoys* (Indian soldiers) made Britain a global land power. India remained the focal point of the British Empire throughout the imperial century, but the changing dynamics of empire and the new imperialism resulting from the West's global expansion also had a transformative impact on the nature of British rule in South Asia and India's role in the newly expanded formal empire.

India was Britain's first major overseas possession to have a non-Western majority. It would have been impossible to conquer and rule millions of people living in such a vast expanse of territory without the assistance of at least a small segment of the subject population. Having figured out how to accomplish this in India, British administrators made India, along with Ireland, the model for governance in the wider empire. Consequently, imperial expansion in the nineteenth century spread India's peoples, products, and cultures around the globe. In many ways the resulting second British Empire was almost as Indian as it was British.

The Origins of British India

The British East India Company, a privately held chartered company that paid the Crown for the exclusive right to monopolize trade in South Asia, was able to acquire sovereignty over India in the eighteenth century because much of the subcontinent was already under foreign rule. The BEIC supplanted the Mughal Empire, which had subjugated most of northern India in the sixteenth century. The Mughals were Islamicized Mongols who, like their British successors, governed India by right of conquest. They ruled the non-Muslim majority by giving Hindu elites important positions in their army and administration, as well as co-opting princes, rajas, and village notables at the local level. As one of the world's great imperial powers in

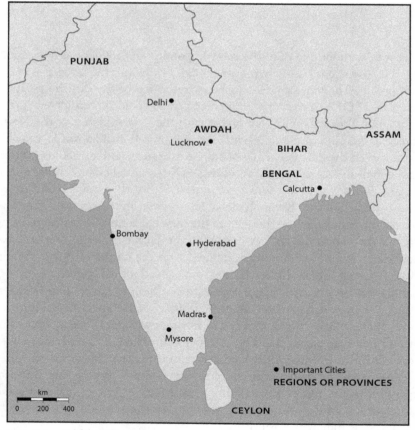

Map 3.1. British India

the seventeenth century, Mughal India used its wealth and administrative genius to produce impressive achievements in science, art, architecture, and literature. By the eighteenth century, however, the peripheral regions of the empire were breaking away. Mughal governors and viceroys used their growing autonomy to become feudal rulers in their own right. Most, however, still acknowledged the emperor's formal authority and continued to pay him a share of their territories' annual revenues to maintain their legitimacy. Nevertheless, this erosion of central authority led the Mughals to lose control of some of their most lucrative holdings in Bengal, Awadh, and the Deccan Plateau.

Initially, the British East India Company's main concern was to impose some sort of order on the periphery of the decaying Mughal Empire to facilitate trade. In time, economic opportunity created by the highly commercialized Indian economy drew its employees into the hinterlands of the subcontinent. Although the BEIC competed, sometimes violently, with French and Dutch chartered companies for control of the most lucrative Asian markets, it had no British rivals. The Company, as the BEIC was commonly known, took up its royal charter in 1600, and within a century it had leased over twenty trading posts near Madras and Bombay from the Mughal emperor. It struggled at first to realize significant profits because it had to import silver to pay for indigo, saltpeter, cotton cloth, silk, and spices. Company officials therefore used their private army to coerce local rulers into giving them the right to collect the Mughal emperor's tribute and taxes. This was an important and highly lucrative concession because these revenue agents had the right to keep a substantial portion of what they collected.

The eastern province of Bengal was the Company's most profitable field of operations. Although technically under the suzerainty of the emperor, Bengal was an autonomous fiefdom ruled by a Mughal vassal known as a *nawab*. Bengali merchants grew wealthy by supplying commodities to the Company's main trading settlement at Calcutta, which enhanced the BEIC's influence and alarmed Nawab Siraj-ud Daula. When the Company violated the terms of its lease by fortifying Calcutta against the French, he tried to drive them out by force of arms. Many Calcutta merchants sided with the British in the ensuing conflict, and Company forces under the command of Robert Clive, formerly a clerk, won a major victory over the nawab at the Battle of Plassey in 1757.

As a result, the emperor granted the Company the right to manage the finances and taxes of Bengal, which made the British East India Company his nominal vassal. Bengal was a rich agricultural region, and Company officials found that their commission on the annual land tax was often more profit-able than trading. Quite a few representatives of the Company amassed great personal fortunes by taking advantage of the monopolies and subsidies that were the perquisites of all Indian administrators in the eighteenth century. As they became more deeply enmeshed in Indian commerce, the Company's influence spread into the interior of the subcontinent.

This prosperity gave the BEIC a vested interest in maintaining Indian political stability to ensure the free flow of commerce and efficient tax col-lection. To this end, the Company sent military garrisons and special am-bassadors, known as Residents, to the courts of their most important Indian allies. These rulers had to pay for their "protection," and the high cost of the garrisons often drove them into bankruptcy. In such cases, Company officials subsequently assumed control of their finances to ensure continued stability. Although the indebted Indian rulers retained a degree of formal autonomy, they became de facto vassals of the Company.

These expansionist policies were largely inspired by the BEIC's economic interests and not a desire for formal or direct imperial rule. However, the Company also sought to ensure that important Indian rulers did not fall under the sway of their French rivals. These tensions embroiled India in the global Seven Years' War, and at the conclusion of the conflict in 1763 the BEIC was the only significant European chartered company left on the subcontinent. Having defeated the powerful Indian states of Mysore and Hy-derabad later in the century, the Company emerged as the dominant political and economic power in India. Although the Sikhs and Marathas were still independent in the central and northwestern regions, Company-ruled India became an integral part of the first British Empire.

For the purposes of administration, the Company divided India into the Bengal, Madras, and Bombay presidencies. Although each had its own separate civil service and army, the governor-general of Bengal coordi-nated Company policy as the senior British official in India. The BEIC based its legitimacy on its status as a symbolic Mughal vassal and contin-ued to pay the emperor a nominal sum as token tribute. The Company was in fact directly responsible to the British government in London. As BEIC holdings in India grew more extensive and profitable, Parliament passed a series of laws in the late eighteenth century that asserted more formal metropolitan control over Company affairs. These acts made the Company responsible to a board of control composed of unpaid councl-ors, with the board's president serving in the British cabinet. East India House, the Company's London headquarters, became a center of power and opulence that dazzled many an Indian visitor: "They call it a house, but it is a palace, containing a great number of apartments and halls, all well furnished. It is the place where the destiny of my sweet native land lies in the hands of twenty-four men, called the Honourable Directors of the Honourable East India Company."[1] The new rules also established a professional Indian civil service, staffed by British revenue collectors and district magistrates.

While the Company still generated substantial revenues from trade at the turn of the nineteenth century, its role as chief tax collector for the Mughal Empire was the main reason for its enormous profitability. Highly efficient Bengali farmers produced the vast majority of this wealth. Before the arrival of the British, Mughal officials in Bengal extracted one-third of the province's gross annual product in the form of land taxes and tribute. After its victory at Plassey, this substantial windfall freed the BEIC from having to import silver to purchase Indian products, and Bengali revenues subsidized dividend payments to the Crown and its British stockholders. Company officials therefore had a vested interest in making Indian agriculture more productive and tax collection more efficient.

Under the Mughals, a class of hereditary tax farmers known as *zamindars* in Bengal and *talukdars* in Awadh and Hyderabad collected the land tax in exchange for 10 percent of all the funds they raised. In the late eighteenth century, Company officials sought to expand India's taxable agricultural output by transforming these tax collectors into a class of hereditary landlords, who would theoretically have a greater incentive to invest in increasing the productivity of the land under their control. Individual rent-paying farmers undertook most of the actual cultivation, and the Company hoped to give the zamindars a stake in improved agricultural production by granting them formal title to the land they administered. This "permanent settlement," as the reforms came to be known, altered substantially the basis of land rights in northeastern India. Most individual farmers became tenants of the zamindars, who now held legal title to the farms.

Although this system allowed the Company to collect almost 50 percent of Bengal's gross annual product in taxes by the beginning of the nineteenth century, the permanent settlement did not live up to expectations. Instead of becoming progressive gentlemanly farmers on the English model, the zamindars behaved more like the absentee rent-collecting English landlords in Ireland. Since many Bengalis had difficulty paying the increased taxes, an estimated one-third of the land in Bengal changed hands in the decades immediately following the settlement.[2] Much of it eventually fell into the hands of the Calcutta merchants who had tied their fortunes to the Company a century earlier.

Consolidation and Expansion in the Imperial Century

The value of the Bengal land revenues, and to a lesser degree the revenues of the Madras and Bombay presidencies, made India Britain's most valuable overseas possession at the start of the nineteenth century. Company bonds paid from 8 to 12 percent per year, and annual revenues, which totaled over £20 million in the first decades of the century, helped balance Britain's trade deficit with China.[3] The Company also transferred a substantial portion of these funds directly to Britain as "home charges" in the form of bullion, administrative salaries, pensions, stock dividends, freight charges, insurance, and banking fees.

Yet in spite of this increased profitability, the BEIC fought to justify its total control of the Indian economy in the face of the metropolitan backlash against the restrictions of the mercantilist system. When the Company's charter came up for renewal in 1813, free traders forced it to surrender its monopoly over Indian trade. The new charter only allowed the Company to retain its local monopolies on salt and opium production. By 1834, the Company's stock ceased to trade, and shareholders received an annual dividend of roughly 10 percent of the total revenues of British India. This was still a tidy sum, but during the era of informal empire the British East India Company had essentially become a political institution. The Company's primary focus was now administration and revenue collection, even though it technically remained a privately held commercial enterprise.

Although the British government gained a much greater say in Company affairs, administrators in India still enjoyed a considerable degree of autonomy because their lucrative tax base allowed them to remain financially independent of the British Treasury. The most effective method of meeting the rising cost of governance and making the Company more profitable was to acquire more taxable territory. To this end, the BEIC freely employed its large standing army to expand its borders and subdue its remaining Indian rivals. During the first decades of the imperial century, Company forces vanquished the powerful Hindu Maratha states on the Deccan Plateau, as well as the Sikhs of the Punjab, and occupied extensive territories on India's northwestern and northeastern frontiers.

On other occasions, the Company expanded its influence by administrative fiat rather than force of arms. It decreed that the rulers of the semiautonomous princely states who had acknowledged the suzerainty of the Company by accepting British Residents into their courts could not designate an adopted heir if they were childless. Under what became known as the "doctrine of lapse," the Company inherited the lands and possessions of these princes and rajas when they died. These tactics allowed the BEIC to subjugate the subcontinent completely by the mid-nineteenth century. Powerful rulers in the interior like the sultan of Mysore and the nizam of Hyderabad survived as British vassals, while the Company had direct control over vast stretches of territory in Bengal, the Northwestern provinces, and India's coasts.

One of the great ironies of India's imperial experience was that the Company's conquest of the subcontinent was carried out largely by South Asians. The Indian army made Britain a great land power, but it was essentially an Indian institution led by a handful of British officers and stiffened by a core of British regular soldiers. In 1848, the army consisted of approximately 29,000 Europeans and 235,000 Indian soldiers known as sepoys.[4] Although it may appear incongruous for Indians to have served foreign conquerors, a large percentage of the Mughals' armies had also been composed of Hindus and other non-Muslims. Company recruiters exploited communal, religious, and class divisions among the subject population, and there was not yet a greater Indian national identity for these soldiers to betray.

Moreover, the Company paid generous salaries, offered pensions for fifteen years of reliable service, and gave its soldiers precedence in civil lawsuits. Sita Ram, the son of a prosperous Brahmin zamindar and one of the few sepoys to publish a formal autobiography, recalled that the wealth and status of his uncle convinced him to join as well. Seeming more prestigious than a nawab, the uncle, who was a "native officer" in the infantry of the Bengal presidency, "had such a splendid necklace of gold beads, and a curious bright red coat, covered with gold buttons; and, above all, he appeared to have an unlimited supply of gold mohurs [Mughal coins]."[5] Sita Ram's mother opposed his enlistment, but his father favored it in the hope that his son's service would give him an edge in a lawsuit over the ownership of a grove of four hundred mango trees.

The British East India Company also relied on Indians at the administrative level because its formal civil service never numbered more than about two thousand Europeans. While the Company was no longer a purely commercial enterprise, it still lacked the personnel and resources to govern India directly. This was particularly true in the countryside where there were rarely more than one or two British officials in a given district. Britain itself did not establish a formal police force until 1829, and the Company did not have the manpower or popular support to create a similar organization for India. Instead, it simply absorbed Indian village watchmen and headmen into its administration. The watchmen, known as *chowkidars* in Bengal, were primarily responsible for suppressing rural banditry. Village headmen interpreted the Company's rules and regulations for the general population and advised

British officials on local affairs. Both groups were poorly paid and had little reason to be loyal to the Company. Consequently, they often enriched themselves by accepting bribes and exercising their authority selectively.

Company administrators generally had to tolerate these practices because they could not afford to meddle too deeply in Indian affairs. The aim was to co-opt local legal and bureaucratic institutions without provoking widespread social unrest. The BEIC governed most of India through adapted Mughal administrative systems and based its law codes on Hindu and Muslim legal texts. It also formalized the residency system to exert greater influence in the princely states. British Residents manipulated their clients by taking informal control of their foreign relations, armed forces, and financial affairs. For the most part, the princes retained their wealth and social status, but the growing influence of the Company's Residents in effect reduced them to ceremonial figureheads.

Although Company officials tried to minimize the social disruption caused by their expanding political role, the importance of land revenues gave them an incentive to intervene more directly in local agrarian and economic affairs. The BEIC derived roughly a quarter of its total income from its monopoly on salt and opium production. Almost 40 percent of its revenue came from land taxes, which amounted to almost £18 million by the mid-nineteenth century. In this sense, the Company emulated its Mughal predecessors by extracting the agricultural surplus of India.

This reliance on Indian agriculture meant that Company officials remained focused on issues relating to taxation and land tenure. To this end, the BEIC built on the permanent settlement by surveying rural India extensively in an attempt to streamline the Mughal revenue collection system. Land assessments consequently increased substantially at the beginning of the imperial century. Most levies averaged half of the annual value of a farmer's crops, and officials allowed no exemptions for drought or insect infestation. The Company taxed Bengal's zamindar landholders under the terms of the permanent settlement but adopted a substantially different policy in the Bombay and Madras presidencies. Instead of trying to turn tax collectors into landlords, officials in southern and western India encouraged free peasants known as *ryots* to improve their land in order to take advantage of greater access to global markets. Finally, in the Punjab and Northwestern provinces, the Company also encouraged individual land ownership but directed peasants to pay their taxes communally as a village unit.

The Company generally did not encourage the development of plantation agriculture in India on the Caribbean model. The one exception was in northeastern India, where European planters grew indigo, opium, and tea in Bengal, Bihar, and Assam. Yet even there the planters did not own large estates. Instead, they loaned Indian peasants money to cover their rent to the zamindars, and, in return, the peasants agreed to grow cash crops on a fixed portion of their land. Large-scale opium growers were relatively well treated because the Company still held a monopoly on opium production, but peasants growing indigo were largely at the mercy of planters who conspired with zamindars and hoodlums to force them into inequitable long-term contracts. This use of excessive force and unfree labor practices embarrassed Company officials at a time when the humanitarian lobby in Britain had just succeeded in abolishing slavery throughout the British Empire. Moreover, rising discontent among the peasant growers threatened to spark expensive social unrest. The BEIC therefore gradually forced the planters out of business as indigo became less profitable.

The limited success of plantation agriculture in India reaffirmed the Company's reliance on Indian farmers. While officials tried to ensure that their agrarian policies did not cause undue social disruption, their attempt to restructure local economies accelerated and distorted profound changes that were already taking place in rural Indian society. In the eighteenth century, a shortage of agricultural labor kept land prices low and ensured that there was usually enough land for any farmer who wanted it. Land became more valuable in the nineteenth century as population growth, expanded cash crop production, rising agricultural prices, better irrigation, improved transportation, and greater access to global markets drew the remaining reserves of unused land into production. The Company did not have the capacity to entirely restructure India's rural economy, but it helped make prime agricultural land a salable commodity by codifying individual land tenure to improve taxation.

These changes had a number of unexpected consequences. Indian moneylenders, who had previously used a peasant's crops as collateral, foreclosed on the farms themselves when a peasant went bankrupt. Company officials feared that these moneylenders were more interested in land speculation than agricultural production but could do little to arrest the process that they themselves had helped set in motion. Instead of reshaping India's rural economy to suit its own ends, the Company simply changed the rules of the game. On the plus side, moneylenders and commodity traders prospered from rising land values and the commercialization of agriculture. Conversely, the old warrior Indian castes, like Sita Ram's family, that derived status from feudalistic systems of landholding declined, while many small farmers lost their land altogether.

In addition to these economic ramifications, mounting political pressure in Britain forced the Company to relax its policy of noninterference in

Indian social affairs as the imperial century progressed. Company officials believed that religion governed all aspects of Indian society and therefore adopted a strict ban on Christian evangelism to avoid social disruption. In an effort to rule by "Indian tradition," the Company based its legal system on Hindu and Muslim scriptures as interpreted by high-caste Brahmans and senior Islamic scholars. In the late eighteenth century, high-ranking Company officials rejected proposals to create an English-based education system in India and instead established the Islamic Calcutta Madrassa and the Hindu Sanskrit College to train young Indians for administrative and legal positions in the Company bureaucracy. To further establish their legitimacy, Company officials emulated their Indian predecessors by posing as protectors of local cemeteries, shrines, and temples.

Although these practices helped minimize the social impact of the Company's invasive economic policies, they provoked widespread condemnation from British evangelicals and humanitarians, who attacked the Company for its tolerance of Indian "barbarism." Initially, would-be British missionaries worked out of the Dutch enclave of Serampore to get around the Company's prohibition on proselytization. In the early nineteenth century, evangelicals joined free traders in attacking the BEIC's monopolistic control of Indian commerce and society. Led by William Wilberforce, a prominent evangelical and abolitionist, the Clapham Sect collected over half a million signatures on petitions demanding an end to the Company's toleration of what they deemed anti-Christian practices in India. These included *sati* (or suttee), the self-immolation of a Hindu widow on her husband's funeral pyre; *thagi*, an itinerant religious sect that allegedly murdered hapless travelers; female infanticide; and human sacrifice. Just as the Company lost its commercial monopoly when its charter was renewed in 1813 and 1833, the British government also forced it to abolish restrictions on Christian proselytization in India.

Although older Company officials considered these changes to be dangerously disruptive, others, influenced by liberal Utilitarian ideals, believed in strengthening British rule by reforming Indian society through free trade, evangelism, Western law, and English education. Many prominent Utilitarians joined the BEIC in the first decades of the nineteenth century as it became less a commercial enterprise and more a governing bureaucracy. Both James Mill and his son John Stuart Mill held clerical and administrative roles in the Company. As advocates of "good government," the Mills and their Utilitarian allies joined evangelicals in condemning what they perceived to be Indian backwardness and moral stagnation. Their cure for India's ills was Western legal reform and the full-scale Anglicization of Indian society.

Unlike their eighteenth-century predecessors, these new Company officials had little respect for Indian cultures and traditions. Thomas Babington Macaulay, who was responsible for educational and legal reform, opined that "a single shelf of a good European library was worth the whole native literature of India and Arabia."[6] Moreover, in a drastic shift from earlier Company policy, he argued in 1835 that "we must at present do our best to form a class who may be interpreters between us and the millions whom we govern, a class of persons Indian in blood and colour, but English in taste, in opinions, in morals and intellect."[7]

Macaulay and the Utilitarians sought to create this new Anglicized middle class by transforming Indian education. They established English-based universities in the main presidency towns. These institutions differed from earlier missionary colleges by using English literature rather than the Bible as the basis of instruction. Evangelicals branded the new secular curriculum atheistic, for it allowed students to acquire a Western education without converting to Christianity. The success of the new universities also allowed the Company to replace Persian, the language of the Mughal court, with English as the primary language of Indian administration.

To some extent, the English-language universities succeeded in creating an Anglicized Indian middle class. Most of the new graduates were the sons of India's literate classes, who embraced an English education for social advancement in British India. The Charter Act of 1833 specifically barred the Company from practicing racial discrimination, and the new graduates filled the lower ranks of its civil service. With their own English-language newspapers and commitment to social reform, they were a dynamic force in Indian society. Most were Hindus because Muslims were less comfortable with the Christian character of Western education, no matter how secular the new universities appeared to be. Dwarkanath Tagore was the first Indian to hold a high position in the Company. A prominent zamindar, he served on the Company's board of customs, founded India's first Western-style bank, and was a leading investor in Indian-owned coal mines and steamship lines. Ram Mohan Roy, another leading Hindu intellectual, became the assistant to the collector of Rangpur and served as the Mughal emperor's representative in London.

Although many students embraced Western education and commerce as a means of improving Indian society, it would be a mistake to see them as "English in taste, in opinions, in morals and intellect." Even though students of the Young Bengal Movement threw beef into the houses of leading Calcutta Brahmans to protest the restrictions of conservative Hinduism, they did not divorce themselves completely from their cultural roots. To many Western-educated Hindus, British education and culture were a means to reform and strengthen Indian society. The Hindu reformers were opposed by conservative scholars, many of whom interpreted Hindu law for the Company and maintained a vested interest in emphasizing the authoritative role of religious texts and scriptures in Indian society.

Many of the practices that India's British critics labeled barbaric were at the center of these debates. When Ram Mohan Roy supported the Company's 1839 ban on sati, he argued the practice of widow burning was not an organic part of Hinduism. Rather, he maintained that sati was primarily an innovation of high-caste Hindu priests who wanted to discipline potentially unfaithful wives. "The ground which I took . . . was, not that of opposition to Brahminism, but to a perversion of it; and I endeavoured to show that the idolatry of the Brahmins was contrary to the practice of their ancestors, and the principles of the ancient books and authorities which they profess to revere and obey."[8] Although Indian conservatives argued that reformers misread and ignored key passages from Hindu scriptures, the Company's tabulation of widow-burning incidents in the years preceding its ban supported Roy's position. Sati appears to have been rarely practiced among the greater Hindu population in the early nineteenth century, but over 60 percent of the 8,134 recorded incidents of sati in 1829 involved upper-caste Hindus living in Calcutta.[9]

British rule thus created a new arena for interpreting, contesting, and even inventing Indian customs. Both conservative religious elites and Westernized reformers sought to exploit the restrictions and opportunities presented by the growing commercialization of Indian society under foreign rule by claiming the potent privilege of defining tradition. The Company administration was not fully aware of this contest, and the success or failure of the competing factions depended largely on their ability to convince British officials of the authenticity of a particular interpretation or definition of an Indian tradition. Thus the introduction of Western education did not "modernize" Indian society as British reformers had intended. Instead, an English-style education provided the new commercial elites with the means to challenge the dominant position of the older, often feudalistic, elites in Indian society.

India under the Raj

Although elements of India's educated and commercial classes successfully exploited the opportunities presented by the new imperial order, the tacit acquiescence of the general populace that enabled a handful of British officials to govern the Indian majority was, in turn, undermined by the significant social and economic tensions produced by a century of interventionist Company rule. These pressures came to a head in April 1857, exactly one hundred years after the Battle of Plassey, when three regiments of the Bengal army stationed at Meerut near Delhi executed their British officers and proclaimed the restoration of the Mughal emperor. The sepoys had numerous grievances, but the immediate cause of the mutiny was a rumor that ammunition for the newly introduced Enfield rifle was greased with a mixture of pork and beef fat. Historians have debated the accuracy of these reports. But if the stories were true, the new cartridges would have contaminated any devout Hindu or Muslim who used them because the soldiers had to rip open the cartridge's paper wrapping with their teeth.

In the past, sepoys had struck occasionally to protest a variety of issues relating to religion, uniforms, and service abroad, but the 1857 mutiny was unique in its scope and severity. The soldiers' open defiance of British authority weakened the coercive bonds that kept the Indian majority in check. Consequently, the military insurrection grew swiftly into a general civil revolt in the Northwestern provinces, the Maratha states, and western Bengal. The most affected areas were key recruiting centers and regions that had experienced a high degree of social and economic dislocation under British rule.[10] Yet there was little to unite the rebels other than an intense dissatisfaction with Company policies. Many landowners, squeezed by high tax rates, lost their holdings to moneylenders. Peasants and nomadic peoples resented their loss of access to communal grazing lands, and the few Indian princes who joined the revolt saw the Doctrine of Lapse as a barely disguised excuse to annex their domains. These multiple grievances make it difficult to categorize the mutiny definitively, and contemporary historians have labeled it variously a rural revolt, a Muslim holy war, a Mughal restoration, a Hindu Maratha revival, and an Indian national movement.

While the violence of the rebellion was spectacular in its ferocity, British forces contained the rebellion because it was limited largely to the Bengal presidency. For the most part, southern and western India remained quiet, and educated Indians and most of the semiautonomous rulers of princely states also stayed largely on the sidelines. Nevertheless, the mutiny remains one of the most bloody and expensive episodes in the history of the British Empire. In one sense, it resembled a civil war because the rebels and mutineers also turned on members of India's newly Anglicized educated and commercial classes. British officials, however, were more alarmed by violent attacks on the small community of resident Britons. The rebels refused to spare European women and children, and the British press popularized sensational, but untrue, stories that female victims were raped before they were killed.

These incidents made Britons living in India acutely aware of their vulnerability. With only forty-five thousand European soldiers in all of India, the Company relied heavily on newly recruited Sikh soldiers, loyal Bengali sepoys, and the Madras and Bombay armies during the fourteen-month-long campaign to reconquer the rebellious north. When the British were ultimately victorious, individual officers sought retribution for the lurid atrocities sensationalized in the popular press. Their revenge, predicated on the assumption that religion ruled Indian society, aimed to defile the mutineers. The victors forced Muslims to eat pork before they were cremated and Hindus to eat beef before they were buried. These wholesale executions were as barbarous as any of the outrages perpetrated by the rebels, and they undermined the paternalistic ideology that legitimized British rule in India. All told, the mutiny cost Britain £50 million and over eleven thousand British soldiers, lost to both fighting and disease. There are no reliable figures for rebel losses, but historians estimate that, at the very least, hundreds of thousands of Indian soldiers and civilians died as a result of the fighting and British reprisals.[11]

The psychological and economic cost of the mutiny forced the metropolitan British government to reevaluate the basic philosophical tenets of imperial governance in India. Prime Minister Benjamin Disraeli told the House of Commons in 1857 that the unrest was due to a reactionary Indian backlash against foreign social engineering. Company officials had hoped to win the support of ordinary Indians through good government and rural prosperity, and they were shocked when such a large segment of the peasantry of central and northeastern India rose against them. Evangelicals and Utilitarians in the 1830s and 1840s believed that they could restructure Indian society, but after 1857 most officials concluded that in general Indians were too superstitious and fanatical to assimilate Western cultural values.

It is now clear, however, that the mutiny was not a backlash against modernity. Many of the areas that revolted had experienced British rule for only a few decades. Calcutta and most of Bengal, which had been governed by the Company for an entire century, experienced little unrest during the mutiny. Moreover, it is hard to attribute the initial sepoy insurrection at Meerut to religious fanaticism, since the same Hindu and Muslim soldiers willingly used the offending cartridges against the British forces. In the final analysis, the soldiers' collective defiance of authority was simply the spark that ignited simmering discontent over fundamental social and economic changes brought on by Company governance. The British rulers of India weathered the storm because only a few areas experienced the full effects of their most invasive policies and because a substantial segment of India's commercial classes, educated elites, and princely rulers benefited from the opportunities presented by the new imperial order.

Nevertheless, the mutiny inspired the government in London to take a more direct hand in governing Britain's most important imperial possession. The era of Company rule in India came to an end in 1858 when Parliament passed the Act for the Better Government of India, which established the India Office as a formal governmental ministry. It was responsible to the secretary of state for India, who presided over a council of fifteen advisors that replaced the Company's old board of control.

In India, the abolition of the Company eliminated the usefulness of the Mughal emperor as a legitimizing figurehead, and the authorities tried and exiled the elderly Bahadur Shah for treason. In his place Prime Minister Disraeli designated Queen Victoria "Empress of India," and India's new imperial government became known as the Raj. The governor-general of Bengal became Victoria's viceroy. To keep the viceroy better apprised of public opinion, the Indian Councils Act of 1861 provided for nominal Indian representation, largely in an advisory capacity, on legislative councils in the three main presidency towns. The Indian Civil Service (ICS), which became the premier bureaucracy in the British Empire, remained responsible for basic administrative functions. A competitive examination system opened the civil service to talent, and high salaries and generous pensions attracted some of the most capable members of the British (and Irish) middle classes.

Imperial strategists also restructured the Indian army to forestall future mutinies. To keep the most potent instruments of war in British hands, they disbanded all Indian artillery units and deployed more battalions of the regular British army to India. The reformers also altered the ethnic composition of the Indian army dramatically. The traumatic recollection of rebellious Indian troops murdering British officers shook their confidence in all non-European soldiers. Even though many Bengali sepoys refused to join the mutineers, senior military officials concluded that the security and prosperity of British rule had made the men of Bengal too selfish and "effeminate" to be reliable soldiers. Consequently, they shifted their recruiting efforts to regions that had yet to experience the full impact of the economic and social dislocations produced by imperial rule. Blind to the economic realities that made military service appealing in impoverished areas, British recruiters assumed that certain communities in remote parts of South Asia were "martial races" who were genetically predisposed to be good soldiers. They therefore restocked the Indian army with Nepalese Gurkhas, Sikhs, and Punjabi Muslims. The Raj also bestowed substantial irrigation projects on the latter two regions to reduce the chance that sepoy grievances over agrarian policies might spark further unrest.

British administrators sought to further apply the apparent lessons of the mutiny by making the new Raj more responsive to "responsible" forces in Indian society. The reformers abandoned the Utilitarians' Anglicization experiment, placed new restrictions on Christian evangelism, and sought to co-opt and reinforce what they deemed usefully conservative Indian customs and traditions. The Raj had little use for the Indian educated and commercial classes, which had supposedly failed to convince the general population of the value of British rule. The new imperial regime therefore instead sought to increase its legitimacy by allying with the forces of "tradition" in the countryside. Assuming that the mutiny was partially a response to land foreclosures by grasping moneylenders, postmutiny administrators tried to appease both landlords and peasants by decreasing the land tax.

Lord Charles Canning, the first British viceroy, rewarded Indian princes who had remained loyal during the revolt by ending the Doctrine of Lapse. Depicting the Raj as a great Indian power, he invented a set of new imperial Indian traditions to legitimize British rule and flatter the princes, who still governed 40 percent of the subcontinent in the 1860s. Canning created the Star of India and the Order of the Indian Empire for loyal princes and senior civil servants, and he awarded cooperative rulers with the titles Raja, Nawab, Rai, and Bahadur. The government's Alqabnamah Register listed the formal titles and privileges of every prince, including his coat of arms, the number of guns in his official salute, and the color of the crest on his official correspondence. The British viceroys staged grand public displays known as durbars to celebrate and nurture these new imperial institutions. The resulting official culture of the Raj was therefore neither exclusively British nor Indian. Rather, it was a hybrid that adapted and invented Indian institutions to legitimize British rule.

The sweeping political and social reforms that gave rise to the Raj were also a product of the changing economic bases of British rule in India. The mutiny took place at a time when British leaders were losing faith in free trade and informal empire in the face of aggressive competition from European rivals. They therefore began to look upon India primarily as a reserved market for British trade and investment rather than as a source of raw materials or land revenues. Although these changes were already under way before 1857, the mutiny accelerated the shift by demonstrating the danger of excessive land taxes and the inefficiency of the British East India Company. Raj officials realized that efforts to increase land revenues by stimulating Indian agricultural production were socially disruptive and that license fees, income taxes, and customs duties were safer sources of revenue.

India's economic relationship with Britain under the Raj cannot be termed mercantilistic because foreigners had access to Indian markets, but the new imperial regime ensured that the Indian economy was structured to favor British interests. In the late nineteenth century, Britain financed almost two-thirds of its growing global trade deficit with Indian exports of jute, cotton, and tea to Europe and rice and opium to the Far East. Furthermore, roughly 85 percent of India's imports in the 1880s and 1890s came from Britain, which amounted to almost 20 percent of all British foreign exports during the period.[12] Most British imports to India consisted of cotton textiles, hardware, iron, and steel. Britain's spinning and weaving industries, which had great difficulty keeping up with their more efficient European competitors, were particularly dependent on Indian markets. By 1913, over 40 percent of all British textile exports went to India. Lancashire manufacturers were acutely aware of this dependence and used their influence in the British Liberal Party to block an attempt by the Raj to raise revenue by increasing Indian tariffs.[13]

Yet India was more than just a prop for Britain's increasingly outmoded and inefficient industrial sector. Its greatest value at the end of the imperial century was as a lucrative outlet for British capital. From 1865 to 1914, London financiers invested over £2.5 million in India, which made the Raj the second most favored investment site in the British Empire, after Canada. The great majority of this capital went into developing the Indian railway network, which encompassed thirty-four thousand miles of track in 1913.[14] The Raj promoted railway construction for a number of reasons. The rail system enhanced security by allowing the small garrison of regular British troops to deal swiftly with civil unrest. Moreover, railways gave British manufacturers greater access to Indian markets and helped Indian farmers sell their produce abroad.

Although the railway did stimulate the Indian economy, its construction was a windfall to British manufacturers and investors. Most of its infrastructure was imported from Britain, and highly paid British workers supplied most of the skilled labor on the project. The Raj raised the enormous sums of money needed to build this vast subcontinental rail system by guaranteeing investors profits of at least 4.5 percent. It therefore had to borrow funds at high rates of interest to make good on this commitment whenever the railways failed to return a sufficient profit. The burden of these subsidies, coupled with the cost of the Indian army and other administrative obligations, inflated the Indian national debt substantially. India's obligations to its creditors amounted to almost half the value of its total exports in the latter half of the nineteenth century, and by 1900 the interest alone on this debt amounted to £10 million per year.[15]

Many Indian intellectuals resented this forced indebtedness and charged that British rule retarded India's development by siphoning off capital that the country needed to industrialize. A former British revenue commissioner for Bombay was actually the first to suggest that imperial policy retarded India's economic development. Romesh Chander Dutt, a onetime lecturer at the University of London and president of the Indian National Congress, took the argument several steps further and made it a central Indian criticism of the Raj. Proponents of this theory of "drain" pointed to the British East India Company's commercial monopoly, excessive land taxes, and unreasonably low tariffs favoring Lancashire textile interests as evidence of India's subordinate economic relationship with Britain. They argued that Indian taxpayers were unfairly saddled with responsibility for these home charges, which included the annual cost of interest on the national debt, government contracts fulfilled in Britain, administrative costs for both the Raj and the London-based India Office, and pensions for retired British officials. Writing in 1904, Dutt calculated that Britain extracted £20 million from India each year. "The richest country on earth stoops to levy this annual contribution from the poorest. Those who earn £42 per head ask for 10s. per head from a nation earning £2 per head. . . . The contribution does not benefit British commerce and trade, while it drains the life-blood of India in a continuous ceaseless flow."[16] Dutt and his allies also complained that the unreasonably large and expensive Indian army absorbed almost 40 percent of the national budget. Not only did Indian taxpayers have to maintain the British garrison in India, they also had to pay for any foreign campaign involving Indian troops that the British government deemed in the general interest of India. As costly as these obligations may have been, there are still debates as to whether they hindered India's industrial development. Indians certainly subsidized the British Empire, but the Raj's defenders have calculated that the home charges constituted only a tiny fraction of India's gross national income.[17]

It is clear, however, that Britain's dependence on India grew considerably in the closing decades of the nineteenth century. The defense and security of the Raj preoccupied strategists in London during the era of the new imperialism, and successive British governments were obsessed with protecting India's borders and links with the rest of the empire. The Company's expansionist policies drew it into two wars in Burma earlier in the nineteenth century that led to the acquisition of some Burmese territory. In 1886, concerns that the Burmese were secretly seeking an alliance with the French led to Burma's outright annexation by the Raj after a largely Indian imperial force was victorious in the Third Anglo-Burmese War. Similarly,

Singapore and the Federated Malay States were well within the Raj's sphere of influence even though they were technically under the jurisdiction of the Colonial Office.

India at the End of the Imperial Century

Domestically, the traumatic memories of 1857 made the Raj acutely concerned with the stability of Indian society. Yet British attempts to co-opt the forces of "tradition" backfired by accelerating the social and economic transformation of India. Ever mindful of the supposed lessons of the Indian Mutiny, administrators now concluded that it was dangerous to try to govern non-Western people by remaking them in their own image. They worried that they had become dangerously detached from the general population and worked to reestablish their legitimacy in the eyes of what they perceived to be India's most influential classes. In practical terms, this meant co-opting influential segments of Indian society by demonstrating the value of participating in the imperial system. But these new policies did not strengthen the Raj because they often harmed more people than they benefited.

In the countryside, the Raj offered significant opportunities to Indian farmers through increased access to world markets via the railway and the development of an extensive irrigation system. The network of canals in the northern Indian province of Uttar Pradesh watered 2.5 million acres of land in times of drought. Although overirrigation waterlogged low-lying lands and reduced soil fertility by raising saline levels, the steady and reliable supply of water enriched efficient Indian farmers by allowing them to switch from subsistence food production to cash crops.

The potential benefits of the Raj's railways and canals were tempered by British attempts to stimulate agricultural production and facilitate tax collection by shifting landholding in rural India from customary communal rights to individual ownership. In other words, British rule offered the prize of private land tenure to farmers and landlords who could afford to pay their taxes. Their fortune often came at the expense of poorer kinsmen and neighbors who lost their claims to the land. In northern India, British officials gave Rajput elites title to 60 percent of Banda district at the beginning of the era of Company rule. By 1874, however, these elites had lost 30 percent of their holdings to foreclosure and public auction. Much of the district was subsequently acquired by Muslim commercial families who used their administrative connections to purchase the land at reduced prices.[18]

In the south, the Raj's insistence that land taxes had to be paid in cash often forced ryots (peasant farmers) to mortgage their land to wealthy rural elites when their crops failed. These rural magnates were far better equipped to exploit the possibilities of the imperial system by producing cash crops for the world market. Many bought up the harvests of individual ryots and made more money as commodity speculators than as actual farmers. Small producers who lost their land faced the unpalatable choice of becoming sharecroppers or moving to the cities to look for paid employment. These changes were due in part to population pressure and a worldwide demand for Indian produce, but the Raj's agricultural policies accelerated the process by making even more rural land a salable commodity rather than a communally held family or community asset.

British rule also created similar opportunities and pitfalls in the commercial and industrial sectors. In the 1850s, Karl Marx expected British imperial rule to industrialize India by sweeping away "feudal" elements in Indian society.[19] In reality, the introduction of low-cost, mass-produced British cotton goods retarded India's industrial development by bankrupting its indigenous textile sector. Although other handicraft industries devoted to leather, metal, and woodworking survived into the twentieth century, all but a few wealthy Indians preferred moneylending and petty trading to manufacturing. Moreover, India's loss of sovereignty deprived would-be Indian manufacturers of the protective tariffs that allowed their European counterparts to defend developing industries from foreign competition. British manufacturing interests often used their political influence to hinder the development of rival Indian enterprises, and officials in London discouraged the Raj from purchasing Indian products. The Indian government could buy locally produced iron only if it cost at least 5 percent less than imported British iron.

Despite these restrictions, a small Indian industrial sector developed by taking advantage of the opportunities offered by British rule. India had ample supplies of coal, and the displacement of peasant farmers in the countryside created a relatively inexpensive wage labor force. Railways provided ready access to both Indian and world markets, and Indian manufacturers profited from Britain's continued commitment to free trade. As a result, hostile Lancashire magnates could not prevent India from becoming the world's fourth largest cotton manufacturer on the eve of the First World War.

As in Britain itself, successful Indian entrepreneurs often used textiles as a launching pad for other industrial ventures. J. N. Tata, who made his fortune in Bombay cotton, founded India's first indigenous steel industry in 1907 after an influx of cheap European imports forced the Raj to abandon its restrictions on Indian industrial development. When British bankers refused to help him raise capital, he sold over £1.5 million in shares to individual Indian investors.[20] Today the Tata Group owns substantial assets throughout the Western world, including Britain's venerable Land Rover and Jaguar automotive brands.

British imperial rule also had profound social, as well as economic, ramifications. British officials tended to base their administrative policies on the assumption that Indian society was defined and ordered by tribe, caste, and religion. With a limited understanding of Indian social practices, these administrators relied primarily on orthodox Hindu and Muslim texts to interpret these categories. Yet Indian identities were far more complex and fluid than the British realized. The designation "tribe," which derives from the Latin term for the three main population segments of the ancient Roman capital, had no cultural or national meaning in India, but British administrators deemed the semi-nomadic clan-based societies on the frontiers of agrarian India to be "tribes." While these early ethnographers assumed tribal identities were fixed and unchangeable, mobile peoples could transform themselves into Muslims or Hindus in the eyes of the Raj simply by adopting a more settled lifestyle.

Similarly, the word "caste" is not of South Asian origin. Based on the Latin *castus* and the Iberian *casta*, it became meaningful in India when the Portuguese used it to describe the various social groupings they encountered in sixteenth-century India. Caste became a powerful administrative tool for classifying and organizing Hindu society under British rule in the nineteenth century.[21] The most influential Hindu scriptures describe four principle castes: Brahman (priest), Kshatriya (warrior), Vaishya (trader), and Sudra (farmer or artisan). This was in addition to a category of social outcasts known to the British as the untouchables, along with over three thousand subcastes based largely on occupation. Whereas British ethnographic experts believed that Hindu castes were primordial and unchanging, there is substantial evidence of frequent intermarriage between the various subcastes before the nineteenth century. The Raj's commitment to codifying tradition, however, encouraged Indian religious experts to rethink and refine what it meant to be Hindu. This was hardly a straightforward or easy process, and the debate over sati demonstrated conflicting interpretations of what constituted religious orthodoxy. Moreover, the hardships and opportunities inherent in these state-backed identities inspired some people to redefine themselves as members of new or different communities. This created complications for imperial officials who sought to slot Indians into easily managed castes and tribes.

The Raj therefore sought to make the relatively fluid caste identities far more rigid. By favoring scripture over customary law, administrators encouraged the development of more rigid and legalistic conceptions of Hinduism and Islam, which tended to fix religion as a social category.[22] Furthermore, the British helped make tribal and caste-based identities more inelastic by setting tradition as the basis of political and social legitimacy. Groups and individuals that successfully depicted themselves as traditional leaders of particular communities were in the best position to manipulate the imperial system. In addition to restricting the lucrative occupation of military service to martial races and warrior castes, British administrators tried to limit the influence of moneylenders in northwestern India by passing the Punjab Land Alienation Act of 1900, which decreed that only members of "agricultural tribes" could purchase land.

On the other hand, groups that had their identities fixed for them by outsiders often suffered under the Raj. The Criminal Tribes Act of 1871 empowered the Indian government to name any "tribe, gang or class of persons" a "criminal tribe." This statute gave the government the authority to confine such groups to a fixed area and to discipline any who resisted with fines, corporal punishment, and imprisonment. Although British officials believed that caste (and even biology) made these groups "natural" criminals, in reality most of the "criminal tribes" were groups like the Banjaras, a subcaste of transportation specialists who took to banditry after the Indian rail system destroyed their livelihood.[23]

The Raj's efforts to use identity to control unrest and punish dissent demonstrates that Indians did not react passively to foreign social and economic meddling. Although the imperial system offered substantial opportunity to a fortunate few, on the whole it was a confining garment that fitted the general Indian population far too tightly. The 1857 mutiny demonstrated the folly of contesting British authority with armed force, but Indians still used their weight of numbers to contest imperial policy.

This was particularly the case in rural areas, as lower-class field laborers, herdsmen, and even village watchmen regularly turned to banditry in times of economic hardship. Lacking the arms and organization to attack the British administration directly, they terrorized landlords and moneylenders who prospered under the imperial system. British authorities attributed these incidents to the "primitive superstitions" of rural India, but in reality, they were a potent form of social protest. Unlike the British East India Company, the Raj did have a small European police force, but its policemen still relied on village watchmen and headmen to assert their authority throughout the vast countryside. As a small and isolated ruling minority, Britons lacked the capacity to discipline the lower levels of Indian society.

Indian peasants learned to exploit this weakness by collectively defying unpopular government policies. With the 1857 mutiny never far from their minds, administrators under the Raj were understandably reluctant to push the peasantry too far in forcing them to meet increased revenue obligations. They tempered their support for the Indian landlord class with legislation designed to offer peasant farmers a measure of protection from the dislocation caused by the Company's efforts to restructure the rural economy. The Rent Act of 1859 granted long-term occupancy rights to sharecroppers who worked a plot of land for more than twelve years, and it limited a landlord's right to confiscate the crops of delinquent tenants. The Deccan Agriculturalists Relief Act of 1879 placed a ceiling on peasant debts and restricted land transfers in order to give moneylenders less of an incentive to foreclose on delinquent farmers. Nevertheless, these palliative measures did not produce significant rural support for the Raj, and large numbers of small landholders simply refused to pay their taxes during the 1896 famine on the Deccan Plateau.

Although these reforms were generally successful in preventing outbreaks of serious rural unrest, the most potent Indian challenge to the legitimacy of the Raj came not from the countryside but from the cities. India's commercial and educated classes rejected their diminished status after the mutiny and became impatient with the discriminatory aspects of the imperial system as the nineteenth century drew to a close. Graduates of India's Western-style universities had few suitable career prospects beyond the limited scope of medicine, law, journalism, or education. They were barred from the upper levels of the government and the military, and the business and manufacturing sectors were dominated by British interests. To make matters worse, the British popular press ridiculed educated Indians as pretentious and semi-civilized "babus" who aped but did not understand Western culture. Most educated elites remained committed to using their familiarity with Western culture to produce a stronger and more economically vigorous India in spite of this abuse and discrimination, but after 1857 many concluded that they could do so without the aid of Britain.

In 1885, educated Hindus in Bombay founded the Indian National Congress (INC) with the assistance of a retired British administrator. The viceroy had hoped the organization would confine itself to providing advice on social issues, but its members used the Congress to publicize their grievances with the Raj. Members called for lower land taxes, a reduction in the size of the Indian army, and greater investment in Indian agriculture, industry, and education. In the administrative field, they wanted civil service exams held in India rather than London and insisted on the right of the Raj's Indian judges to hear cases concerning Europeans. Before the First World War, a few Congress members adopted a more explicitly anti-imperial agenda. In a 1907 address, Bal Gangadhar Tilak declared that self-government could be won by refusing to cooperate with British rule. "At present, we are clerks and willing instruments of our own oppression in the hands of an alien government. . . . We shall not give them assistance to collect revenue and keep peace. We shall not assist them in fighting beyond the frontier. . . . We shall not assist them in carrying on the administration of justice."[24] While the Raj could not be overthrown by force of arms, most congressmen hoped to take it over by opening its institutions to qualified Indians.

Mindful of this very real threat, British administrators tried to buy time and appease the nationalists through gradual constitutional concessions. The Indian Councils Act of 1892 granted Indians increased representation on both central and provincial legislative councils. When the Indian National Congress grew more influential after the turn of the century, the Morley-Minto Reforms of 1909 increased Indian representation yet again, allowing directly elected Indian legislators to propose resolutions and initiate debate on legislative matters. But the Raj's strategy of isolating the most radical nationalists by giving moderate Indians a stake in the imperial system floundered because it refused to surrender its monopoly on politics. In spite of the reforms, British officials retained a majority on all legislative councils and diluted the influence of the Hindu majority by reserving a specific number of seats for Muslims. While the reforms made some political concessions, India would never become a dominion on the model of Canada, Australia, or New Zealand.

British rule would certainly have become untenable had the Indian National Congress been able to acquire a broad popular following, but its influence was limited by the religious and social background of its members. Prominent congressmen were certainly able to mobilize large segments of Hindu society to protest unpopular government policies. Surendranath Banerjea, for example, challenged the privileged status accorded British economic interests by founding the *swadeshi* ("of our own country") movement, which organized a successful mass boycott of British products. Yet the Congress had difficulty forming ties with the Indian peasantry because many congressmen were products of the moneylending classes. These individuals opposed legislation to improve tenant rights and blamed rural unrest on the "drain" of Indian wealth to Britain.

More significantly, many Muslims considered the Congress a predominately Hindu body. A radical faction of congressmen led by Tilak, who was also a prominent Brahman attorney, openly called for a Hindu revival based on a romanticized image of India in the "golden age" before Muslim rule. The revivalists founded the "cow protection" movement to oppose the slaughter and consumption of Hinduism's most revered animal, and riots broke out in many cities when Hindus tried to block the slaughter of cattle during

Muslim holy days. These incidents led prominent Muslims like Sir Sayyid Ahmad Khan to conclude that they might need the Raj as protection from the Hindu majority. Moderate Congress members responded that these fears were unfounded and accused the Raj of intentionally fostering communal unrest to divide the Indian nationalist movement.

Mounting Hindu–Muslim tensions at the close of the imperial century were a prelude to the tragic communal strife that tore India apart at independence in 1947. Although British administrators certainly exploited class, caste, religious, and tribal divisions to prevent the Indians from uniting against them, they did not set out to make India ungovernable by turning these identities into rigid and antagonistic social categories. Most Britons in India were only dimly aware of the risks of attempting to codify collective identities to facilitate imperial rule. India's Hindu–Muslim tensions predated British rule, but the intensification of communal antagonism in India under the Raj was primarily an unforeseen consequence of the administrative tactics needed to rule so many people with such limited manpower. These tactics were so effective that Britain exported them to Africa, and in doing so, saddled their African subjects with many of the same problems that confronted Indians.

Notes

1. Lutfullah, *Autobiography of Lutfullah, a Mohamedan Gentleman: And His Transactions with His Fellow-creatures: Interspersed with Remarks on the Habits, Customs, and Character of the People with Whom He Had to Deal*, ed. Edward Eastwick (London: Smith, Elder and Co, 1857), 410.

2. Neil Charlesworth, *British Rule and the Indian Economy, 1800–1914* (London: Macmillan Press, 1982), 19; C. A. Bayly, *Indian Society and the Making of the British Empire* (New York: Cambridge University Press, 1990), 108–9.

3. Frederic Wakeman, "The Canton Trade and the Opium War," in *The Cambridge History of China*, volume 10: *Late Ch'ing, 1800–1911, Part I*, ed. John Fairbank (Cambridge: Cambridge University Press, 1978), 173; Bayly, *Indian Society and the Making of the British Empire*, 116.

4. A. N. Porter, ed., *Atlas of British Overseas Expansion* (New York: Simon & Schuster, 1991), 119.

5. D. C. Phillott, ed., *From Sepoy to Subadar: Being the Life and Adventures of a Native Officer of the Bengal Army Written and Related by Himself*, translated by Lieutenant-Colonel Norgate (Calcutta: Baptist Mission Press, 1911), 1–3.

6. G. M. Young, ed., *Macaulay Prose and Poetry* (London: Rupert Hart-Davis, 1861), 722.

7. Young, *Macaulay Prose and Poetry*, 729.

8. Jogendra Chunder Ghose, ed., *The English Works of Raja Rammohun Roy*, volume 1 (Calcutta: Srikanta Roy, 1901), 319.

9. Lata Mani, "Contentious Traditions: The Debate on Sati in Colonial India," in *Recasting Women*, ed. K. Sangari and S. Vaid (New Brunswick, NJ: Rutgers University Press, 1990), 88.

10. Crispin Bates, Introduction to *Mutiny at the Margins: New Perspectives on the Indian Uprising of 1857*, volume 1: *Anticipations and Experiences in the Locality*, ed. Crispin Bates (New Delhi: Sage Publications, 2013), xxii.

11. Bayly, *Indian Society and the Making of the British Empire*, 195; Kaushik Roy, "The Beginning of 'The People's War' in India," *Economic and Political Weekly* 42 (2007): 1725.

12. P. J. Cain, and A. G. Hopkins, *British Imperialism: Innovation and Expansion, 1688–1914* (London: Longman, 1993), 333.

13. Cain and Hopkins, *British Imperialism*, 338; Charlesworth, *British Rule and the Indian Economy*, 36.

14. Cain and Hopkins, *British Imperialism*, 338; Charlesworth, *British Rule and the Indian Economy*, 36; R. J. Moore, "India and the British Empire," in *British Imperialism in the Nineteenth Century*, ed. C. C. Eldridge (New York: St Martin's Press, 1984), 80.

15. Moore, "India and the British Empire," 80.

16. Romesh Dutt, *India in the Victorian Age: An Economic History of the People* (London: Kegan Paul, Trench Trübner & Co, 1904), xiv.

17. Charlesworth, *British Rule and the Indian Economy*, 53.

18. Eric Stokes, "Peasants, Moneylenders and Colonial Rule: An Excursion into Central India," in *Credit, Markets and the Agrarian Economy in Colonial India*, ed. Sugata Bose (Delhi: Oxford University Press, 1994), 60.

19. "England has a double mission in India: one destructive, the other regenerating—the annihilation of old Asiatic society and the laying [of] the material foundations of Western society in Asia." Karl Marx, "Future Results of British Rule in India," *New York Daily Tribune* (8 August 1853).

20. Daniel Headrick, *The Tentacles of Progress: Technology Transfer in the Age of Imperialism, 1850–1940* (New York: Oxford University Press, 1988), 290.

21. Susan Bayly, *Caste, Society and Politics in India from the Eighteenth Century to the Modern Age* (Cambridge: Cambridge University Press, 1999), 121–23.

22. Brian Pennington, *Was Hinduism Invented? Britons, Indians, and the Colonial Construction of Religion* (New York: Oxford University Press, 2005), 172.

23. Anand Yang, "Dangerous Castes and Tribes: The Criminal Tribes Act and the Maghiya Doms of Northeast India," in *Crime and Criminality in British India*, ed. A. Yang (Tucson: University of Arizona Press, 1985), 116.

24. Bal Gangadhar Tilak, "Address to the Indian National Congress, 1907," in *Sources of Indian Tradition*, ed. William T. de Bary et al. (New York: Columbia University Press, 1958), 719–23.

CHAPTER FOUR

~

Africa

One of the greatest paradoxes of the imperial century was Britain's acquisition of extensive tracts of marginally valuable territory in Africa. Whereas India made substantial contributions of wealth and manpower to the British Empire, with the exception of South Africa and Egypt, few of the new African colonies and protectorates paid substantive dividends. India had value because the Mughal Empire's extensive bureaucracy had already organized the trade and administration of most of the subcontinent, thereby making tax collection efficient and lucrative. The British East India Company merely had to co-opt this system to tap India's wealth. Much of continental Africa, however, was divided into small kingdoms and stateless societies whose social and economic institutions could not be as easily captured or restructured. There were no lucrative land taxes to be collected in Africa because many of these societies were organized around communal systems of tenure. In most cases, they had a surplus of land and a shortage of labor, which made it difficult to adapt Indian economic policies to Africa.

Britain had trading contacts with West African coastal states dating back to the sixteenth century, but the few chartered companies operating in the region never remotely approached the success of the British East India Company. Britain did not acquire extensive territories in Africa until the later third of the imperial century, when it reached a sufficiently advanced state of financial, industrial, and technological development to intervene more effectively in African economic and social affairs. The impact of this new imperialism on Britain's African subjects was profound. For most people, the loss of sovereignty during the European "scramble" for the continent was traumatic, and the attempts of British empire builders to make their African territories more profitable often had tragic results. Hamstrung by extremely limited revenue bases, the new colonial regimes did not have the capacity to govern directly. British administrators therefore adapted the Indian system of indirect rule to Africa. Consequently, as in India, certain groups and individuals could benefit themselves or at least lessen the disruptive aspects of foreign conquest by exploiting the contradictions and limitations of British rule.

Africa before the Partition

One of the main reasons the imperial powers had little difficulty conquering Africa in the 1880s was that few Africans realized the full implications of the industrial changes taking place in Europe during the imperial century. Direct European contacts with Africa date back to the maritime revolution of the late fifteenth century, when the Portuguese established forts and coastal commercial enclaves throughout the continent. Their attempts to replicate the success of the Spanish conquistadors in the Americas were largely un-successful because most African societies were able to defend themselves adequately. Although Dutch settlers known as Afrikaners established a per-manent colony on the southern tip of Africa in the 1600s, generally speaking, Europeans trading with Africans before the nineteenth century had to do so on African terms. The Scottish explorer Mungo Park, who sought new routes into the West African savanna at the turn of the nineteenth century, noted that the kingdom of Barra had the capacity to tax European merchants on the Gambia River. "The number of canoes and people constantly em-ployed . . . makes the king of Barra more formidable to Europeans than any other chieftain on the river; and this circumstance probably encouraged him to establish those exorbitant duties which traders of all nations are obliged to pay at entry, amounting to nearly £20 on every vessel, great and small."[1] Moreover, infectious diseases kept most foreigners confined to the coasts of tropical Africa, which meant that few peoples living in the interior of the continent had direct contact with Westerners.

British merchants initially concentrated on West Africa after the mari-time revolution. Lacking significant governmental support, they needed the consent of local rulers to trade for gold, ivory, animal skins, spices, and slaves. African states made considerable profits by monopolizing the production and transportation of these commodities. Without military backing, British trad-ers had to pay local rulers like the king of Barra substantial bribes, rents, and tariffs to gain access to coastal markets. Africans therefore had little reason to view the British and their European contemporaries as anything more than profitable trading partners.

The Napoleonic Wars and the British abolitionist movement marked the first substantial changes in these relationships. During the conflict with France, Britain occupied the Dutch overseas empire to keep it out of French hands after Napoleon seized the Netherlands. Of particular concern was the Cape Town naval base, which sat astride the strategically important sea-lanes to India. Britain therefore annexed the Cape Colony as a permanent possession during the Congress of Vienna in 1814. The plan was to Anglicize the territory by encouraging increased British settlement. But most Afrikaners held fast to their language and culture, and they bitterly resented the British abolition of slavery in 1833. Seeking political autonomy, the most anti-British Afrikaners made several "great treks" inland and in doing so defeated or displaced the Khoisan- and Bantu-speaking populations of central and eastern South Africa.

In West Africa, the British government had to intervene more directly in African affairs to enforce its 1807 ban on the export of slaves from territories north of the equator. The political influence of the domestic abolitionist lobby made the elimination of slavery a fundamental goal of British foreign policy, and Britain used its influence at the Congress of Vienna to force the Western maritime nations to sign treaties banning slave trading. After the blanket abolition of slavery in the 1830s, the British government compensated West Indian planters for their losses, but the abolitionists could not offer exporters like Ghezo's Dahomey an economically viable substitute for the slave trade. As a result, most Africans refused to recognize Britain's right to regulate their commerce. Brodie Cruickshank, the British envoy to Dahomey, unquestionably blamed Ghezo and his like for refusing to accept that the slave trade was ending. "What principally struck me upon this occasion was the animus displayed by every [Dahomean] present, from the king to the meanest of his people. . . . There was no palliating, no softening down, no attempt to conceal their real sentiments under the plea of necessity for undertaking their slave-hunting wars."[2] Thus the abolitionist movement shifted the responsibility for the inhuman transatlantic commerce in human beings from the Western nations that reaped the benefits of cheap African labor to the Africans themselves.

While the British government had no intention of fighting wars in Africa at this time, the Royal Navy put some teeth in the antislavery treaties by stopping and searching the vessels of suspected smugglers. Its West African antislavery squadron at one time constituted a sixth of Britain's total naval force and cost as much as £750,000 per year. Yet the squadron interdicted only 8 percent of the total Atlantic slave trade.[3] The Atlantic Ocean was enormous, and the Royal Navy's deep-keeled sailing ships had difficulty operating in the shallow estuaries of the West African coast. Abolitionists therefore pressured the British government to stem the slave trade at its source. Depicting slavery as an African problem, they created a humanitarian excuse to intervene in African affairs. Operating from Freetown in Sierra Leone and a handful of strategic ports on the West African coast, British envoys offered generous subsidies to local rulers willing to sign antislaving treaties.

While Britain had formally abolished slavery throughout its empire, it remained legal in the United States until the 1860s and in Brazil until the 1880s. Few of the European nations that Britain coerced into signing antislavery treaties put much effort into enforcing them, and the abolitionists' moral arguments against slavery carried little weight with European slave traders and African exporters. As the son of the Ibo King Obi sagely noted on being reminded of the evils of slave trading by a visiting abolitionist delegation: "Well, if White people give up buying, Black people will give up selling slaves."[4] Given this reality, it was little wonder that the Royal Navy had such limited success in reducing the overall volume of slave exports from Africa in the early decades of the imperial century.

Moreover, British attempts to choke off the West African slave trade simply shifted it to other parts of Africa. Portuguese slave traders, who controlled most of the trans-Atlantic slave traffic in the mid-nineteenth century, exploited a loophole in the antislaving treaties that allowed them to continue to operate south of the equator. They exported approximately three hundred thousand slaves from Portuguese East Africa (Mozambique) to Brazil, Cuba, and the sugar-producing islands in the Indian Ocean in the 1830s and 1840s. Furthermore, Arab merchants continued to supply Middle Eastern markets with large numbers of East African slaves. The Royal Navy's patrols in the Indian Ocean rarely amounted to more than a handful of small ships, which helps to explain why slave exports from East Africa actually increased after British intervention in the early nineteenth century.

The relative ineffectiveness of the antislavery squadrons led British abolitionists to conclude that the key to eliminating the slave trade in Africa was to provide Africans with suitable economic alternatives to trafficking in slaves. The leading abolitionist Thomas Buxton was the most influential voice in this campaign. Arguing that Christianity and increased trade were the keys to suppressing African slavery, Buxton and the proponents of free trade sought to convince coastal African rulers to embrace "legitimate commerce." They were also forthright in admitting that such a shift worked to Britain's economic advantage. Reflecting the close ties between British evangelical and commercial interests, Buxton and his allies called on their government to encourage Africans to produce inexpensive exports of cotton, cocoa, palm oil, peanuts, and cloves for British consumption. Furthermore, British manufacturers expected to tap new African markets by producing cheap industrial wares to barter for these commodities.

Many Africans willingly embraced legitimate commerce as global prices for tropical raw materials increased over the course of the imperial century. West African palm oil went into soaps and candles and lubricated industrial machinery. In the 1860s, the total value of Britain's palm oil imports alone amounted to almost £1.5 million. Unfortunately, legitimate commerce did not reduce slavery as much as the abolitionists had hoped. In the first place, many successful African planters had never been involved in the slave trade. Moreover, although the gradual abolition of slavery in the Americas eventually weakened powerful African slave-exporting societies, the closure of foreign slave markets simply produced a glut of slaves in Africa. The resulting drop in local slave prices on the African coasts encouraged some entrepreneurs to rely on slave labor to produce commodities for export.

In East Africa, the growing European demand for African products actually stimulated the expansion of the slave trade by encouraging ivory hunters to push inland in search of dwindling elephant herds. Ivory was not an industrial raw material, but the demand for combs, piano keys, billiard balls, and other consumer goods among the growing middle classes of Europe and North America could only be met by the wholesale slaughter of African elephants with advanced firearms. The expansion of this hunting frontier sparked political instability and epidemics by introducing guns and infectious disease into previously isolated societies of the East African hinterland.

Highland communities were particularly vulnerable to smallpox and other endemic old-world diseases because, until this point, they had few direct links to the wider world. Moreover, the hunters often used their guns to prey upon militarily vulnerable societies. They had little difficulty enslaving the survivors of these catastrophic wars and epidemics, and slave caravans carried most of their ivory to the East African coastal trading ports. Muhammad bin Hamid, popularly known as Tippu Tib, was one of the predatory traders. Born into a Zanzibari commercial family, he took pride in his ruthless rounding up of captive laborers: "They called me *Kingugwa*—the 'leopard'—because the leopard attacks indiscriminately."[5] By the 1870s, Tippu Tib was so powerful that he controlled a vast stretch of territory in Central Africa. Horrified by these developments, famous evangelist and explorer David Livingstone concluded that slave raiding was a product of Muslim greed and

African barbarism. He did not understand that it was actually an unforeseen consequence of growing European consumerism.

Yet the social and political consequences of legitimate commerce were not entirely negative. Many African producers and traders successfully exploited the increasing international appetite for tropical raw materials. Palm oil exports from the West African Niger Delta enriched a new class of influential traders who used their wealth and their access to firearms to create new states. Legitimate commerce also often empowered those enterprising African women who played a pivotal role in the production and marketing of the new commodities. These developments demonstrate the inaccuracy of the widely held European assumption that African societies on the supposedly "dark continent" were static and unchanging. Whereas much of the African interior was still isolated from the changes taking place in Europe and the Americas, coastal entrepreneurs with access to international markets often took advantage of the opportunities presented by global processes of industrialization.

Inspired by the rising value of African markets and raw materials, Westerners sought firsthand knowledge of the continent in order to exploit its full economic potential. The Royal Geographic Society, founded in 1788 to explore and classify the uncharted regions of the world, sponsored adventurers like Mungo Park to fill in the blank spaces on European maps of Africa. Although many of these explorers were driven by a quest for knowledge and a romantic love of adventure, the merchants and industrialists who funded their expeditions were also interested in gathering useful economic intelligence about the African interior. These entrepreneurs hoped to bypass the powerful coastal societies that had previously monopolized Africa's international trade.

It is therefore not surprising that Park and his contemporaries concentrated their efforts on mapping major African rivers that had the potential to become lucrative commercial arteries. Park, along with Hugh Clapperton, charted the upper and lower reaches of the Niger in the early decades of the nineteenth century. In East Africa, Richard Burton and John Speke reached Lake Tanganyika in the 1850s, and Samuel Baker confirmed that Lake Victoria/Nyanza was the source of the Nile in 1862. Lest there be any doubt that these expeditions had a commercial dimension, David Livingstone carefully noted regions that were well suited to sugar and cotton production during his exploration of Central Africa in the 1850s. British-born explorers like Henry Stanley, who charted the Congo Basin for King Leopold of Belgium in the 1880s, saw no conflict of interest in working for foreign governments because they were confident that they were opening Africa for British commerce during the era of free trade.

Park, Clapperton, and Livingstone all died of disease or misadventure on their travels, and most of the explorers who survived did so with the aid of cooperative Africans who provided them with food and guidance. Yet this hospitality did not mean that African states and societies were willing to allow the Western merchants who followed in the explorers' wake to shift the terms of trade in their favor. In Central Africa, competition between the African Lakes Company and Afro-Arab traders in what is now northern Malawi led to the Slavers War of 1887. Although the Lakes Company depicted the conflict as a crusade against slavery, in reality it was a struggle for control of the region's lucrative ivory trade.

Similarly, almost as soon as Park and Clapperton had established that the Niger River was navigable, a Liverpool commercial consortium made plans to bypass coastal middlemen by using steamships to deal directly with commodity producers further up the river. The Africa Inland Commercial Company's first expedition was almost wiped out by disease in 1832, but twenty years later British river steamers became so prevalent in the Niger Delta that they were attacked by outraged African traders. Protesting this flagrant violation of the principles of free trade, British palm oil traders convinced their government to provide military support. A Royal Navy gunboat destroyed the offending villages, and by the 1870s armed steamers patrolled the river to discourage African attempts to reassert their commercial monopoly. These military advantages did not, however, allow British merchants to dictate the terms of the palm oil trade entirely. When they attempted to form a cartel to reduce palm oil prices, African producers retaliated with a trade embargo. Africans could therefore deal with European commercial interests on relatively equal terms as long as they retained their sovereignty.

While British merchants and manufacturers with commercial interests in Africa often lobbied for greater government support in dealing with troublesome trading partners, few in Britain favored annexing African territory before the late nineteenth century. During the era of free trade, they calculated that even with the expansion of legitimate commerce, the potential economic value of African colonies did not justify the overall cost of their conquest and administration. Informal influence was still the most cost-effective means of protecting British interests in Africa during the middle decades of the nineteenth century. The judicious application of military force backed up this "soft power." In East Africa, menacing Royal Navy warships convinced the sultans of Zanzibar to renounce slave trading, and in 1890 Lord Salisbury's government transformed Zanzibar into a British protectorate by using military intimidation to compel the sultan to follow the advice of a British consul general. The arrangement was essentially an extension of the inexpensive resident system that the British East India Company used to maintain its authority in the Indian princely states.

With the exception of the Cape Colony in southern Africa, Britain's only formal African possessions at midcentury were in coastal West Africa. British merchants had extensive commercial interests in the Gambia, Sierra Leone, Lagos, and the Gold Coast, but the decision to transform these regions into formal Crown Colonies was based primarily on the logistical requirements of the antislavery campaign. British abolitionists and Clapham philanthropists established the settlement at Freetown in Sierra Leone as a home for liberated slaves and the "black poor" of London in 1787. The latter group consisted largely of peoples of African descent who sided with loyalists during the American Revolution. Although the settlement initially faced considerable financial difficulties, it developed into the main center of operations for the West African antislaving campaign and became a Crown Colony in 1808.

Similarly, in the eighteenth century, British merchants had abandoned their long-standing trading enclaves on the Gambia River due to the French military threat and the intransigence of local African rulers like the king of Barra. In 1816, the Royal Navy returned to the river to transform Banjul Island, renamed Bathurst after a British colonial secretary, into a base for the antislavery squadron. The territory subsequently became a Crown Colony in 1821. In what was to become Nigeria, similar commercial and strategic interests led Britain to annex the port town of Lagos three decades later. The town and its hinterlands achieved Crown Colony status in the 1860s when an alliance of palm oil traders and abolitionists won official support in London for their plans to push their operations further into the interior.

On the Gold Coast, Britain became embroiled in a conflict with the powerful Asante Confederation over the administration of coastal trading forts in the 1820s. The confederation controlled the Akan goldfields, but by the nineteenth century, Asante elites were also heavily involved in the slave trade. Angered by the attempts of British merchants and abolitionists to break their commercial monopoly by making alliances with their Fante rivals, the Asante fought several major wars with Britain during the middle decades of the nineteenth century. The confederation's acquisition of advanced firearms through trade and rent on the coastal trading forts made it a potent foe. Therefore, successive British governments did not try to subdue the Asante until the era of informal empire drew to a close. The region became a Crown Colony only after a major British military expedition ended the confederation's hold on the coast in 1874.

Humanitarian or strategic arguments were the means of overcoming Britain's reluctance to acquire African territory during the era of informal empire. British merchants had extensive trading interests up and down the West African coast, but they could only convince the government to intervene on their behalf if they demonstrated that a region served a larger national interest. As noted in chapter 2, Sir Charles Adderley argued in Parliament that the four West African colonies were an unacceptable drain on the Treasury because they only benefited a small group of exporters and traders. Adderley's anti-imperialist allies were equally unmoved by the commercial lobby's attempt to make a moral and Christian argument for seizing territory. As Lord Stanley put it: "If we talk of civilising the Africans I am afraid we had better first look at home. We have not to go five miles from the place in which we are sitting [in London] to find plenty of persons who stand as much in need of civilising and who have as little done for them as the negro."[6] Adderley's anti-imperial campaign was unsuccessful, but he ensured that the four African Crown Colonies received very little financial support from London. As a result, the administration of the West African territories was left largely in the hands of merchants, missionaries, and a handful of soldiers and officials. One of the main reasons for British expansion in Africa during the era of informal empire was that these "men on the spot" often exceeded their authority by embroiling the British government in local affairs in which it had no official interest.

The West African colonies survived in this climate of financial austerity and official indifference with the assistance of an influential class of Westernized Africans who served as interpreters, commercial agents, commodity brokers, doctors, lawyers, and civil servants. Many of these highly educated people came from well-established Afro-European communities that were the product of three centuries of interaction between European traders and the peoples of the West African coast.[7] It was not unusual for visiting British sailors and merchants to marry local women, and African merchants often learned English and converted to Christianity to serve as middlemen in West Africa's international system of trade. One of the most successful of these families were the Brews of the Cold Coast, who traced their ancestry to an eighteenth-century Irish merchant. These globally minded people often sent their children to school in Britain as they became more prosperous, and so they were well equipped to exploit the opportunities presented by the expansion of British influence on the West African coast.

This Anglicized African community grew considerably in the nineteenth century with the establishment of Sierra Leone as a settlement for liberated slaves. The Africans rescued by the Royal Navy presented the abolitionists with a dilemma because few could return to their original homes. Some were enslaved as children, and others had been criminals or social outcasts. British evangelists hoped to use these displaced people to spread the gospel in Africa and purchased the land for the original settlement that became the city of Freetown. Over the course of the nineteenth century, this community grew substantially with the return of former Yoruba slaves from Brazil and the Caribbean. British missionary societies established an extensive system of Western-style primary and secondary schools in Sierra Leone and the Gold Coast to facilitate their conversion and to prove that Africans were capable of assimilating Christian values. By midcentury, these schools had produced a class of "Afro-Victorians" who embraced the values and material trappings of British culture.

Over time the diverse people of Sierra Leone fashioned a common identity that became known as Krio. Most of them were Christians, and in the 1790s they founded the first Western-style Christian church in Africa, predating the arrival of the first European missionaries by almost twenty years. Members of this Krio Church used high English for their religious services but spoke a hybrid of English and local African languages in their daily lives. They also followed African customs in circumcision and burial rites. These modifications made Christianity more accessible to the general African population, and the Afro-Victorians played a key role in spreading their faith throughout the continent.

The Church Missionary Society's mission to Nigeria was under the leadership of Samuel Ajayi Crowther. Crowther, the first African bishop ordained in the Anglican Church, was born in the Yoruba region of Nigeria and enslaved by a hostile neighboring community in 1821 at the age of eleven. Having been rescued by the Royal Navy and educated by the Anglicans, Crowther took legitimate commerce seriously. In his view, the primary goal of Christian evangelism in Nigeria was to persuade King Obi and other political leaders to "give up the dreadful practice of burning each others' towns, and stealing and selling their poor countrymen for slaves." Instead he wanted them to learn "how to raise corn, and sugar, and cotton, and other things."[8] At midcentury, Crowther saw British soft power in West Africa as a progressive Christian influence.

The Afro-Victorians clearly did not participate in the colonial venture because they were the unwitting pawns of British imperial interests. They helped build Britain's informal African empire because they assumed, with good reason, that they would be its primary beneficiaries. Before Social Darwinism and pseudoscientific racism became popular in the late nineteenth century, Afro-Victorians made up a substantial segment of the colonial bureaucracy in Britain's small coastal colonies. They were cheaper to pay and less vulnerable to disease than metropolitan civil servants, and many achieved senior positions in the colonial administration. Barrister Samuel Lewis was the first African to receive a knighthood, and James Africanus Horton rose to the rank of lieutenant-colonel in the British army's medical service. Many of these Anglicized people believed that it was entirely possible to be both Western and African. Most genuinely assumed that Africa would benefit from the "civilizing" influence of British rule, and editorials in African papers in the 1870s and 1880s joined with British merchants in calling on the government to annex the hinterlands of the West African colonies.

Britain and the Partition of Africa

Most Africans were caught off guard by the European conquest and partition of Africa. Until the late nineteenth century, Britain and its rivals had given no indication that they planned to divide up the entire continent. Even British imperial enthusiasts seemed unable to explain their sudden desire to acquire vast expanses of new territory with no apparent immediate value. Most were inspired primarily by changes taking place in Europe rather than in Africa. Faced with the daunting prospect of the global depression and increased competition from foreign rivals discussed in chapter 2, British merchants and manufacturers lobbied the government to take an active role in protecting and expanding their overseas markets.

It would therefore be tempting to explain Britain's active role in the partition of Africa as an effort to defend its informal empire by formal means. But sub-Saharan Africa was of little actual value even after the economic panic of the 1870s for it never accounted for more than 5 percent of Britain's total exports in the late nineteenth century.[9] To be sure, desperate textile magnates hard hit by the depression did hope that new African colonies might become captive and protected markets for their products, but they lacked the political influence to dictate such a drastic revision in British strategic and imperial policy. Although it might appear that Britain annexed Egypt and South Africa to protect extensive financial interests in these territories, this explanation does not work for the rest of Africa because British investors avoided risking their capital in the less developed regions of the continent.

Britain's annexation of large sections of the African interior was most likely inspired by a combination of economic and strategic considerations linked to the increasing level of commercial and political competition in western Europe in the late nineteenth century. As the declining British manufacturing sector lost ground to continental, North American, and even Japanese rivals, Britain became more dependent on international banking and other "invisible exports" to finance imports of food and raw materials.

Although British bankers and investors concentrated on the developing industrial economies in Europe, the Americas, and Australia, the pressure of increased international competition beginning in the 1870s forced them to consider the economic potential of sub-Saharan Africa and the other tropical regions of the world.

Yet few African societies were equipped structurally to provide suitable outlets for Western trade and capitalist investment. With the exception of a handful of states on the West African coast, they lacked a uniform system of convertible currency, and most of their productive labor was devoted to pastoralism or subsistence agriculture. Unlike the South Asian case, there was no Mughal Empire to do the messy work of organizing trade, imposing a standardized currency, and, most important, setting up an efficient system of tax collection. Most Africans had complex systems of exchange that provided for their material wants, but they had little interest in wage labor, government loans, or railways. Thus the new imperialism in Africa was a largely speculative gamble by Western empire builders that African societies could be forcibly restructured to make them more suitable for capitalist trade and investment. The African interior offered few prospects for immediate riches, but the British proponents of formal empire considered their share of the continent to be a long-term investment. Merchants, long frustrated by the restrictive trade policies of coastal African states, were particularly vocal in supporting the new imperialism. Charging that Africans could not manage commodity production on their own, they called for military intervention to force African societies to abolish their internal tariffs and honor commercial contracts and debts.

Nevertheless, lobbying by commercial and financial interests was not enough to convince the British government to abandon its long-standing hostility to formal empire. It took the pressure of French and German imperialism to force Britain to defend its African interests. Egypt and South Africa attracted substantial levels of British investment, but they also sat astride strategically important routes to India. An influential interpretation of British imperial history holds that the British occupation of Egypt in 1882 touched off the "scramble for Africa" by signaling to the French and the Germans that Britain intended to acquire an extensive African empire.[10] With the discovery of extensive gold and diamond deposits in South Africa, no imperial power was willing to risk missing out on similar riches in other corners of the continent. Moreover, the popularity of protective tariffs in continental Europe and North America raised the possibility that Britain's rivals would no longer abide by the principles of free trade in Africa. These fears compelled British strategists, investors, and merchants to resort to formal empire to defend their interests, both real and speculative, in the African hinterland.

One of the main differences between Britain's conquest of India and its empire-building ventures in Africa was that it never sought to control the entire continent. Imperialists only coveted regions that had strategic value, economic potential, or existing commercial ties to Britain. Although the British and their rivals competed to acquire promising territories, they were not willing to allow their differences in Africa to lead to war in Europe. The major European powers therefore met in Berlin in 1884 to set the ground rules for the partition of Africa. The Berlin Conference established that an imperial power had to substantiate its territorial claims by demonstrating "effective administration" of the area in question, meaning that they had to convince African rulers to acknowledge their authority by signing a "treaty of protection."

Few Africans realized the full implications of these treaties. Those who lived in coastal regions fully understood that the terms of their long-standing commercial relations with Europe were about to change drastically. Africans in the interior, however, were initially more inclined to view the British and their contemporaries as profitable trading partners and useful allies against local enemies. For example, in August 1889, a supposed "chief" named M'Boli in what is now Kenya made an X mark on a treaty signifying that he placed "himself and all his territories, countries, and people, and subjects under the protection" of the Imperial British East Africa Company.[11] M'Boli's Kamba community was a stateless society, which meant that they had no chiefs. M'Boli was actually an influential ivory trader, but signing the treaty with the British chartered company gave him significant political authority. Thus, one should not assume that his illiteracy, which led him to sign the treaty with an X, made him stupid or foolish. But it is safe to say that few of the influential figures who signed the protection treaties fully understood that their signatures (or thumbprints that represented their signatures) meant that they were surrendering sovereignty to a foreign power.

The fact that signatories like M'Boli rarely had the authority to make such concessions helps to explain why empire builders often had to use violence to force African states and stateless communities to abide by the terms of the treaties of protection. Whereas the British East India Company had needed vast sums of money and several hundred thousand soldiers to complete its century-long conquest of the Indian subcontinent, Britain and the other new imperialist powers used late nineteenth-century advances in military technology to carve out African colonies at a fraction of the cost in manpower and resources. Repeating rifles, lightweight field artillery, and maxim guns allowed a handful of European adventurers to kill vast numbers of Africans at little risk to themselves. Imperial conquerors further reduced the cost of these operations by employing large numbers of inexpensive African soldiers and auxiliaries. As was the case in India, they exploited local social and political tensions to convince marginalized Africans to help colonize themselves.

Although many African states tried to keep pace with advances in military technology, the Brussels Treaty of 1890 banned the sale of modern rifles in sub-Saharan Africa. Thus in 1893 it took fifty members of the British South African Police just ninety minutes to slaughter approximately three thousand Ndebele warriors in what is now Zimbabwe. When the Ndebele tried to throw off foreign rule three years later they had only a few antiquated guns and short stabbing spears and shields. As Ndansi Kumalo recalled, the South Africans' maxim guns were the deciding factor: "We charged them at close quarters: we thought we had a good chance to kill them but the Maxims were too much for us. . . . We made many charges but each time we were beaten off. . . . But for the Maxims, it would have been different."[12] During the Anglo-Egyptian conquest of the Sudan in 1898, a young war correspondent named Winston Churchill noted the devastating effectiveness of these new weapons against massed Sudanese soldiers at the Battle of Omdurman.

> The infantry fired steadily and stolidly, without hurry or excitement, for the enemy were far away and the officers careful. Besides, the soldiers were interested in the work and took great pains. . . . The empty cartridge-cases, tinkling to the ground, formed a small but growing heap beside each man. And all the time out on the plain on the other side bullets were shearing through flesh, smashing and splintering bone; blood spouted from terrible wounds; valiant men were struggling on through a hell of whistling metal, exploding shells, and spurting dust—suffering, despairing, dying.[13]

On the other hand, Africans could still compensate for the sudden imbalance in military power by strategy, bravery, and exploiting weak Western leadership. In 1879, the Zulu killed some sixteen hundred British troops at the Battle of Isandlwana after General Lord Chelmsford foolishly overextended his forces. These victories were short-lived, however, and no African state (save Ethiopia) was able to preserve its sovereignty by force of arms.

The relative ease with which British forces defeated Africans on the battlefield helped provide ideological legitimacy for the new imperialism. Imperial apologists cited their military and technological supremacy to support the Social Darwinists' depiction of Africans as culturally inferior. In their view, Britain's conquest of Africa was part of the process of "natural selection" by which superior nations dominated the "backward races" of the world. Even evangelicals tended to accept this stereotype in arguing that formal British rule would protect "childlike" Africans from unscrupulous European speculators and adventurers. This argument allowed empire builders to portray themselves, particularly to the metropolitan British public, as altruistic humanitarians rather than self-interested conquerors.

Britain's African subjects faced a difficult task in determining how to coexist with the new imperial order. In West Africa, Britain made little effort to expand its coastal enclaves in the Gambia and Sierra Leone but acquired the hinterlands of Lagos and the Gold Coast to protect its expanding commercial interests. In the former case, Sir George Goldie's Royal Niger Company imposed "effective administration" on what was to become Nigeria. Adhering to the terms of the Berlin Conference agreement, company employees convinced "chiefs" in the region to sign treaties that declared, among other things, that "We understand that the ... Royal Niger Company ... [has] full power to mine, farm, and build in any portion of our country."[14] Frederick Lugard, a former Indian army officer, used the West African Frontier Force, which was essentially the Royal Niger Company's private army, to subdue the emirates of the Sokoto caliphate in 1897. After that, Goldie turned a profit by wresting control of the palm oil trade from local African merchants. The British government in London tolerated these decidedly unfree trade practices because Goldie checked French designs on the region and paid for the costs of its conquest and administration with company funds.

In comparison, Britain could not rely on a chartered company to conquer the Gold Coast because the Asante Confederation, which was essentially an empire in its own right, was a much more formidable enemy. The Asante mustered an army of twenty thousand men, and in 1874 it took three battalions of the regular British army to break their hold on the coast. The resulting Treaty of Fomena forced the confederation to pay Britain an indemnity of fifty thousand ounces of gold, but the Asante retained their sovereignty for the time being. Even so, the magnitude of the defeat sparked a crisis of confidence in Asante society. An influential segment of the ruling elite concluded that the only way to cope with the British threat was to depose the reigning Asantehene (head of state) and remodel the confederation along European lines.

Unfortunately, the new Asantehene Prempeh I's attempts to update the army and reform the penal code provoked serious social instability. The military and economic innovations that made British imperial expansion possible had significant social costs and could not be readily grafted onto existing African societies. Although reformers might eventually have succeeded in strengthening the confederation, they never got the chance to see their experiment through to the end. British empire builders exploited the confederation's weaknesses by making alliances with its restive vassal states, who did not have any great allegiance to the confederation, and the Asante had no choice but to submit to British protection in 1890.

Most East African societies were even less equipped to cope with the new imperialism. There were no European commercial enclaves in the region, and the coastal Swahili peoples were linked to the Islamic Middle East by religion and commerce. As in West Africa, the authorities in London had little interest in bearing the expense of acquiring formal colonies. Having fixed the boundaries of what was to become British East Africa with its German rivals, the British government turned the administration of the territory over to Sir William MacKinnon's Imperial British East Africa Company (IBEAC). MacKinnon had vague but ambitious plans to develop the East African highlands, and his employees were the envoys who convinced M'Boli to sign a treaty of protection. The IBEAC, however, teetered on the brink of bankruptcy because the region lacked easily exploitable mineral resources, and local African economies could not be easily taxed. Few East Africans in the interior produced commodities for the world market, and MacKinnon could not emulate Goldie's success by capturing preexisting trade networks. He therefore hoped to secure a government subsidy for his empire-building activities. Normally, the British government would have refused to commit scarce public revenues to support such an unprofitable and ill-conceived private enterprise, but it needed MacKinnon to supply "effective administration" to establish Britain's claim to the region under the terms of the Berlin Conference.

More specifically, it hoped to use the IBEAC to extend British influence to Lake Victoria/Nyanza and the headwaters of the Nile. The kingdom of Buganda, a centralized African state on the northwestern shore of the lake, was a prize that attracted both Britain and France. In an effort to acquire Western technology and balance the growing influence of Muslim traders at his court, the *kabaka* (king) Mutesa opened his kingdom to the Christian missions. His invitation attracted French and British missionaries who hoped to convert all of Bugandan society by gaining influence over the kabaka and his nobles. A popular story in Buganda, which is probably apocryphal, holds that Mutesa's Muslim counselors warned him not to trust the missionaries: "In a short time you will indeed be poor and will become a mere peasant for the Europeans do not teach their religion alone."[15] In the late 1880s, the resulting struggle between Protestant, Catholic, and Muslim factions among the Bugandan nobility plunged the kingdom into civil war. As was the case with the Asante, the kabaka's attempts to strengthen his realm by using

Christianity and Western technology produced serious social tensions that left his kingdom vulnerable during the new imperial era.

Frederick Lugard, who worked for the IBEAC before shifting to George Goldie's employ in Nigeria, took advantage of these divisions to impose British authority on Buganda by using a small African force backed by maxim guns to win the civil war for the Protestant faction. MacKinnon then pressured Lord Rosebery's government to help develop his holdings by subsidizing the construction of a railway from the East African coast to Lake Victoria/Nyanza, and he threatened to withdraw from this strategically important region if he did not get assistance. Concluding that the security of British rule in Egypt depended on control of the Nile headwaters, Prime Minister Lord Rosebery declared Buganda a British protectorate in 1892. MacKinnon did not get his subsidy, but the British government rescued him from further losses by buying him out three years later.

The Imperial British East Africa Company begot the Uganda Protectorate and the East Africa Protectorate, which subsequently became Kenya in 1920. The collapse of MacKinnon's chartered company left the administration of these territories in the hands of the British government. Lacking a monetarized economy and well-established international trade links that could be tapped through taxes and tariffs, both colonies threatened to become serious burdens to the British taxpayer. Colonial administrators therefore decided to accelerate the economic transformation of East Africa by using government funds to build MacKinnon's railway. Furthermore, they encouraged Europeans, mostly minor British aristocrats, to settle in the cool and fertile highlands to ensure that the Uganda Railway would have paying customers.

This radical settlement policy required the subjugation of the peoples of the Kenyan hinterland. Most of these societies had economies based on pastoralism or subsistence agriculture, and on the surface they appeared to be much less able than the Gandans to come to terms with British imperial expansion. But in practice their decentralized institutions of authority proved an advantage as there was no powerful head of state like the kabaka to sign away their sovereignty. Furthermore, they retained a higher degree of internal cohesion because, unlike the Gandans and the Asante, they did not try to borrow socially divisive elements of Western culture and technology. These advantages were offset by Britain's military superiority and the unintentional introduction of infectious diseases. The resulting famine and epidemics reduced the population of certain communities by as much as 50 percent.

Some decentralized East African societies were better equipped than others to cope with these crises. The Maasai and Nandi peoples, for example, adopted substantially different tactics to deal with the expansion of British authority despite their shared reliance on pastoralism. The Maasai, long-standing rivals of the Nandi, dominated the broad grasslands of the Rift Valley throughout most of the nineteenth century. Yet on the eve of the British conquest they were weakened substantially by a crippling civil war and a virulent cattle virus, known as rinderpest, which all but wiped out their primary means of subsistence. As a result, many Maasai warriors rebuilt their herds by serving as "native auxiliaries" in the IBEAC's private army in return for a share of the livestock they captured. The Maasai became one of the few African societies to have their relations with Britain codified by treaty. Kenyan administrators subsequently broke these treaties by appropriating the central Rift Valley for British settlement, but the Maasai retained title to the largest reserve of fertile land in the territory despite the fact that they were one of the colony's smallest communities.

The Nandi, on the other hand, refused to compromise. Even though their herds were also reduced by the rinderpest epidemic, the legacy of the Afro-Arab slave traders left them suspicious of strangers. Inspired by a charismatic leader known as an *orkoiyot*, Nandi warriors opposed the construction of tele-graph lines and the Uganda Railway. After numerous "punitive expeditions" failed to convince the Nandi to cooperate, it took almost four thousand colonial soldiers and one thousand Maasai auxiliaries to break their resis-tance. In addition to killing six hundred Nandi warriors in 1905, the "Nandi field force" carried off approximately ten thousand head of cattle and almost twenty thousand sheep and goats. The Nandi had the choice of surrender or starvation, and in their capitulation they lost so much of their land to European settlement that many Nandi had to turn to wage labor to survive.

The formal expansion of British imperial rule in southern Africa followed a substantially different trajectory. Throughout most of the nineteenth century the government of the Cape Colony struggled to find a means of assimilating the Afrikaner population it had inherited from the Dutch. The Afrikaners vehemently opposed the abolition of slavery and attempts to Anglicize them by making English the language of administration. As pros-perous ranchers and farmers, they considered British humanitarian criticism of their treatment of local Africans a threat to their way of life. Katie Jacobs, a ninety-six-year-old former slave who shared her life story with interview-ers in 1910, recalled that her husband's owner was enraged by the British meddling: "He was mad with rage on the day of our emancipation. Early in the morning he armed himself with a gun, mounted a horse, and drove every ex-slave off his farm. At the boundary he warned them that the first that was found trespassing on his land would be shot down."[16] This angry reaction was a key factor in the decision by fourteen thousand pioneers, known as *voortrekkers*, to flee to the high grasslands of southeastern Africa in the 1830s. After defeating a powerful Zulu force at the Battle of Blood River in 1839, they founded the Transvaal and the Orange Free State as separate republics.

Although Britain recognized the independence of these governments under the Sand River Convention of 1852, imperial planners were unwilling to allow them enough autonomy to threaten the strategically important Cape Colony. One tactic was to deny the Afrikaners an outlet to the sea by encouraging British immigration in Natal, which enabled Britain to claim most of the southwest African coast as a Crown Colony. Humanitarian concerns over the poor treatment of local African societies also provided an excuse to intervene in the affairs of the Transvaal and the Orange Free State.

This concern for "native welfare," however, did not prevent Britain from fighting a series of wars with the people of Natal and the eastern Cape to protect settlers and block the further expansion of Afrikaner influence. Hardships resulting from this imposition of foreign rule were a key factor in the civil strife that led the Xhosa people to slaughter their cattle and abandon their farms in 1856. Acting on the warning of a teenaged girl named Nongqawuse that their livestock had been "reared with defiled hands, as the people handle witchcraft," the Xhosa accepted the prophetess's guarantee that if they took this drastic step their ancestors would return from the dead and the Westerners would be driven into the sea.[17] Consequently, as many as forty thousand people starved to death, and those who did not often had to accept poorly paid work on European farms to survive.

Other southern Africans were more astute in dealing with the imperial threat. Acting on the advice of British missionaries, both the Sotho and Tswana voluntarily sought British protection as the lesser of two evils when faced with the prospect of conquest by the Afrikaners or the largely autonomous Cape Colony government. Most famously, a delegation of Tswana leaders visited London in 1895 to personally petition Queen Victoria to make Bechuanaland a British protectorate. But this was not an act of blind submission. Kgosi Khama, the leader of the Tswana delegation, qualified his declaration that "we love the government of the Queen," by saying "we do not love the government of the Cape [Colony]." He also insisted that Britain should recognize that "our law which declares that [our] lands are not saleable."[18] Several decades earlier, Moshoeshoe, the founder of the Basutoland kingdom, similarly warned off potential settlers by telling the Cape Colony government: "The selling, or renting of lands, has been hitherto a practice wholly unknown to us. . . . I could not according to the custom of my tribe, to alienate any portion of my territory without the consent of the people."[19]

This willingness to claim parts of southern African at midcentury did not mean that Britain had overcome its aversion to formal empire. Annexing coastal territory and establishing protectorates over Basutoland, Swaziland, and Bechuanaland was a relatively low-cost method of hemming in the Afrikaners. These measures were largely successful until prospectors discovered extensive deposits of diamonds and gold in the Transvaal and the Orange Free State in 1869 and 1886 respectively. This led British strategists to become concerned that the Afrikaner republics might eclipse the Cape Colony as the dominant political force in southern Africa as their lucrative mineral reserves attracted substantial foreign investment. They therefore sought to annex the two republics into a British-led South African federation in the 1870s. Yet the voortrekkers were no more willing to live under British rule at this point than they had been in the 1830s. Three years later the Afrikaners regained control of local affairs in the Transvaal by defeating a British force at Majuba Hill, but under the terms of the Pretoria Convention of 1881 Britain retained a nominal say over their foreign relations.

This was the situation in southern Africa when Britain adopted a more expansionist imperial policy after the Conference of Berlin in the late 1880s. Although there were considerable cultural differences between the Afrikaners and their African neighbors, empire builders treated the Afrikaners as another African "tribe" whose economy required restructuring to favor British commercial interests. British investors supplied most of the capital to develop the southern African gold and diamond fields, but they were frustrated by restrictions that the republics placed on the mining industry. Led by Cecil Rhodes, the director of the British South Africa Company and prime minister of the Cape Colony, they pressed the government in London to force the Afrikaners to be more accommodating to foreign investment.

As the most influential of the mining magnates, Rhodes often pursued an independent imperialist agenda. He monopolized the Kimberley diamond mines in the Orange Free State and held a controlling interest in the Transvaal's Witwatersrand goldfields. In an effort to find more gold deposits and further isolate the Afrikaners, Rhodes secured an imperial charter for the central African territories that came to be known as Northern and Southern Rhodesia (Zambia and Zimbabwe). It was his company's private army of European adventurers and African policemen that subdued the Shona and Ndansi Kumalo's Ndebele and, unlike Goldie and MacKinnon, Rhodes realized substantial profits by developing the region's gold, copper, and coal deposits. Believing that his personal fortune was tied to the expansion of the British Empire, he dreamed of a transcontinental railway linking Britain's African possessions from Cape Town to Cairo.

The Afrikaner governments of the Transvaal and Orange Free State stood in the way of these grand plans. In 1895 Rhodes did his best to create an opportunity for Britain to annex the republics by having one of his underlings, Leander Starr Jameson, instigate an uprising of foreign miners (known as Uitlanders) in the Transvaal. The Jameson Raid was a total failure because most miners were more interested in looking for gold than fighting Afrikaners, but it was still tempting to blame Rhodes for the Anglo–South African War of 1899–1902. J. A. Hobson, a contemporary journalist and critic of empire, charged that Rhodes and a shadowy cabal of capitalist investors instigated the war to protect their narrow economic interests.[20] There is little evidence to support this conclusion. The Afrikaners did not threaten the mines, and many of Rhodes's fellow mining magnates did their best to avert the conflict because they correctly recognized that it would disrupt production.

Instead, Britain's decision to go to war with the Afrikaners was based primarily on strategic concerns that its imperial rivals, particularly Germany, were gaining too much influence in the Transvaal and Orange Free State. The Germans had loaned the government of the Transvaal several million pounds to purchase weapons, there were over five thousand German immigrants in the republics, and the kaiser publicly congratulated the Afrikaners on defeating the Jameson Raid. Imperial strategists feared that this foreign support and the republics' vast mineral wealth would allow the Afrikaners to create a powerful South African union that would swallow the Cape Colony and Natal. Having failed to control the Afrikaners by less formal means, Prime Minister Lord Salisbury resorted to armed force to unite southern Africa under a friendly government that he hoped would safeguard Britain's considerable economic and strategic interests in the region.

The war itself was a powerful lesson on the risks of formal empire. Although numerically superior, the British army was able to defeat the highly mobile and self-sufficient Afrikaner mounted forces only by cordoning off the countryside with barbed wire and fortified blockhouses and by incarcerating Afrikaner families in detention camps. Almost thirty-four thousand Afrikaner soldiers were killed in the fighting, and approximately twenty thousand of their women and children died of disease and neglect in the camps. The war cost Britain twenty-two thousand casualties and over £200 million, roughly 14 percent of its national income in 1902. It took fifteen pence per head to subdue each of Britain's African subjects but over £1,000 for each Afrikaner defeated during the Anglo-Boer War.[21] Britain's superior military technology made conquest relatively easy, but the expense of the South African war in human life and economic resources invoked a key lesson of the Indian Mutiny: the security and stability of an overseas empire depended on convincing at least a small percentage of colonial subjects to participate willingly in the imperial enterprise.

Africa under British Rule

As the conquest era drew to a close at the turn of the twentieth century, the British were left with the problem of how to govern their new African empire. With the exception of the annexation of Egypt and South Africa, Britain's acquisition of territory during the "scramble for Africa" was largely speculative. Although Cecil Rhodes and a handful of his contemporaries profited from the new imperialism, few African colonies offered much chance of an immediate return on the British government's imperial investment. The Treasury therefore issued an emphatic prohibition on the use of metropolitan funds to subsidize colonial rule, which weakened the new African administrations severely.

With limited resources to hire civil servants, policemen, and soldiers from metropolitan Britain, colonial administrators faced the difficult task of transforming the colonies into profitable enterprises without provoking an unmanageable backlash from their African subjects. In 1898, the three-year anticolonial uprising known as the Hut Tax War in Sierra Leone cost £45,000. Between 1895 and 1905, the East Africa Protectorate (Kenya) spent one-third of its total domestic revenues on "punitive operations" to force groups like the Nandi to pay their taxes.[22] Most colonial governments did not have the resources to fight prolonged pacification wars. These financial limitations thus softened the impact of partition by creating substantial opportunities for Africans who could exploit the inherent contradictions in the imperial system.

Cost and utility were the key factors that shaped British Africa's administrative systems. Lacking even a rudimentary tax base, most colonies struggled to make do with extremely limited financial resources. With the exception of South Africa, few of Britain's new possessions attracted significant amounts of foreign investment. Only the West African territories had the basis of a viable export economy, and this was because of the pioneering efforts of African entrepreneurs who took advantage of the opportunities offered by the global demand for tropical raw materials. Moreover, Britain's attempt to acquire an African empire on the cheap by relying on men like Goldie, MacKinnon, and Rhodes failed because their companies could rarely survive without substantial subsidies. While chartered companies spared metropolitan taxpayers the expense of conquest and administration, these outmoded

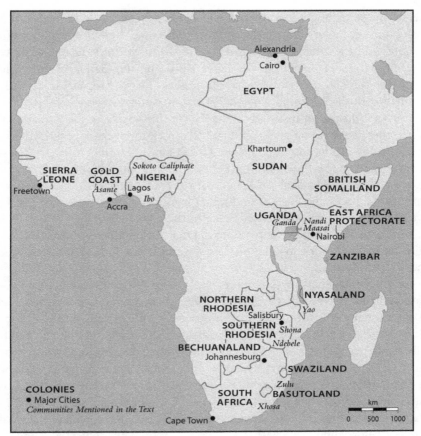

Map 4.1.   British Africa, c. 1914

throwbacks to the "old" imperialism of the early modern era were hardly the modernizing agents that some historians have imagined them to be. Furthermore, the tendency of profit-seeking companies to put the interests of their shareholders ahead of the rights of African subjects undermined the humanitarian ideals that legitimized the conquest and partition. By the turn of the century, mounting criticism over these private governments' excessive use of force compelled the government in London to assume direct responsibility for its African colonies.

Whenever possible, British administrators, many of whom had served in the Raj, adapted Indian models of indirect rule to Africa. Theophilus Shepstone pioneered these practices to govern the Zulu in Natal by co-opting influential local rulers and appointing new ones from the ranks of men who seemed most willing to work with the colonial regime. From the British standpoint, the rulers of strong centralized states like the Northern Nigerian emirates and the kingdom of Buganda were the most easily assimilated into the colonial bureaucracy. But the Fulbe emirs and the Gandan kabaka did not enjoy the autonomy of the Indian princes. These African leaders only retained control of local affairs, and British Residents reserved the right to suppress any custom or institution that they deemed barbarous or uncivilized. When there were no sufficiently amendable institutions of local authority to co-opt, colonial administrators adapted the system of indirect rule to stateless African societies by transforming cooperative local dignitaries into "chiefs" and "headmen." Although they maintained the fiction that these "native authorities" had some form of traditional legitimacy, most won their offices because they were willing to participate in the colonial system.

It is particularly telling that Britain did not rely on Afro-Victorians to administer its West African colonies. Just as the leaders of the Raj blamed the Indian Mutiny at least partially on the failure of Western-educated Indians to convince the general population of the benefits of British rule, African colonial officials decided that Anglicized Africans were illegitimate in the eyes of traditional African society. The "trousered" African thus joined the Indian "babu" as a subject of scorn and ridicule. Although this shift can be attributed in part to the rise of pseudoscientific racism in Britain, it was equally due to the fact that the very existence of the Afro-Victorians punctured the myth of African backwardness that legitimized British imperialism. Successful African doctors, lawyers, journalists, and businessmen made it hard to argue that primitive African societies needed a period of benevolent Western tutelage before they could withstand integration into the global economy.

Furthermore, humanitarian rhetoric about protecting backward tribesmen did not prevent the British government from delegating its administrative responsibilities to British settlers in east and central Africa. Colonial officials encouraged European immigration to the East Africa Protectorate, Nyasaland, and the Rhodesias to build a viable economic base and offset the costs of colonial administration. Although the existence of an African majority prevented them from granting these European communities responsible government on the dominion model, the settlers enjoyed unofficial representation on colonial legislative councils. The Uganda Protectorate, which never had a significant settler population, was the only territory in the region in which British officials openly favored African interests.

In South Africa, the expense and bloodshed of the Anglo–South African War forced the British government to seek an accommodation with the Afrikaners at the expense of their African subjects. Under the terms of the

1902 Peace of Vereeniging, Britain granted the Afrikaners amnesty, civil autonomy, and £3 million in compensation for lost property in return for an oath of allegiance to the king of Britain. Sir Alfred Milner, the high commissioner for South Africa, was willing to be magnanimous because he hoped increased British immigration and the expansion of English-style education would diminish the Afrikaners' political influence. His optimism was unfounded, however, because the Great Trek of 1836 had already shown that the Afrikaners were thoroughly resistant to Anglicization.

Moreover, as tensions in Europe mounted in the decades before the First World War, Britain could not afford to maintain a large and expensive military garrison in South Africa. Imperial strategists therefore came to terms with the Afrikaners. In 1910, Britain allowed the Afrikaner majority to dominate the new Union of South Africa, which finally combined the Cape Colony, Natal, Transvaal, and the Orange Free State into a single federated administrative entity that soon achieved dominion status. Ironically, General Louis Botha, who had been commander in chief of Afrikaner forces during the war, became the Union's first prime minister. Political expedience also forced Britain to withdraw its protection of local African societies and allow the Afrikaners to settle the "native question" on their own terms. This retreat had severe repercussions in the Cape Colony, since the territory's property-based, nonracial franchise gave almost 5 percent of the non-European population the right to vote. The new Union government refused to recognize the citizenship of these elites and gradually phased out their voting rights.

Britain's retreat from its humanitarian ideals in South Africa reflected one of the fundamental contradictions of the imperial system in Africa. Empire builders needed productive and reliable sources of revenue to govern their colonies effectively, but they did not have the means to impose their will on their Afrikaner and African subjects. With imperial subsidies out of the question, administrators desperately needed to develop the infrastructure of the colonies to attract foreign investment. Yet the political influence of metropolitan commercial and manufacturing interests barred them from promoting any African enterprise that might compete with British trade or industry. Colonial officials had to concentrate their efforts on developing export-driven economies that produced minerals and agricultural commodities for the world market. This strategy was scarcely in keeping with the imperial lobby's promise to modernize the new colonies, and the legacy of Britain's neomercantile policies continues to hamper the economic development of Africa in the twenty-first century. Although some administrators hoped that British settlers might provide a sustainable tax base, most colonial ventures were so undercapitalized that they had to rely on large amounts of inexpensive African labor to remain viable. This placed the colonial governments in the difficult position of trying to stimulate economic development without provoking widespread social disruption and unrest.

In West Africa, it did not take much effort for colonial officials to convince African farmers to grow cocoa, palm oil, and peanuts for export because rising commodity prices in the early nineteenth century had already inspired many West Africans to embrace legitimate commerce. This trend continued into the first decades of the next century, and by 1915, Nigeria and the Gold Coast accounted for almost a quarter of the world's cocoa output. West African farmers were so efficient that the British government turned down Sir William Lever's request to establish palm oil plantations in Nigeria. The revenue generated by African commodity production created better markets for Britain's industrial exports and allowed colonial governments to rely on customs and export duties to cover the cost of administration.

This system worked so well that the Gold Coast and Nigeria did not have to introduce direct taxation until the 1930s, but it was not easily adapted to Britain's other African colonies. With the exception of clove production on Zanzibar, few East African societies had grown commodities for export before the colonial era. In Uganda, British administrators tried to transform Gandan notables into progressive landlords by granting them title to large tracts of land, but the Gandans preferred to collect rents from tenant farmers and proved no more responsive to the experiment than the Bengali zamindars. The Ugandan government was free to encourage African agricultural production because the protectorate did not have a substantial European population. In the rest of British east and central Africa, however, colonial officials tailored development policies to serve the needs of European settlers and international mining interests.

The authorities in London came to accept a settler-based agricultural economy in the East Africa Protectorate (Kenya) for a variety of political and economic reasons. It cost the Treasury almost £9 million to build the Uganda railway, and settlers appeared to be best equipped to make the railway a viable enterprise by buying tickets and shipping agricultural commodities to global markets. But settlement meant the expropriation of large sections of the territory's fertile central highlands. Imperial apologists justified the move by claiming that the land was largely uninhabited, but in reality, the region's Kikuyu, Kalenjin (a large umbrella identity that includes the Nandi), and Kamba communities had been reduced substantially by colonial wars, epidemics, and famine. Joseph Chamberlain, the British colonial secretary, even went so far as to offer the highlands to Theodor Herzl's Zionists, but influential settler leaders, many of whom were unapologetically anti-Semitic, used their connections in the House of Lords to convince colonial officials to favor members of the English gentry. By the turn of the century, would-be immigrants to the East Africa Protectorate had to demonstrate financial resources of at least £1,000. Few of these wealthy settlers had much practical agricultural experience, and the protectorate would probably have generated greater revenue through African commodity production because, as in West Africa, the peoples of the East African highlands were entirely capable of producing marketable products for global markets. They also had a better understanding of local growing conditions and had less difficulty organizing labor for commercial agriculture.

In southern Africa, Rhodes's British South Africa Company governed the Rhodesias until the 1920s. Although the region's substantial mineral deposits helped the company retain its charter after the metropolitan government bought out MacKinnon and Goldie, these deposits were not substantial enough to keep the territories solvent. Company officials therefore seized large tracts of African land to promote the development of a European agricultural sector. They made it easy for middle-class Britons to settle Southern Rhodesia because they worried that the colony might be absorbed into the Union of South Africa as large numbers of Afrikaners migrated north after the Anglo–South African War. Similarly, British planters acquired extensive coffee and cotton estates in the Shire highlands of the Nyasaland Protectorate (Malawi) by purchasing large tracts of land, which had been depopulated by a half century of slave raiding, from local Yao chiefs who, like M'Boli in Kenya, did not actually have the authority to enter into such transactions. The South African and Northern Rhodesian economies, by comparison, remained tied primarily to the mining industry.

British administrators hoped European agricultural and mining interests would provide a solid foundation for colonial economic development. Few of these enterprises lived up to expectations. They were undercapitalized and lacked the basic infrastructure to produce reasonably priced exports for the world market. Their only hope of compensating for prohibitively high production and transportation costs was to rely on cheap African labor. Even South African mining companies, which controlled some of the world's richest gold and diamond reserves, depended on poorly paid African miners to turn a profit. Furthermore, the colonial governments themselves had to rely on low-cost African labor to make up for their lack of funding for public works. They needed colonial subjects to build, largely by hand, the roads, railways, and harbors that constituted the infrastructure of an export-based economy.

However, most Africans in the early colonial era had little interest in paid employment. With the exception of the small class of West African commodity producers, many came from relatively self-sufficient pastoral and subsistence-oriented agricultural societies and were willing to sell their labor only to acquire specific material luxuries like bicycles, gramophones, and fine clothing. Colonial officials therefore often resorted to drastic measures to produce laborers for settler farms, mines, and public works. In the first decades after partition, they simply forced Africans to work. Udo Akpabio, a Nigerian warrant chief, recalled being under intense pressure to coerce the people in his community into working as unpaid laborers: "We used to build all the houses the Government required without payment. . . . We were compelled to clear the bush, make roads through the towns and keep them clean. Everybody was employed in this work, men, women and children. . . . If a road was bad, or anyone refused to go and work, the chief of the village and that person were arrested and fined or imprisoned."[23] Most colonial governments even tolerated the continued existence of slavery out of fear that universal emancipation would disrupt commodity production. Colonial administrators thus postponed the moral crusade of the abolitionists, which was one of the main legitimizing ideologies of the imperial enterprise, to achieve specific economic goals. Ultimately, they let the various institutions of slavery die a gradual death by outlawing slave trading and encouraging individual slaves to purchase their freedom.

Colonial administrators developed more acceptable methods of encouraging Africans to work as humanitarian criticism of forced labor mounted. This was particularly necessary in the first decades of the twentieth century after much more brutal behavior by chartered companies in the Congo Free State came to light. The new more supposedly humane labor policies focused on restructuring local African economies through land seizures, punitive fines, and coercive taxation. Most British colonies imposed head taxes on able-bodied adults and hut taxes on African residences to increase government revenues and force Africans to earn money. As a whole, these taxes usually amounted to the equivalent of one to two months of paid labor. But not everyone was willing to work to pay their taxes. As the Nigerian chief Udo lamented: "When the time comes to pay the tax there seems to be a plague of thieving."[24]

In eastern and southern Africa, where settler and mine owner demand for labor was particularly intense, colonial officials adopted even more invasive tactics. Military pacification campaigns punished tax resisters by seizing their livestock and burning their crops. Potential starvation created a powerful incentive to look for paid employment. Additionally, the East Africa

Protectorate and the Union of South Africa established a system of "native reserves" not unlike Native American reservations in the United States. The South African Natives Land Act of 1913 confined the African majority, which constituted over 70 percent of the population, to just 13 percent of the Union's arable land. Africans were over 80 percent of the population of the East Africa Protectorate, but only 20 percent of the colony's productive land was devoted to native reserves. The small European settler community did not actually need these vast stretches of territory and most of the "white highlands" lay fallow in the decades before the First World War. The primary function of the native reserve system was to force Africans to become wage laborers by restricting their ability to practice subsistence agriculture.

By restructuring regional economies through taxation and land appropriation, the colonial governments set in place a system that compelled Africans to travel great distances to earn enough money to pay taxes and provide for basic needs. Their main destinations were settler farms, plantations owned by international corporations, and the southern African gold and diamond mines. Strict racial segregation, known as the "colour bar," prevented African labor migrants from settling with their families in the European areas in which they worked. Colonial administrators argued that this policy protected backward tribal societies from the corrosive impact of modernity, but in reality, it kept wages low by forcing Africans to maintain ties to their rural homes. In other words, the wives and families of African labor migrants had to grow enough food to absolve European farmers and mine owners from having to pay their workers a living wage.

The Consequences of Britain's African Empire

The expansion of the formal British Empire was traumatic for many people. Caught off guard by the unexpected shift in their relations with Europe and the wider world and by the sudden intrusion of militaristic Europeans (in the case of many inland societies), Africans struggled to cope with the alien nature of imperial rule. Many shared the profound sense of dislocation and loss experienced by the Ibo village of Umuofia in Chinua Achebe's classic *Things Fall Apart*. In the novel, Okonkwo, a man of considerable means and influence, is stripped of his status and dignity by the new imperial order and finally commits suicide after murdering an African servant of the new colonial regime.[25]

Yet African experiences in the new imperial era were far from uniform. Some societies rebelled violently when confronted with the colonial state's demand for land, taxes, and forced labor. In 1896, Ndansi Kumalo and the

Ndebele killed over six hundred Europeans in a bloody guerrilla war, known as the Chimurenga, against the British South Africa Company. The Asante followed a similar course in 1900 after learning the full implications of being a British protectorate. Although these anticolonial uprisings occasionally managed to force administrators to temper specific policies, they also exposed rebellious African societies to the full retaliatory force of armed British imperialism. Over nine thousand men, women, and children died during the Chimurenga, which was a heavy price to pay for temporarily slowing the rate of European settlement in the colony.

The Afro-Victorians, on the other hand, had more success in using British humanitarian ideology to oppose the most invidious aspects of imperial rule. The Aborigines Rights Protection Society and the Peoples Union of Lagos lobbied the metropolitan British government successfully to block attempts by colonial administrators to appropriate all uncultivated land in the Gold Coast and Nigeria. In southern Africa, however, humanitarian appeals had far less impact on the Afrikaner-dominated government of the Union of South Africa, and the South African National Congress made little headway in blocking the Natives Land Act of 1913. Faced with increased discrimination under the colour bar, frustrated African intellectuals turned to religion and racial solidarity to oppose colonial rule. In West Africa, James Africanus Horton and Edward Blyden embraced Pan-Africanism as a response to the colonial depiction of Africans as racially inferior. Educated Christians also founded their own independent churches as an alternative to the European missions.

Although this physical and intellectual resistance to foreign rule was widespread and often intense, it was too dispersed and uncoordinated to threaten the security of British rule. In spite of the best efforts of the Pan-Africanists, distinctions in language, religion, and ethnicity limited the scope of their movement. Furthermore, the weakness of most territorial governments actually strengthened the colonial system. Without the financial resources and manpower to rule directly, British administrators could not govern without the cooperation of at least a segment of African society. African chiefs and headmen like Udo Akpabio filled the lower levels of the colonial bureaucracy, and the Christian missions, which ran more than 80 percent of the schools in Anglophone Africa, provided a new class of educated Africans with the means to advance in colonial society. Even the African poor found opportunities in the restructured colonial economy. Taxation and forced labor were oppressive, but British rule also gave some farmers greater access to world markets and ultimately raised the price of African labor. It is illustrative that large numbers of people willingly migrated to Britain's West African colonies from neighboring French territories and, in Central Africa, from Portuguese Mozambique to British Nyasaland.

Indirect rule in particular created real opportunities for people who managed to convince the colonial authorities that they were traditional rulers. British ethnographers and administrators believed all Africans belonged to a tribe, which they defined as a lower order of political and social organization that was less than a nation. They also assumed that tribal characteristics were inborn and largely unchangeable. In reality, precolonial ethnicity was largely shaped by specific economic and environmental circumstances, with Africans acquiring new collective identities through intermarriage, drought, migration, and slavery. Indirect rule ended this flexibility by making the tribe the main unit of colonial administration. As in India, rigid ethnic categories helped the British understand the beliefs and values of their non-Western subjects. This was particularly true in the case of stateless African societies, where multiple individuals and institutions held a measure of authority. Confident in their ethnographic expertise, colonial administrators barely realized that certain individuals were manipulating tribal identities and cultures to unlock the opportunities of indirect rule. The chiefs and headmen who successfully interpreted African traditions for their British sponsors opportunistically redefined and codified marriage and inheritance customs to give themselves authority over women and younger men.

By creating incentives for a limited number of subject people to participate in the colonial system, British administrators simultaneously reduced the cost of imperial rule and diluted the effectiveness of African resistance. Those who worked with the imperial regime often found themselves in the difficult position of having to enforce unpopular policies, particularly in regards to forced labor and taxation. Although British administrators and an earlier generation of historians celebrated these African chiefs and bureaucrats as sensible modernizers who recognized the value of European civilization, many nationalist historians in the postcolonial era branded them as traitors.[26] In hindsight, neither description was particularly accurate. British imperial rule destroyed the preconquest political and social order, so there was little left to betray. Faced with the unexpected loss of sovereignty, African individuals and communities had to find new ways to cope with the realities of alien rule. What nationalist historians have described as "collaboration" was instead an attempt to retain as much autonomy as possible under the new imperial order. Although the British Empire appeared powerful and indestructible at the turn of the twentieth century, its inherent contradictions meant the era of British rule in Africa was largely over by the 1960s.

Notes

1. Mungo Park, *Travels* (New York: E. P. Dutton & Co, 1939), 3.

2. Brodie Cruickshank, "The King of Dahomey and the Slave Trade," *Chamber's Edinburgh Journal* 292 (4 August 1849): 71.

3. Oliver Furley, "The Humanitarian Impact," in *Britain Pre-Eminent: Studies of British World Influence in the Nineteenth Century*, ed. C. J. Bartlett (London: Macmillan, 1969), 130.

4. James Frederick Schön and Samuel Crowther, *Journals of the Rev. James Frederick Schön and Mr. Samuel Crowther* (London: Hatchard and Son, 1842), 48.

5. Quoted in *Africa and the West: A Documentary History from the Slave Trade to Independence*, William Worger, Nancy Clark, Edward Alpers, eds. (Phoenix, AZ: Oryx Press, 2001), 105.

6. Great Britain Parliament, *Hansard's Parliamentary Debates*, Third Series, vol. 177, 7 February–20 March 1865 (New York: Kraus Reprint Co., 1971), 551.

7. David Northrup, *Africa's Discovery of Europe, 1450–1850* (New York: Oxford University Press, 2002), 145–48.

8. Samuel Crowther, *The African Slave Boy: A Memoir* (London: Wertheim & MacIntosh, 1852), 30–31.

9. P. J. Cain and A. G. Hopkins, *British Imperialism: Innovation and Expansion, 1688–1914* (London: Longman, 1993), 359.

10. Ronald Robinson and John Gallagher, *Africa and the Victorians* (New York: St. Martin's Press, 1961), 162.

11. "Treaty of the Imperial British East Africa Company with M'Boli of Ivati, 4 August 1889," in *Kenya: Select Historical Documents*, ed. G. H. Mungheam (Nairobi: EA Publishing House, 1978), 45–46.

12. Margery Perham, ed., *Ten Africans* (London: Faber and Faber, 1936), 71–72.

13. Winston Churchill, *The River War: An Historical Account of the Reconquest of the Soudan* (London: Longmans, Green, 1899), 247–48.

14. waado.org/UrhoboHistory/NigerDelta/ColonialTreaties/RoyalNigerTreaties/ProForma.html.

15. Ham Mukasa, "Some Notes on the Reign of Mutesa," *Uganda Journal* 2 (1934): 69–70.

16. Susan Martin, Caroline Daley, Elizabeth Dimock, Cheryl Cassidy, and Cecily Devereux, eds., *Women and Empire 1750–1939*, volume 3: *Africa* (New York: Routledge, 2009), 43–44.

17. William W. Gqoba. "The Cause of the Cattle-Killing at the Nongqawuse Period," in *Intellectual Traditions of Pre-Colonial Africa*, ed. Constance Hilliard (Boston: McGraw Hill, 1998), 452–53.

18. Quoted in Louise Torr Knight-Bruce, *The Story of an African Chief: Being the Life of Khama* (London: Kegan Paul, Trench, Trübner & Co, 1893), 48–49.

19. "Chief Moshesh (Moshoeshoe) to Secretary to the Government, Cape Colony, 1845," *Basutoland Records*, volume 1: *1833–1852*, ed. G. M. Theal (Cape Town: C. Struik, 1964), 85–86.

20. J. A. Hobson, *The War in South Africa: Its Causes and Effects*, 2nd ed. (London: James Nisbet and Co, 1900), 189.

21. John Lonsdale, "The European Scramble and Conquest in African History," in *The Cambridge History of Africa*, volume 6, ed. Roland Oliver and G. N. Sanderson (Cambridge: Cambridge University Press, 1985), 718; Iain Smith, "The Origins of the South African War (1899–1902): A Reappraisal," *South African Historical Journal* 22 (1990): 25–26.

22. Lance Davis and Robert Huttenback, *Mammon and the Pursuit of Empire: The Political Economy of British Imperialism, 1860–1912* (Cambridge: Cambridge University Press, 1986), 149; John Lonsdale and Bruce Berman, *Unhappy Valley: Conflict in Kenya and Africa* (London: James Curry, 1992), 18.

23. "The Story of Udo Akpabio of the Anang Tribe, Southern Nigeria," in Perham, *Ten Africans*, 62–63.

24. "The Story of Udo Akpabio," 64–65.

25. Chinua Achebe, *Things Fall Apart* (New York: Fawcett Crest, 1984).

26. For example, see M. Semakula Kiwanuka, "Colonial Policies and Administrations in Africa: The Myths of the Contrasts," *African Historical Studies* 3 (1970): 297.

CHAPTER FIVE

~

Imperial Influence

An imperial enthusiast in London might well have gazed approvingly at how much a nineteenth-century globe in a school, office, or gentlemen's club was colored red or pink, the most common colors mapmakers used to designate British territory. In reality, however, this marker of imperial greatness was misleading. As seen in chapter 4, the new territories in British Africa were not particularly valuable, and it is questionable how many Africans were actually ruled directly by the new weak and undermanned colonial regimes in the decades before the First World War. More significantly, some of the most important and lucrative regions that fell under Britain's imperial sway by the end of the imperial century were not colored in pink at all on the maps in London. The Chinese, Ottomans, Persians, and most Latin Americans all retained their formal sovereignty during the era of the new imperialism, but this did not keep them outside Britain's sphere of influence.

The same factors that led to direct imperial rule in India and Africa also inspired British speculators, merchants, diplomats, missionaries, and adventurers to seek greater influence in South America and the great land empires of continental Asia. With the exception of Egypt and South Africa, Britain had significantly more important economic and strategic interests in Latin America and Asia than in any of its new African colonies. In theory, the Royal Navy and the Indian army gave Britain the capacity to color these regions pink on the maps in London. The substantial standing armies in Asia were so antiquated by the mid-nineteenth century that they were easily vanquished by smaller European forces equipped with advanced weapons, and the relatively new Latin American nations were scarcely able to defend themselves. At first glance, political instability, economic dependence, and social strife made these regions appear ripe for partition and annexation under the new imperialism, particularly given that the British East India Company had been so successful in exploiting the weaknesses of the Mughal Empire.

Although the Chinese, Ottoman, and Persian Empires eventually fell victim to their own internal tensions in the early twentieth century, they lost little territory to Britain. Similarly, although many observers described Argentina as a de facto British colony, the nation retained its sovereignty. Ironically, Britain's military and political support was actually a useful tool in resisting partition by rival imperial powers. There are a number of explanations for the reluctance of successive British prime ministers to add China, Persia, or the Ottomans to the formal British Empire. The advocates of informal influence may have opposed taking on the responsibility for governing more non-Europeans after the trauma of the Indian Mutiny, but this aversion to the expense of formal rule did not prevent Britain's active role in the partition of Africa. The Anglo–South African War also showed that imperial strategists were ready to fight conventional wars to protect significant British interests. One might argue that the Asian and Latin American economies did not require substantial restructuring to become suitable outlets for British commerce and finance, but British merchants in these regions often echoed their West African colleagues in demanding intervention to force open markets and punish governments that did not adequately respect the rules of free trade.

All of these explanations are unsatisfactory because they focus on British motives rather than local responses to the new imperialism. Indians and Africans were divided by ethnicity, caste, and religion, but the social cohesion of Chinese, Ottomans, and Persians, not to mention the growing sense of nationalism in Latin America, offered considerable protection against Western imperial expansion. While the Asian empires were in advanced stages of political decay during the imperial century, they retained enough economic and social vitality to give the majority of their citizens insufficient incentives to cooperate with foreign empire builders. Although Britain had the capacity to win wars (and did so on many occasions in China, with the assistance of the Indian army), cultural solidarity and a better developed sense of nationalism made it difficult for empire builders to deploy the instruments of indirect rule effectively. Without the aid of a sufficient number of locally recruited soldiers, policemen, clerks, and headmen, Britain did not have the resources or manpower to establish formal governance in these parts of the world. Instead, British merchants, investors, generals, and missionaries continued to rely on imperial soft power to protect their interests at a time when adventurers like Cecil Rhodes, George Goldie, and William MacKinnon convinced the government in London to take an active part in the conquest and partition of Africa. In hindsight, either social cohesion based on older identities like Islam or Confucianism or an emerging sense of national identity and pride were the best ways to keep empire builders at bay during the imperial century. Conversely, one could argue that the British taxpayer was better served by not coloring these lands in British red on imperial maps for it was more profitable to exert influence than it was to conquer and rule.

Asian Empires

Although there were substantial differences between the great Asian empires of the nineteenth century, these societies shared a number of characteristics that allowed them to resist formal imperial annexation. Boasting populations of thirty-five million Ottomans, roughly ten million Persians, and over four hundred million Chinese in the nineteenth century, they had complex economies based on subsistence and commercial agriculture, extensive internal markets, sophisticated handicraft industries, and well-developed global commercial ties. These economies became lucrative outlets for British trade and investment, but they were highly resistant, particularly in the case of China, to forced restructuring by external interests. While the Mughal example showed that imperial states were vulnerable to takeover by other empire builders, the remaining Asian empires that survived into the nineteenth century had strong unifying ideologies that made it difficult for foreign conquerors to find sufficient local allies to make direct rule practical.

Historically, the Chinese considered themselves culturally superior to foreign visitors. With a sense of continuity generated by a culture that had existed for thousands of years, they believed that their numbers, military power, economic vitality, technological achievements, and Confucian ideals made their culture the embodiment of global civilization. In the early modern era, China acted as a magnet for precious metals as merchants from around the world arrived to purchase its ceramics, silk, cotton textiles, and spices. Much of the silver from the Spanish American colonies was spent this way, with hundreds of tons arriving annually from the West and Japan during the seventeenth century.[1] Confident in their wealth and security, the Chinese viewed every other society, regardless of its accomplishments, as barbarous in comparison to their Middle Kingdom.

The few foreign invaders who managed to conquer China during the course of its long history largely had to abandon their own language and cultural institutions to govern the vast Chinese population, as illustrated by the Manchu nomads who overthrew the Ming dynasty in the mid-seventeenth century. The resulting Ch'ing (now Qing) dynasty co-opted Confucianism as a ruling ideology and governed through the existing Chinese bureaucracy. Although the Ch'ing emperors never lost the taint of foreignness in the eyes of the general population, it took only a few generations for them to become culturally Chinese. In turn, Chinese elites rarely questioned Ch'ing legitimacy while China was the supreme East Asian economic and political power in the seventeenth and eighteenth centuries, particularly as it also became an imperial land power by expanding westward into Central Asia.

The considerable cultural self-confidence of the Chinese was a powerful counterweight to Western imperial pressure. Assuming that the desirability of high-quality Chinese products would force foreign merchants to trade on their terms, the Ch'ings adopted a xenophobic commercial policy that quarantined European traders in the southern port of Canton (now Guangzhou). As barbarians, British merchants had no rights or status in China and had to contract with local Cantonese agents, known as Hongs, to acquire the goods they sought. Confined to specific trading factories the Chinese called barbarian houses, British merchants had little contact with the general population. They could have only eight Chinese male servants, were barred from learning Chinese, and could communicate with governmental officials only through the head Chinese commercial agent in Canton. These restrictions served two purposes. First, they allowed the Ch'ing regime and its agents to levy substantial fees and tariffs on foreign trade, and second, they limited the contaminating influence of the Europeans.

The Ottomans could not match the sheer size of the Chinese Empire but derived a similar degree of cultural self-confidence from their Muslim faith. In addition to creating a sense of moral and spiritual superiority over Christian Europe, Islam provided the Turkish sultans with the political legitimacy to rule a diverse multiethnic population. Taking their name from Osman, a thirteenth-century clan leader in Asia Minor, the Ottomans captured Constantinople in 1453 and built a realm stretching from North Africa to the Black Sea. Their siege of Vienna in 1683 demonstrated that Ottoman armies were a match for any contemporary European power. This military dominance was built on a three-legged economic base of tribute, subsistence and commercial agriculture, and control of eastern Mediterranean trade routes.

The Ottoman Empire was ethnically diverse and included a substantial number of Jews and Christians. Although Islam was the political cornerstone of the empire, Islamic law did not require the sultans to convert these "peoples of the book" (*dhimmis*) to Islam. The main exception was the Corps of Janissaries, which formed the core of the Ottoman military. It was composed of military slaves captured as children in the Christian Balkans and raised as Muslims. To govern the majority of their non-Muslim subjects, the Ottomans developed a pragmatic system that granted limited administrative autonomy to the Greek Orthodox, Armenian Christian, and Jewish minorities. Each community, known as a *millet*, paid higher taxes in return for local control over their educational institutions, legal system, and religious affairs.

In contrast to Mughal India, which was also an Islamic state, the millets gave the Ottoman Empire a degree of internal cohesion by making it possible for Jews and Christians to be loyal subjects of the Ottoman sultan. Confident in their moral and military superiority, the Ottomans allowed Western merchants to establish tax-exempt commercial enclaves throughout the empire. With the aim of stimulating trade, they put these foreigners outside Ottoman law by placing them under the extraterritorial legal protection of their own ambassadors and consuls. These concessions, which came to be known as capitulations, were considerably less burdensome than China's Canton system, but the Ottomans did not worry about their potentially divisive impact as long as they enjoyed economic and technological parity with Europe.

Under the Qajar dynasty, Persia (Iran) had fallen far behind the Ottomans in terms of wealth and influence by the turn of the nineteenth century. Successors to the much more powerful Safavid Empire, the Qajar shahs struggled to extend their authority beyond the capital city of Tehran and relied on provincial nobles and tribal leaders to remain in power. Their hold on the northern territories in the Caucasus and Central Asia was particularly tenuous. Nevertheless, the enormously influential Shi'a clergy gave Qajar Iran a strong sense of cultural solidarity. Claiming that their authority to interpret Islamic law gave them the right and obligation to intervene in the public sphere, the Shi'a clerics controlled the judiciary, ran most schools, collected and distributed the charitable offerings (*zakat*) required of all Muslims, and registered births, marriages, and deaths. In this capacity, they were both a check on the power of the Qajar shahs and Western empire builders.

While the Chinese and Ottomans were significantly more powerful than the Qajars on the eve of the imperial century, their systems for controlling foreigners began to crumble as internal economic and political tensions made it harder to keep pace with the burgeoning commercial and industrial power of Europe. Population pressure in China led to the division of peasant farms into small parcels that were not economically viable, which forced many peasants to become tenant farmers for powerful landowners. By the beginning of the nineteenth century, a handful of rich families controlled more than half of the arable land in China.[2] The Ch'ing emperors did not interfere because they could not afford to alienate the landlord class, which produced the scholarly bureaucrats who ran the empire. The Ch'ing were so preoccupied with these internal problems that they considered the expansion of British influence in Asia a relatively minor matter. Alarmed by growing unrest in the countryside, the Ch'ing concentrated on maintaining the support of the landlord-scholar ruling elites. In doing so, they neglected China's extensive irrigation and transportation infrastructure and failed to keep its armed forces up-to-date.

By comparison, the Ottomans' internal problems were even more pronounced. By the late eighteenth century, the Janissaries had become a well-entrenched interest group that blocked all attempts to keep the Ottoman armed forces on par with their European rivals. This was a serious development because much of the empire's prosperity depended on the tribute generated by new conquests. The second and third legs of their economic base also grew weaker as Europeans opened new maritime trade routes to Asia that bypassed the eastern Mediterranean.

This social and economic stagnation had dangerous political repercussions. Provincial Ottoman bureaucrats often became autonomous rulers as the sultans lost control of their more remote possessions. In the early nineteenth century, Muhammad Ali, an Albanian-born Ottoman general, transformed Egypt into a powerful state that remained a province of the empire in name only. At the same time, many of the millet leaders began to assert their autonomy. The Ottomans were uncomfortably close to a powerfully resurgent Europe at the turn of the nineteenth century and could not prevent the major Western powers from supporting the nationalist aspirations of their non-Muslim subjects in the Balkans.

This growing weakness of the Asian land empires created new opportunities for Britain. British commercial interests hoped to tap the vast internal markets of the Asian empires once the administrative and social barriers that had previously restricted European merchants to isolated enclaves began to crumble. Although their industrial supremacy gave them the means to win battlefield victories, few British imperial enthusiasts seriously considered annexing the Ottomans, Chinese, or Persians. More pragmatically, they sought to use diplomatic influence and the judicious application of military force, or at least the threat of it, to wring specific economic and strategic concessions from the weakened powers in the east.

Influence in China

Although China was never part of the British Empire, it played an integral role in Britain's informal network of imperial finance. In the eighteenth century, British merchants had difficulty finding the resources to meet the public's growing taste for Chinese tea. Lacking sufficiently enticing products, the British East India Company purchased Chinese goods with silver bullion. The Company alleviated this imbalance, which amounted to several million pounds per year at the turn of the nineteenth century, by exporting Indian commodities to China. Just as the Chinese government maintained total control over all foreign trade in Canton, the Company monopolized Sino–Indian commerce by virtue of its royal charter. Any private British merchant wishing to carry Indian goods to China in what was known as the "country trade" had to purchase a special license. More importantly, Company officials used their commercial contacts to export Indian revenues to Britain in the form of Chinese tea and textiles.

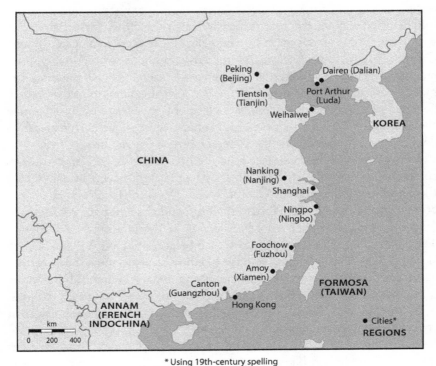

* Using 19th-century spelling

Map 5.1. British Influence in China

India's primary exports to China included raw cotton, ivory, sandalwood, and, most important, opium. Blessed with an enormous internal economy and a sophisticated indigenous handicraft industry that produced valuable export commodities like silk and porcelains, the Chinese had little interest in trading for the simple manufactures of preindustrial Europe. It took a highly addictive drug like opium to redress Britain's Chinese trade deficit. The British East India Company loaned Indian peasants money to grow poppies and circumvented China's ban on opium imports by using the private country traders to sell the processed narcotic to Chinese middlemen. This illicit commerce earned the Company thirty million rupees in 1838; by the 1850s, opium sales accounted for almost 12 percent of the BEIC's total revenues.[3]

The Company's opium dealing attracted little criticism outside of evangelical circles because the narcotic was legal in Britain. Indeed, British grocers and druggists sold opium (most of which was imported from the Ottoman Empire) mixed with chalk, vinegar, and alcohol as a cure for a variety of ailments including influenza, ear aches, and heart disease. There were even opiates especially formulated for children. Having few moral qualms about trafficking in opium, the free traders attacked the BEIC for collaborating with the Chinese government in channeling all foreign commerce through Canton. Hoping to gain access to hundreds of millions of potential customers, they became less interested in China as a source of raw materials and more interested in it as an outlet for British manufacturers. Missionaries, confined to Canton and the coastal enclave of Portuguese Macao, supported these efforts in the hope that increased commerce would lead to greater freedom to seek converts among the general Chinese population.

Free traders and their allies stripped the British East India Company of its commercial monopoly in 1833, but they had far less success in convincing the Chinese to dismantle the Canton system. With the Company finally out of the picture, independent British traders founded aggressive profit-seeking firms that had little patience for bureaucratic restrictions on their activities. They lobbied London to intervene on their behalf, and Lord William Napier, Britain's chief superintendent of trade in China, tried to force the governor-general of Canton to relax the restrictions on foreign merchants. In response, the Chinese quarantined Britain's commercial enclaves. Faced with the prospect of bankruptcy, British merchants had no choice but to convince their government to recall Napier.

Free traders might have had more success prying open Chinese markets if their primary import had not been opium. As millions of Chinese became addicts, China's international balance of trade shifted from a $26 million surplus in the 1810s to a $38 million deficit just twenty years later.[4] The Chinese government therefore had little choice but to crack down on the illegal opium trade. In 1839, it prosecuted Chinese dealers, executed addicts, and blockaded the Canton trading enclaves to force foreign merchants to surrender their stocks of the narcotic. Lin Tse-hsu, the imperial commissioner in Canton, wrote an impassioned letter to Queen Victoria in 1840 defending his government's actions: "Suppose there were people from another country who carried opium for sale to England and seduced your people into buying and smoking it: certainly your honorable ruler would deeply hate it and be bitterly aroused."[5] In taking this defiant stance, the Chinese made the same miscalculation that many African rulers would make forty years later. Unaware that industrial developments in Europe had tipped the military balance of power against them, they did not see the British Empire as a significant military threat. Moreover, they assumed Britain's insatiable appetite for Chinese products would force the British government to back down.

British merchants and politicians, on the other hand, depicted the dispute as a defense of free trade rather than a moral question of a sovereign nation's right to control opium smuggling. Encouraged by petitions from over three hundred metropolitan commercial firms, Lord Palmerston, the British foreign secretary, answered Chinese criticisms by protesting that the authorities in Canton were hypocritically discriminating against British interests by tolerating commerce in opium by Chinese traders. "If a Government makes a Law which applies both to its own Subjects and to Foreigners, such Government ought to enforce that Law impartially or not at all."[6] Palmerston therefore had little reservation in ordering the Royal Navy to blockade the coast to force the Chinese government to pay reparations for the destroyed opium. In 1842, backed by sepoys of the Indian army, armored steamers forced their way up the Yangtze River to blockade China's major inland waterway, known as the Grand Canal. Facing a severe disruption of its internal commerce, the Chinese government negotiated a settlement with Britain.

Under the terms of the 1842 Treaty of Nanking and the 1843 Treaty of the Bogue, the Chinese paid an indemnity of $21 million ($6 million specifically for opium losses), abolished the Canton system, opened four new trading ports (Annoy, Foochow, Ningpo, and Shanghai), and ceded Hong Kong directly to Britain. The treaties also set import tariffs at a uniform 5 percent and, most important, granted all British citizens extraterritorial legal protection. This last measure became a cornerstone of informal British influence in China. It allowed merchants and missionaries to operate freely without the threat of persecution by the Chinese government.

The Chinese did not surrender such a large measure of their sovereignty willingly, and renewed tensions over these extraterritorial concessions were inevitable. In 1856, the Royal Navy shelled and occupied Canton in response to the Chinese government's seizure of a vessel flying a British flag. Although Britain had to postpone further military action to deal with the Indian Mutiny, in 1858 it mounted a joint expedition with the French to force the Chinese to stop interfering with European merchants. The Anglo-French force seized the Teku forts at the mouth of the Hai River, thereby laying Beijing open to a "barbarian" invasion. The resulting Treaty of Tientsin forced the Chinese to open ten more ports to foreign trade, pay substantial indemnities, and allow all Westerners (including missionaries) to travel freely in China.

The collapse of the Canton system opened new opportunities for British commercial interests. Under British rule, Hong Kong became an important entrepôt for goods destined for the Chinese hinterland. In just sixty years it grew from a population of just fifteen thousand (in 1841) to almost three hundred thousand residents, most of whom were not Chinese, and was home to new and influential banks like the Hongkong and Shanghai Banking Corporation (now HSBC). In Canton and the fourteen other treaty ports, powerful British trading houses like Dent and Company and Jardine, Matheson and Company diversified their interests, moving into tea processing, silk reeling, shipping, brewing, insurance, and money lending.

Even though China retained nominal sovereignty over these Western commercial bridgeheads, European merchants and consuls quickly took responsibility for their day-to-day administration. The foreign community in Shanghai grew into an eight-acre "international settlement" with the local British consul and the expatriate Shanghai Municipal Council assuming most of the responsibilities of city government. When a rebel Chinese group known as the Small Sword Society drove Ch'ing customs officials from the city in 1854, the British consul and the local U.S. commissioner collected the Chinese government's customs duties from Western merchants operating in the region. Recognizing the need for a central authority to organize trade, British officials expanded the scope of this maritime customs service to include the entire coast. The Chinese government saw no contradiction in relying on foreigners to control foreigners and found the service's employees less prone to smuggling and embezzlement than its own customs officials. By the end of the nineteenth century, the customs service's British director and staff of three thousand (composed of both Chinese and Westerners) provided the Chinese government with approximately 20 percent of its total revenues.

Yet the treaty ports would not have been economically viable without Chinese assistance. All of the great trading houses depended on a staff of Chinese *compradors* to serve as brokers, translators, and clerks. The term "comprador" came from the Portuguese word *compra* "to buy." Chinese middlemen had played an important intermediary role in the Canton system for centuries but had little freedom to branch out on their own. The expansion of foreign authority in the treaty ports gave them much greater autonomy. The most successful compradors like Tong King-sing, a key intermediary for Jardine Matheson, transformed themselves from employees of British commercial firms into independent brokers who collected Chinese commodities for export and helped local buyers secure credit to purchase foreign goods. Many learned English and adopted Western styles of dress to build cultural ties with their foreign partners. In doing so, they also acquired British nationality to secure extraterritorial protection from the Chinese government, which still sought to curtail the spread of Western influence.

It is difficult to determine the long-term influence of the compradors and the treaty ports on Chinese history. One school of thought holds that the Western commercial enclaves were "beachheads of imperialism" that broke down trade barriers and eroded China's sovereignty by allowing foreign interests access to its internal markets. Yet the overall impact of the treaty ports was quite limited. Powerful British trading houses made substantial profits in China, but their influence rarely extended beyond the coast. Moreover, although the treaties of Nanking and Tientsin allowed Christian missionaries to operate freely in China, the evangelists won few converts among the general population. Chinese compradors were the true beneficiaries of the treaty port system as it gave them greater opportunity to profitably exploit their position as economic and cultural intermediaries.

Many British merchants wanted to use military force to open China's enormous internal markets. But the main commercial firms in the treaty ports had very little political influence in metropolitan Britain because China never became an important outlet for British products. British consuls in the treaty ports could call upon Royal Navy squadrons in times of crisis, but they usually ignored pleas for armed support from frustrated merchants seeking commercial advantages. China's vast internal economy was largely self-contained throughout the imperial century, and opium remained Britain's most profitable Chinese import until the 1890s. In the absence of a viable transportation and distribution system for foreign goods, regional Chinese handicraft industries competed successfully with British manufacturers because they had better access to local markets. In 1903, almost 50 percent of China's imports came from the greater British Empire (including India), but this amounted to an extremely small fraction of Britain's total international trade.[7] Therefore, few British politicians were willing to incur the considerable expense of adding large sections of Chinese territory to the formal empire.

Moreover, although Royal Navy gunboats could dominate the lower reaches of China's major rivers, Britain did not have the manpower (even with the Indian army), resources, or inclination to fight a major war on the Chinese mainland. On the contrary, most imperial strategists recognized the value of preserving the viability of the Ch'ing dynasty. With no desire to assume responsibility for governing millions of Chinese, their goal was to coerce the Ch'ing emperors into opening their markets without destabilizing the Chinese government any more than necessary. Having dismantled the Canton system, Britain worked actively to defend the Ch'ing from their internal enemies and rival European imperial powers instead of further exploiting the regime's weaknesses.

This British aid was significant because the Ch'ing faced far more pressing internal threats as their hold on China started to slip. Beginning in 1850, they began to lose control over large sections of southeastern China as a result of the Taiping Rebellion. Rebel leader Hung Hsiu-ch'uan (now Hong Xiuquan), a failed Confucian scholar and a former student at an American Baptist mission, attracted hundreds of thousands of followers to a movement that embodied the cultural ramifications of foreign influence by combining a peasant revolt, an anti-Ch'ing backlash, and a pseudo-Christian crusade. Drawing on his partial exposure to Christian ideology in a mission school, the Taiping leader proclaimed himself semidivine: "Great and majestic is the Heavenly Father, belonging to all nations. . . . After sending down Jesus to give his life for the redemption of sins, He also sent Ch'uan to proclaim the truth of the Way."[8] It is not clear how many people accepted such pronouncements, but Ch'uan was able to mobilize a substantial army by tapping into popular resentment over Ch'ing policies. Over the course of the fourteen-year uprising, the Taipings caused the death of approximately twenty million people in sixteen provinces, destroyed hundreds of cities, and held Nanking for almost eleven years.

The Taiping Rebellion provided an ideal opportunity for a foreign power to exploit the sudden weakness of the Chinese Empire, but the British government was more interested in maintaining stability in China. British traders disliked the Taiping's ban on opium, and missionaries distrusted their mixing of Christian and Confucian ideology. Recognizing that the Ch'ing bureaucracy served a useful purpose, Britain backed the efforts of a Chinese militia under the command of Charles Gordon, a British adventurer who would later gain fame and martyrdom in the Sudan, to protect Shanghai from the Taipings.

Britain's commitment to informal influence allowed the Chinese to deal with the Taiping rebels without having to worry about foreign threats. Yet, as noted in previous chapters, British empire builders could not rely on informal measures alone to protect their interests when faced with serious competition from rival powers. As latecomers to the imperial contest, France, Russia, Germany, and Japan did not share Britain's aversion to formal empire. By the 1880s, all four nations began to exploit China's military weakness by annexing peripheral territories. France seized the Vietnamese province of Annam in 1884, while the Russians expanded their influence in Sinkiang (a western region). The Japanese, former vassals of the Ming dynasty, followed a particularly aggressive policy toward China. After invading the island of Formosa (modern Taiwan) in 1874, they went to war with China over Korea in 1894. The Chinese were troubled by the loss of these outlying regions, but the real threat came in the peace treaties that followed each military defeat. The victorious imperial powers invariably demanded exorbitant indemnities and exclusive economic concessions that undermined China's sovereignty substantially.

British strategists therefore concluded that they had little choice but to join in this "scramble for concessions." Foreign traders of every nationality profited when Britain forcibly dismantled the Canton system after the Opium Wars, but the new concessions won by its imperial rivals threatened to exclude British merchants and investors. In 1897, Germany used the murder of a pair of German missionaries to extort a ninety-nine-year lease on the northern Chinese port of Kiaochow (now Jiaozhou), and the Russians seized Port Arthur and Dairen (now Dalian). Both powers laid claim to the immediate hinterland of these ports as their exclusive "sphere of influence." The French and Japanese followed suit by acquiring similar concessions in Kwangchow Bay (now Guangzhouwan) and Fukien province respectively.

These spheres of influence were a direct threat to British influence in China, particularly the great trading houses that had diversified their interests by developing shipping, insurance, and banking interests along the Chinese coast. Moreover, London financiers hoped to loan the Chinese government money to pay its indemnities. Faced with demands for intervention from merchants and investors, Lord Salisbury's government leased the port of Weihaiwei (now Weihai) and the Kowloon New Territories adjoining Hong Kong. This forward policy also secured an exclusive railway concession for British investment in the Yangtze River valley. Even so, imperial strategists were still not interested in acquiring formal control over Chinese territory, and the British government supported the U.S. open-door policy toward commerce in China. As the colonial secretary, Joseph Chamberlain, explained in 1900: "We are not likely ever to want to take possession of any territory in the interior ourselves but we ought to try for some understanding which will keep off all others."[9]

Although most of the imperial powers formally accepted the free trade ideals of the open-door policy, the scramble for Chinese concessions continued unabated. By the eve of the First World War, China had lost effective control of almost all of its economically significant coastal regions. Foreign investors held one-third of its cotton spinning industries, over three-fourths of its shipping, and almost all of its iron production and railways.[10] Unlike the case in Africa, China's spheres of influence never became formal colonies. For the most part, the Chinese retained enough political and social cohesion to retain their overall sovereignty.

Recognizing that a reasonably unified China was the best protector of Britain's economic interests, British diplomats and merchants supported the Chinese government's efforts to update its antiquated armed forces by adopting a Western-style economy. Reform-minded Chinese officials used their influence during the reign of the child-emperor T'ung-chih (now Tongzhi) in the 1860s and 1870s to institute a "self-strengthening program" that sought to acquire Western firearms, artillery, and gunboats. They founded a translation institute to gather information on Western economies, political thought, and culture, and broke with China's long-standing xenophobia and isolationism by sending Chinese students and diplomatic missions to Europe and the United States. Recognizing that Europe's military supremacy was a product of its industrial base, the reformers also established government-supervised shipping, mining, telegraph, and railway ventures to reduce the influence of foreign investors in China.

Rather than seeing these independent ventures as a threat to their Chinese interests, British merchants and consuls were strong supporters of the reformers. Robert Hart, head of the maritime customs service, wrote, "I want to make China strong, and I want to make England her best friend."[11] Sympathetic British officials helped run China's new arsenals, dockyards, factories, and schools, and they welcomed visiting Chinese missions to metropolitan Britain. Wisely, the Chinese were careful not to become too dependent on any single source of assistance, and they balanced their ties to Britain by employing private technical advisors from almost every major European power.

Although the Chinese managed to develop a small Western-style arms industry, they were no more successful than African rulers in emulating the West's economic and military success. Most of China's state-run industrial ventures were undercapitalized, and their products were often inferior and prohibitively expensive. Many of the foreign technical experts were more concerned with enriching themselves than with providing useful advice to the Chinese. Horatio Lay, the first inspector general of the customs service, was commissioned by the Chinese government to purchase a fleet of eight

British-built gunboats in 1862. When Lay and his handpicked British naval commander claimed jurisdiction over China's entire navy, the Chinese government disbanded their entire flotilla at a loss of over half a million pounds.

These sorts of fiascoes were expensive and humiliating, but the failure of the self-strengthening program was due primarily, as was often the case in Africa, to opposition from conservative forces within Chinese society. The introduction of Western-style education required reform of the Confucian-based examination system that was the basis of the entire Chinese bureaucracy. Conservatives worried that it would not be possible to acquire Western military technology without also opening China to the divisive influence of Christianity and Western culture. Confident that the foreign imperialists could be safely confined to the coast as long as China maintained its social cohesion, they used popular support to force most of the reformers to resign in disgrace. In time, a reactionary faction of Ch'ing elites recaptured the most influential positions in the imperial court.

While their hold on the government remained secure, the conservatives still did not have an effective strategy to prevent the imperial powers from further dividing China into spheres of influence. Frustrated by their inability to halt the erosion of Chinese sovereignty, in 1900 senior Chinese officials rashly lent their support to a secret society known as the Righteous and Harmonious Fists, an organization dedicated to driving all foreigners from China. The leaders of the movement promoted a regimen of special calisthenics that they guaranteed would render their followers invulnerable to bullets. Reactionary Ch'ing officials promised the Boxers, as the society came to be known in the West, a bounty for each foreigner they killed. Most Chinese Christians in Beijing were slaughtered during the course of the Boxer Rebellion. European missionaries and diplomats barricaded themselves in their consulates and waited until a multinational relief force of eighteen thousand men (one-sixth of which was British) rescued them several months later.

The victorious imperial powers imposed an extremely harsh punitive settlement on the Chinese. In addition to demanding an indemnity of almost £70 million, they forced China to dismantle most of its maritime defenses and imposed a five-year suspension of the prestigious civil service exams in every major city that supported the Boxers. Although the British government took an active role in drafting the terms of China's capitulation, it also used its diplomatic influence to prevent its partners, particularly Russia and Japan, from annexing extensive amounts of Chinese territory. Nevertheless, the humiliation of having foreign troops occupying Beijing played a role in the Ch'ing dynasty's demise. In 1911, it was replaced by Sun Yat-sen's shaky republic, which was too weak to prevent China from collapsing into civil war and warlordism in the decades to come.

Britain did not profit from the disintegration of the Chinese Empire. The anarchy in China's hinterland disrupted trade, threatened foreign investment, and made it harder to protect British interests through influence and informal methods. Yet it would have been a Herculean task for an outside force to impose order on the turbulent Chinese countryside, and the Chinese nationalists never would have tolerated such a high degree of interference. British strategists instead used their military resources and informal influence to ensure that the treaty ports remained stable. The Chinese case clearly demonstrates that political and economic turmoil did not always create opportunities for British empire building.

Influence in the Ottoman Empire and Central Asia

Throughout most of the imperial century, Britain was equally committed to maintaining the territorial integrity and internal stability of the Ottoman and Persian Empires. Yet unlike the Chinese case, Britain's interests in the Near East and Central Asia were as much strategic as they were economic. British merchants had commercial ties to the region dating back to the sixteenth century, but in the nineteenth century the Ottoman Empire's primary value to Britain was as a strategic buffer that protected vital transportation and communication links to India. Similarly, a reasonably strong Persia prevented the Russians from skirting Afghanistan to threaten the Raj through Herat and Kandahar. British strategists wanted the Ottomans to be strong enough to keep the French and Russians out of the eastern Mediterranean but not strong enough to close the Middle Eastern overland and maritime routes to Asia. As was the case in China, they supported Ottoman "modernizers" who sought to revitalize the empire through political and economic reform.

Faced with Austrian and Russian expansion in the Balkans, the Ottomans adopted their own version of a self-strengthening program almost a full century before the Chinese. In the late eighteenth century, Sultan Selim III sent diplomatic missions to London and the other major European capitals to secure Western military technology. Yet, as the Chinese were also to discover, it was virtually impossible to emulate Europe's technical achievements without also spreading Western culture. Islamic intellectuals were wary of the reforms, and Selim was murdered by outraged Janissaries who refused to tolerate the creation of a new, Westernized corps of soldiers.

Nevertheless, Sultan Mahmud II, Selim's successor, recognized the desperate need to strengthen the empire's armed forces and orchestrated a

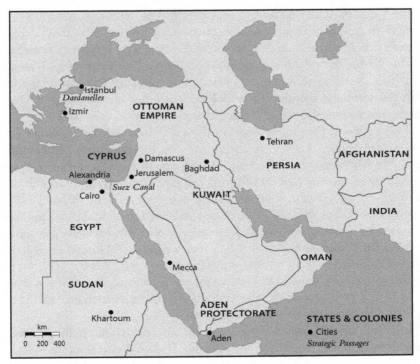

Map 5.2.   British Influence in the Ottoman Empire, c. 1914

massacre of the Janissaries in 1826. He also resumed the quest for Western technology, which had been suspended on Selim's death, by sending student missions to Europe and establishing a translation bureau. These initiatives produced a small faction of Western-oriented bureaucrats and army officers who sought to reinvigorate the empire by strengthening its military, social, and economic institutions. Although they had little popular support, they spearheaded an era of reform known as the Tanzimat ("reorganization"), which lasted from the 1830s until the 1870s. Having begun their careers in the embassies of Paris and London, these bureaucratic elites received support and encouragement from Britain and other Western governments with a stake in preserving the Ottoman Empire.

Recognizing that the great powers used the non-Muslim minorities as an excuse to intervene in Ottoman affairs, the reformers sought to create a more socially unified state. By resolving this "Eastern question" they hoped to end foreign interference in their internal affairs. This was a difficult task because the status of the millets was determined by Islamic law, and Muslim clerics strongly criticized the Tanzimat movement. The reformers used Western support to help overcome this conservative opposition, but they did not abandon their Islamic ideals to espouse Western-style secular nationalism. Midhat Pasha, one of the leading architects of the Tanzimat reforms, argued that Islam was representative and democratic and thus entirely compatible with the reformist agenda. Nevertheless, it was not possible to grant non-Muslim minorities the rights of full citizenship in an Islamic state.

The success of the Greek revolt in the 1820s exposed the growing weakness of the empire. Unable to defeat the Greeks on his own, Mahmud II turned to Muhammad Ali for help. As the autonomous governor of Egypt, the Ottoman viceroy had transformed the Egyptian army into an efficient, Western-style force. Egyptian assistance came too late to forestall Greek independence, but in 1831 Muhammad Ali exploited Mahmud's military weakness by invading Syria with the intention of setting himself up as sultan. Lacking the resources to defeat the Egyptian menace, Mahmud appealed to Britain for protection. In return for driving Muhammad Ali out of Syria, the British government pressed the Ottomans to support the Tanzimat reformers. In 1839, the sultan issued the Hatti-Sharif of Gulhane, which guaranteed full rights for the empire's non-Muslim minorities.

British diplomats hoped these measures would strengthen the Ottoman Empire by reducing the ethnic tensions that had produced the Greek revolt. Lord Palmerston spoke of rejuvenating their "rotten empire" through the introduction of Western-style administrative reforms, for even pro-Ottoman British statesmen believed that the corrupting effects of the harem and "oriental despotism" had robbed the empire of its martial vigor. Led by Stratford Canning, Britain's ambassador in Istanbul, they considered themselves the Ottomans' tutors. Most British merchants supported these efforts in the hope that the Tanzimat reforms would make it easier to enforce contracts and collect debts.

Yet Britain's strategic goals in the Middle East often conflicted with its economic interests. Although British policy aimed to help the Ottomans preserve their territorial integrity, the free traders were not willing to allow them to close their markets to British goods. Generally speaking, the Ottoman Empire exported cereals, raw cotton, dyes, silk, and opium and imported finished textiles, iron, and machinery. The British Levant Company, which held a royal monopoly on commerce in the eastern Mediterranean until 1825, captured most of this trade during the Napoleonic Wars after the Royal Navy drove off its continental competitors. When peacetime commerce resumed, Britain's share of the Ottoman market amounted to over 10 percent of the empire's exports and almost 20 percent of its imports.[12]

Although this trade was only a small part of Britain's total international commerce, it had a corrosive effect on the Ottoman Empire. As in India, the bulk of British imports were inexpensive cotton goods that undercut Ottoman spinners and weavers. Moreover, European merchants of all nationalities relied on local intermediaries known as *dragomans*. Like the Chinese comprador, the Ottoman dragoman was a translator, broker, and intelligence collector. Most shifted their allegiance to their foreign employers because they were often Jews and Christians with little personal stake in the survival of the Ottoman regime. Thus Western commerce had a much greater impact in the Ottoman Empire than it did in China because it damaged indigenous handicraft industries and inflamed existing social divisions.

Recognizing the deleterious effects of unrestricted foreign trade, the Ottoman government tried to assume greater control over its internal economy. In the 1820s, it established state monopolies on key commodities and industries in an effort to generate enough revenue to update the armed forces. It also restricted the activities of foreign merchants and set strict limits on what they could export. Although British diplomats supported the overall goals of this program, they could not tolerate its means. State monopolies flew in the face of the principles of free trade. This is why the British government insisted on their abolition as a condition of its military support against Muhammad Ali. The 1838 Treaty of Balta Liman forced the Ottomans to dismantle the state monopolies and fix tariffs on foreign imports at just 3 percent. As an Egyptian vassal, Muhammad Ali was also bound by the treaty, and Britain insisted that he disband his own system of Egyptian state monopolies as well.

British diplomats further undermined the stability of the Ottoman Empire by insisting on extraterritorial protection for their citizens and local allies. Arguing that the Ottoman legal system was too barbarous for British subjects, they used the old capitulation agreements to undermine Ottoman sovereignty. Joining with the other great powers, British consuls sold British passports and protection to their dragomans and Ottoman clients, many of whom were non-Muslims. Although these special privileges served British economic interests, they weakened the Tanzimat reformers by reinforcing the ethnic and communal tensions that divided Ottoman society. British consuls had so much influence by the end of the nineteenth century that even Muslim businessmen sought their aid in resolving commercial disputes.

Britain also used its informal influence to suppress the Middle Eastern slave trade, which amounted to at least ten thousand slaves per year in the 1840s.[13] The British government forced the Ottomans to allow the Royal Navy to search and seize slaving vessels flying an Ottoman flag. Palmerston was reluctant to interfere so deeply in Ottoman affairs, but the abolitionists successfully pressured him into doing so. British consuls in the Middle East warned him that direct intervention would destabilize the empire because they believed (incorrectly) that slavery was an integral part of Islam. Most Ottomans, who were largely ignorant of the workings of the slave trade, suspected the British abolitionists were exaggerating its horrors to gain further concessions.

The ease with which Britain and the other great powers intervened in Ottoman affairs indicates how simple it would have been to partition the empire. Yet very few British imperial enthusiasts favored such a drastic step. As in China, they were hesitant to assume the responsibility of governing another large non-European population. Russia, on the other hand, had no such reservations. Depicting themselves as the protectors of Orthodox Christians and Slavic peoples, the Russians invaded the Ottoman Romanian provinces in 1854. British strategists considered this invasion intolerable because an Ottoman collapse would have given Russia direct access to the eastern Mediterranean. Joining with France, which was equally concerned with maintaining the diplomatic balance of power in Europe, the British government went to war with Russia in 1854 to defend the Ottoman Empire in what became the Crimean War.

To the east, Britain had similar motivations in protecting Persia from Russian encroachment. In the first decades of the nineteenth century, Russian empire builders seized much of the territory in Central Asia and the Caucasus that had been under the sway of Safavid Persia. A string of military defeats forced the Safavid's Qajar successors, whose standing army only numbered three thousand men, to sign a pair of treaties acknowledging these territorial losses and granting the Russians favorable tariff and extraterritorial legal rights on par with the Chinese and Ottoman concessions. This alarmed British strategists, who viewed Persia and Afghanistan as key buffer states in the defense of India.

Although the Qajars were militarily impotent, they were adept at playing the British and Russians off against each other in what Rudyard Kipling and other popular writers of the time described as "the great game" in Central Asia. Dost Muhammad and the various rulers of Afghanistan were equally proficient participants in the contest. While the Afghans and Persians could not stand up to the military might of the Russian and British empires, they had sufficient strength to compel the Westerners to court them as potential clients and allies. In 1856, an Anglo-Indian expeditionary force blocked Shah Naser al-Din's attempt to seize the western Afghan province of Herat, a defeat which required the Persians to grant even broader extraterritorial concessions to British and Russian subjects. In time, a comprador class developed on the Ottoman model as local merchants adopted foreign citizenship to gain access to markets and escape tariffs. While these "capitulations" were humiliating, they gave the Qajar regime a measure of security by ensuring that neither imperial power would allow its rival to claim too much influence in Persia. In 1879, the Russians went so far as to provide the funding and officers for a two-thousand-man Cossack Brigade, which was the most efficient and professional unit in the shah's forces.

The Ottomans, by comparison, were much less adept at playing the Western powers off against each other. This was particularly true after Britain's marginal victory in the Crimean War diminished their usefulness as a check on Russian expansion. Having expended considerable resources to keep the Ottoman Empire intact, the British government pressed the sultan to issue the Hatti-Humayun of 1856. This "self-strengthening" decree modernized tax collection and reaffirmed the judicial equality of non-Muslims in Ottoman society. Yet the reforms failed to appease Slavic minorities in the Balkans. In 1875, the Russians used a Christian revolt in Bosnia as an excuse to renew their attack on the Ottomans. Faced with the prospect of another Crimean War, the Tanzimat reformers deposed Sultan Abdulaziz and convinced his successor, Abdulhamid, to accept a limited constitution.

The British government supported these reforms and used the threat of war to keep the Russians from dismantling the empire. It could not, however, prevent the great powers from recognizing most of the Ottoman Balkan territories as independent states at the 1878 Congress of Berlin. Moreover, Abdulhamid ended the Tanzimat period that same year by disbanding the first Ottoman parliament and freezing the constitution. The steady loss of Ottoman territory in the Balkans removed the incentive to accommodate his Christian subjects, and Abdulhamid sought to strengthen his hold on the remaining Islamic heartland by emphasizing his titular role as the worldwide leader of the Muslim community.

British consuls blamed the Ottomans' weakness on their inability to implement reforms, but in reality, Britain's economic interests in the Ottoman Empire undermined the goals of the Tanzimat program substantially. Until the Crimean War, the Ottomans had wisely refrained from borrowing large sums of money to fund their modernization efforts. Recognizing that heavy national debts led to dependency, the sultan had ordered his grand viziers to repudiate several unauthorized foreign loans despite the heavy penalties that came from early cancellation. The Crimean War, however, forced the Ottomans to borrow extensively from Britain and France on extremely unfavorable terms. They borrowed 241,900,000 Turkish lira between 1854 and 1874, but received only 52 percent of that sum after the London financial houses that brokered the loans deducted their expenses and commissions.[14] Consequently, by the 1870s the Ottoman regime was borrowing extensively just to keep up the interest payments. This mounting national debt forced the Ottomans into default in 1876. Three years later, they declared formal bankruptcy. European creditors refused to accept these tactics and attended the Congress of Berlin to demand protection for their investments. Even though British bondholders held less than 15 percent of the Ottoman public debt (the French held 60 percent), the British government was unwilling to allow the Ottomans to disrupt the capitalist international network of credit and finance. In 1879, it sent warships of the Royal Navy into the eastern Mediterranean to remind them of their fiscal responsibilities.

More significantly, three years later Britain joined with France in forming the Ottoman Public Debt Commission to manage the empire's finances. Led by a seven-member council representing the major European creditors, the commission assumed control of the empire's taxes and tariffs on salt, stamps, spirits, fish, tobacco, and silk, as well as the tribute of several major provinces, to fund the Ottomans' national debt. From 1881 to 1914 it appropriated approximately one-quarter of all government revenues. With a staff of almost ten thousand employees on the eve of the First World War, the commission undermined Ottoman sovereignty severely by capturing the most viable sectors of their economy.

Imperial strategists therefore began to reconsider their support for the Ottomans as the empire grew markedly weaker in the final decades of the nineteenth century. In 1878, Britain annexed Cyprus, abandoning its long-standing reluctance to acquire Ottoman territory. The island itself had little inherent economic value, but its strategic location in the eastern Mediterranean gave Britain the capacity to close the Dardanelles to the Russian navy in time of war. Moreover, the opening of the Suez Canal in 1869 shortened the passage to India markedly and shifted Britain's strategic focus in the Middle East from defending Turkey and the Dardanelles to ensuring that Egypt remained open to British commerce and influence.

British diplomats therefore began to take a much greater interest in Egyptian affairs. Although the heirs of Muhammad Ali remained nominal vassals of the Ottoman sultan, by midcentury they secured the hereditary right to rule Egypt as autonomous *khedives* (a Persian title meaning lord or master). In the 1860s, Khedive Ismail presided over an economic boom driven primarily by rising cotton prices brought on by the U.S. Civil War. Ismail continued his grandfather's efforts to remake Egypt along Western lines, declaring: "My country is no longer in Africa, we are now part of Europe." Ismail borrowed heavily on future cotton earnings to introduce Western technology and amenities into Egypt but was caught off-guard when global cotton prices dropped after peace returned to the United States. By the 1870s, the khedive was so deeply in debt that, as was the case with his Ottoman suzerain, he had to borrow continuously to pay the interest on his previous loans.

Ismail's insolvency allowed Britain to acquire considerable influence in Egyptian internal affairs. In 1875, Prime Minister Benjamin Disraeli bought the Egyptian government's 44 percent share of the Suez Canal for just £4 million. The purchase made sense from a strategic point of view because 80 percent of canal traffic in the 1870s was British. When Ismail finally defaulted on his loans in 1876, the British government joined with his other European creditors in forming a debt commission to take control of Egypt's economic affairs. They diverted revenues from state railways, telegraphs, and customs receipts, as well as taxes from four provinces (which amounted to almost 60 percent of the national budget in 1880), to service the Egyptian national debt of almost £100 million.[15] In addition to managing Egypt's finances, Europeans also organized and ran its cotton trade, banking sector, and telegraph and postal systems. By 1881, there were over ninety thousand foreigners living in Egypt, most of whom enjoyed extraterritorial legal protection under the Ottoman capitulation treaties.

While a growing number of Egyptians came to view the extraterritorial concessions as humiliating and debilitating, Shah Naser al-Din and the Qajar elites were adept at profiting from their supposed weakness. Under the terms of the capitulations spelled out in the 1857 Treaty of Paris that ended the Anglo-Persian War, British and Russian subjects were exempt from high import tariffs and the jurisdiction of the Islamic courts. In 1872, Baron Julius de Reuter, a nationalized Briton who founded the Reuters news service, negotiated an agreement with Naser al-Din that gave him the exclusive right to collect customs duties, finance a state bank, develop all nonprecious metal deposits in Persia, and broker the construction of railways, canals, telegraph lines, and irrigation systems. In return, the shah was to receive a flat payment of £40,000 and 60 percent of all profits on the concessions. Russian opposition and an intense public backlash forced Naser al-Din to cancel Reuter's concession, but that was the point. Knowing the arrangement was unworkable, the shah and his ambassador in London pocketed Reuter's "faith money," plus as much as £50,000 Reuter spent on presents and other sorts of bribes. Far from being helpless pawns of foreign speculators and empire builders, the Qajar elites were, to use John Galbraith's phrase, experts at "fleecing would-be fleecers."[16]

Reuter's gamble reflected the growing interest of British investors and merchants in Persia in the final decades of the nineteenth century. Their hope was that an improved railway network would create new outlets for British goods and capital. But this increased speculation and commercial activity did not bring about a substantial shift in British foreign or imperial policy. The British government was entirely unmoved by Reuter's pleas to pressure the shah on his behalf, as were the Russians when the hapless speculator approached them for support. And when the British and Russians became more circumspect about investing in Persia, Naser al-Din simply encouraged American and French speculators to consider bidding for his railway concessions.

Most of these revenues went to fund Naser al-Din's lavish court life, which led the Shi'a clergy and most ordinary Persians to lose patience with his corrupt rule. Needing revenue to upgrade the military, bureaucracy, and infrastructure, Naser al-Din raised additional money through the crass sale of titles, the right to collect taxes, and even high administrative offices. In 1891, the shah went too far by selling a fifty-year monopoly on the sale and export of tobacco to an Englishman named Major Talbott in return for a personal "gift" of £25,000. The state was to receive an annual rent of £15,000 and 25 percent of the profits. The Shi'a imams responded by issuing a religious ruling (*fatwa*) declaring that the consumption of tobacco was sinful, and they forced the annulment of Talbott's concession by organizing a highly successful boycott of the product. This hostility made Persia a risky place to invest, and when a Belgian firm actually managed to construct a railway line to a prominent Shi'a shrine a crowd ripped it up after one of the trams accidentally ran over a pilgrim. While the concessions may have been profitable for connected persons, they undercut Naser al-Din's legitimacy. In 1896, a militant reformer assassinated him during public prayers, and a decade later an alliance of intellectuals, reformers, clerics, merchants, artisans, and other groups that had been hurt by the capitulations forced his son and successor Mozaffar al-Din to call a national assembly and accept constitutional limits on his rule.

Similar grievances led Egyptians to challenge Khedive Ismail over his tolerance of increased foreign interference. Ismail himself was deposed by his European creditors (who acted with the tacit assent of Sultan Abdulhamid) for trying to regain control of his finances in 1879. His son Tewfiq had considerable difficulty containing the growing hostility of native-born Egyptians (who considered the Turkish-speaking khedives foreigners) toward his government and the restrictive policies of the debt commission he was bound to uphold. In 1882, Colonel Urabi Pasha led middle-ranking Egyptian army officers in a popular revolt that forced Tewfiq to accept a council of nationalist Egyptian ministers.

Faced with the prospect that the new regime might repudiate its financial responsibilities, British bondholders, who held the majority of the Egyptian debt, lobbied their government for protection. British politicians of both parties usually refused to use state resources to support private economic interests, but Prime Minister William Gladstone made an exception in Egypt. Fearing that French investors would acquire too much influence if he hesitated, the Liberal prime minister sent the Royal Navy to the Egyptian port of Alexandria to demonstrate Britain's resolve. Gladstone did not intend to add Egypt to Britain's formal empire. He had originally hoped to work in cooperation with the French but was forced to act alone when the French Chamber of Deputies refused to take part in the operation. Gladstone's primary goal was to strengthen Britain's informal influence in Egypt through the threat of military intervention, not to expand the formal empire.

Nevertheless, Britain found itself in the difficult position of having to occupy Egypt in the summer of 1882. Although Gladstone denied having imperial designs on Egypt, the men on the spot had other ideas. The commander of the Royal Navy flotilla ignited a wave of violent antiforeign riots in Alexandria by opening fire on the city after its shore batteries refused his demands to surrender. Claiming to be the protector of Tewfiq and the Suez Canal, a British expeditionary force landed in Egypt to restore order and expel Urabi Pasha from the Egyptian government. While imperial strategists claimed that they had acted to defend the canal, it was never in much danger. The Suez Canal was over a hundred miles from Alexandria and was never threatened by Urabi and the nationalists. In hindsight, the canal and the riots provided the supporters of the bondholders with an excuse to gain government protection for their Egyptian investments.

Gladstone promised that the British occupation was a temporary measure intended only to reestablish Egyptian financial responsibility. But he could not follow through on the promise to withdraw because outraged French officials blocked his attempt to secure international recognition for Britain's informal role as the primary tutor and sponsor of the Egyptian government. More importantly, no British politician was willing to surrender the strategically important Suez Canal. Thus the Gladstone government grudgingly assumed greater responsibility for governing Egypt.

This commitment also forced Britain to extend its influence into the Sudan. Imperial strategists had previously been content to leave the territory in the hands of Muhammad Ahmed, commonly known as the Mahdi, even though in 1885 he had massacred the famous general Sir Charles Gordon (who rose to fame defending Shanghai from the Taipings) along with the Egyptian garrison of Khartoum. Yet, as the unofficial rulers of Egypt, British officials in Cairo had to send an Anglo-Egyptian force to reoccupy the region in the late 1890s to prevent France and the other imperial rivals from controlling the upper reaches of the Nile.

In governing Egypt, Britain preserved the khedival administration to reduce costs and avoid provoking the nation's other European creditors. Tewfiq and his ministers retained their nominal authority but were now responsible to the consul general Lord Cromer. A British advisor ran each Egyptian government ministry, and by the turn of the century, there were over one thousand generously paid British civil servants in the country. Britain administered the Sudan, which was technically an Egyptian colony, through a cadre of British advisors and a bureaucracy paid for and staffed by the Egyptian government. Egypt itself technically remained an autonomous province of the Ottoman Empire until the eve of the First World War, but by this point it was essentially an informal British protectorate.

The failure of the Tanzimat reforms allowed British imperialists to justify these blatant infringements of Ottoman sovereignty on moralistic grounds. Adbulhamid's suspension of the constitution of 1876 and his brutal suppression of a Christian uprising in Bulgaria in the 1880s angered humanitarians in Britain. Arguing in favor of a moral basis for British foreign policy, Gladstone branded the Ottomans inhumane oppressors of non-Muslim minorities. The International Anti-Slavery Society, incensed by the continued toleration of slavery in the empire, issued its "Address to Electors of Great Britain" during the elections of 1880, which pressed politicians of both parties to revise their pro-Ottoman foreign policies. Palmerston and Canning styled themselves as "tutors" of the Tanzimat reformers, but their successors considered Abdulhamid an illiberal Asian despot who trampled on the freedom of his subjects.

Britain's declining economic interests in the eastern Mediterranean made it relatively easy for imperial strategists to abandon the Ottomans. In 1880, 45 percent of the Ottomans' imports came from Britain, but in the first decade of the twentieth century British manufacturers supplied less than a quarter of the empire's imports. Overall, the Ottomans accounted for less than 2 percent of Britain's overseas exports during this period.[17] A community of British speculators held a substantial stake in the production of dyes, raw cotton, grapes, and opium around the Turkish port of Izmir, and India-based shippers and traders had extensive interests in the Persian Gulf. Yet, for the most part, British investors generally avoided the Ottoman Empire. Put off by the empire's default in 1876, London financiers sold most of their Ottoman holdings to French and German concerns by the turn of the century. The British government tried to preserve its influence in the eastern Mediterranean and the Middle East by lending unofficial support to the

National Bank of Turkey, but the bank failed in 1913 when British investors refused to risk their money in the Ottoman Empire.

Anglo-Ottoman relations declined even further after the revolt of the Young Turks in 1908. They forced Abdulhamid to restore the 1876 constitution and then replaced him one year later with his younger brother, who was little more than a figurehead. The Young Turks were primarily young army officers and political refugees who imbibed the lessons of revolutionary nationalism during exile in the major capitals of Europe. Their goal was to prevent the further dismemberment of the empire, particularly in the Balkans, through a renewed program of political and military reform. Unlike their Tanzimat predecessors, however, they did so by emphasizing secular (which in practice meant Turkish) nationalism over the Pan-Islamicism of Abdulhamid. Their Committee of Union and Progress, which governed the empire during the final years of the imperial century, suppressed all alternative political associations based on ethnic or religious identities, essentially spelling the end of the millet system. This was a pragmatic step, for the seemingly endless series of revolts and uprisings in the Balkans demonstrated that there was little possibility of winning the allegiance of the empire's remaining non-Muslim minorities.

At first glance, it might have appeared that Britain would have welcomed the Young Turks' efforts to strengthen what was left of the empire. This was not the case. With the acquisition of Egypt, imperial planners no longer felt the need to defend the routes to India by propping up the Ottomans. On the contrary, both Abdulhamid and the Committee of Union and Progress endangered British interests in the Middle East by forming close relations with Germany. British strategists saw German plans for a Berlin-to-Baghdad railway as a threat to their influence in the Persian Gulf and, by extension, the security of India. It therefore became more practical for the British government to ally itself with Russia, an Ottoman foe of long standing, than to continue to support the territorial integrity of the empire. This Anglo-Russian entente, coupled with British meddling in Arabia, brought the Young Turks into the First World War on the side of the Germans. As a result, Britain willingly participated in the final dissolution of the Ottoman Empire after the defeat of the Central Powers in 1918.

Similarly, the political turmoil ensuing from Shah Mozaffar al-Din's constitutional concessions led British strategists to put aside their long-running competition with Russia for imperial influence in Persia and Afghanistan. Fed up with decades of foreign meddling, a wide segment of the Persian population came to embrace political reform, self-strengthening, and a growing sense of nationalism. The German threat gave British strategists the opportunity to bring the great game in Central Asia to an end once the tsarist government became more accommodative after its defeat by the Japanese in the Russo-Japanese war and the ensuing 1905 Russian revolution. In 1907, an Anglo-Russian Convention divided Persia into British, Russian, and "neutral" spheres of influence, which brought southern Persia into the informal subempire of the Raj. Political officers posted from the Government of India's Foreign Department imposed a measure of stability in the region by helping the local civil authorities, tribal leaders, clerical elites, and large landowners manage their finances, uphold law and order, and develop its natural resources. These British consuls were largely removed from the revolutionary turmoil taking place in Teheran (which fell in the Russian sphere), but their activities undermined the legitimacy of the Qajar regime and thus contributed indirectly to its demise.

Influence in South America

While many South American nations also fell within the British imperial sphere of influence in the nineteenth century, their relations with Britain differed substantially from those of the Asian empires. In contrast to the venerable Chinese, Ottoman, and Persian Empires, the South American nations were new states born of the breakup of the Spanish and Portuguese overseas empires. While they suffered from deep social divisions that often resulted in tyranny and civil war, their ability to avoid annexation into the formal British Empire over the course of the nineteenth century stemmed from an emerging sense of nationalism that would have made long-term rule by a foreign power violently difficult and thus uneconomical.

Equally significant, British strategists saw little reason to burden Britain with expensive wars of conquest in South America. In the first decades of the nineteenth century, their main goals were to get the new nations in the Western hemisphere to renounce slavery and grant Britain most favored nation status in terms of trade. British views of Latin America were mixed during this period. Philanthropically minded Britons took pride in helping to break up the allegedly despotic Spanish and Portuguese empires, but conservatives viewed the rulers of the new republics as semicivilized radicals who required constant discipline. Once the threat of American and French intervention in the region helped overcome this hesitancy to recognize the former colonies as sovereign nations, the main aim of British foreign policy was to protect British commercial interests by promoting political stability. Having abandoned a plan to annex the estuary of the River Platt, Britain's only significant territorial acquisition in nineteenth-century South America was its reassertion of sovereignty over the Falkland Islands (which had been a bone of contention with Spain since the 1770s) to establish a naval base and claim fishing rights in the area.

This lack of significant strategic interests in the region meant that, as was norm during most of the imperial century, British merchants and investors could not expect the metropolitan government to intervene on their behalf if they undertook risky speculative ventures. So long as the South American republics respected international law and did not threaten British lives or property, they were safe from British empire builders. Such intervention was rarely necessary, and the continent became a lucrative destination for British trade and investment. South Americans sold Britain cereal crops, beef, coffee, and minerals and in return purchased British textiles, railway equipment, and other capital goods. In the 1820s, South America accounted for 13 percent of Britain's total exports. By the eve of the First World War, the total value of this trade was £1.1 billion, which was more than any other colony or region in the British Empire except India. Similarly, Britons owned two-thirds of all foreign investment in South America by 1913.[18]

This did not mean, however, that Britons and South Americans were equal partners. British merchants, bankers, insurance brokers, and speculators played an intermediary role in the South Americans' access to global markets for most of the nineteenth century. When governments sought to sell bonds or secure a loan they usually hired a London firm, which generally inflated prices on top of claiming a commission. This arrangement was not entirely exploitive, for in return for their business the South Americans got British help in disciplining indigenous peoples, organizing labor, protecting trade and investment, and developing their urban and rural infrastructure. There was a "scramble for influence" at the end of the nineteenth century, which corresponded to the new imperial era in Africa and Asia, that saw Americans and continental Europeans claim a greater share of South America's trade. But this increased competition did not substantially diminish the value or influence of British investment in the region.

These extensive economic links led to intimate social connections between Britons and South Americans. British investors, merchants, and engineers often married into elite local families and occasionally surrendered their British citizenship to become naturalized Brazilians, Chileans, Venezuelans, and Argentines. Distinctions between Catholicism and Protestantism put limits on this assimilation, and most expatriates preserved their cultural identity by founding British churches, schools, newspapers, and clubs in key port cities and mining towns. It is tempting to view these diasporic Britons as agents of British imperialism, but this was not always the case. Some wealthy merchants and landowners in Brazil paid little heed to the metropolitan abolitionist crusade and openly owned slaves. In Argentina, British volunteers manned shore batteries aimed at ships of the Royal Navy during one of several outbreaks of diplomatic tension between the two governments.[19] Conversely, Latin American elites often embraced British culture by hiring British governesses for their children, sending their sons to British schools, founding their own British-style clubs, and taking up British games like football (soccer) and cricket.

While this sort of elite cultural Anglophilia was common throughout South America, British influence was strongest in Argentina, so much so that historians and contemporary observers often deemed it an "honorary dominion." While the expatriate British community only numbered twenty-one thousand people out of a total population of three million in 1895, they owned key elements of Argentina's infrastructure, including banks, railways, port facilities, and cattle ranches (where the herds consisted of imported Aberdeen Angus, Hereford, and Shorthorn British cattle).[20] These entrepreneurs found willing partners among the roughly four hundred elite Argentine families who embraced the cultural trappings of the British upper classes.

To some extent, this was a mutually beneficial relationship. British merchants and bankers needed local contacts and legal protection. In return, they were generous patrons to their local clients. While they never intervened directly in local politics, they had the capacity to exert influence on the government through their ability to alter the terms of Argentina's credit in London. But this was rarely necessary because the Argentine oligarchs profited from their British partnerships. The losers in this relationship were peasants and Amerindians who lost land to capitalist speculators and artisans who could not compete with cheap British manufactured goods. On the other hand, low-cost Argentine grain and copper had an equally negative impact on farmers and miners in Britain. While some nationally minded Argentines came to question their subordination to Britain at the turn of the twentieth century, British influence in Argentina and the other South American nations was far less disruptive than it was in the more diverse and unstable Asian empires.

Influence

Although the Asian empires eventually fell under the weight of their own internal problems, they still managed to preserve their sovereignty throughout the imperial century. Their survival was due in part to Britain's commitment to maintaining their territorial integrity. Rather than resort to the expense of partition, British imperialists used informal influence, backed by military force when necessary, to push the Ottomans, Persians, and Chinese into instituting economic and social reforms that served Britain's economic and strategic interests. The new South American nations, by comparison, rarely required such a push because their ties with Britain were generally more profitable.

In both regions, British strategists deemed it unnecessary and impractical to annex large sections of territory to their formal empire. Using their advantages judiciously, they claimed Hong Kong, Cyprus, and the Falkland Islands to achieve narrow economic and strategic goals. Egypt only fell under British rule after it became an autonomous Ottoman province. This self-restraint was due primarily to the realization that cooperative states were more valuable intact. The Chinese and South American governments maintained a relatively favorable environment for foreign commerce and investment, and the Ottoman and Persian Empires were useful strategic buffers against Britain's imperial rivals.

However, Britain's self-restraint was also due to the relative cohesion of Chinese and Muslim societies and emerging South American national solidarity. Although compradors and dragomans aligned themselves with European imperial interests in Asia, they were culturally isolated and had little overall influence in their host societies. In China, the scope and influence of Christian missionaries was limited by cultural self-confidence and general xenophobia, and in the Ottoman and Persian Empires by the viability of Islam. Western missions in China had to offer cash rewards to win converts, and missionary evangelists in the Middle East faced considerable hostility in Persia and made little headway among Muslims and the Ottomans' Jewish and Orthodox Christian subjects. Catholicism limited the influence of British missionaries in Latin America. Unlike Indians and Africans, the Chinese, Persians, and Ottomans avoided becoming subjects of the British Empire because their cohesiveness rendered indirect rule largely unworkable. Empire building in South America would have required formal wars of conquest and the subjugation of a populace whose hostility to foreign rule would have been fanned by nationalist sentiments. Without local allies to serve as colonial intermediaries, Britain would have had to occupy and hold such territories by military force. In such cases, it was cheaper and more practical to rely on soft power and influence to protect Britain's strategic and economic interests, which, in contrast to India and the new African colonies, entailed respecting existing political and economic institutions.

Notes

1. Dennis Flynn and Arturo Giraldez, "Cycles of Silver: Global Economic Unity through the Mid-Eighteenth Century," *Journal of World History* 13 (2002): 402–3.

2. Immanuel C. Y. Hsu, *The Rise of Modern China*, 5th ed. (New York: Oxford University Press, 1995), 222–23.

3. Hsu, *The Rise of Modern China*, 172–73.

4. Frederic Wakeman, "The Canton Trade and the Opium War," *The Cambridge History of China*, volume 10: *Late Ch'ing, 1800–1911*, ed. John Fairbank (Cambridge: Cambridge University Press, 1978), 173.

5. "Lin Tse-Hsu's Moral Advice to Queen Victoria," in *China's Response to the West*, ed. Ssu-yü Teng (New York: Atheneum, 1966), 25–26.

6. "Lord Palmerston to the Minister of the Emperor of China, 20 February 1840," in *The Search for Modern China: A Documentary Collection*, ed. Pei-kai Cheng, Michael Lestz, and Jonathan Spence (New York: W. W. Norton & Company, 1999), 124–25.

7. Albert Feuerwerker, "Economic Trends in the Late Ch'ing Empire, 1870–1911," in *The Cambridge History of China*, volume 10: *Late Ch'ing, 1800–1911, Part II*, ed. John Fairbank (Cambridge: Cambridge University Press, 1978), 52.

8. Hung Hsiu-ch'uan, "Ode Praising the Lord," in *The Taiping Rebellion: History and Documents*, volume 2, ed. Franz Michael (Seattle: University of Washington Press, 1971), 49.

9. C. J. Lowe, *The Reluctant Imperialists: British Foreign Policy 1878–1902*, volume 2 (London: Routledge & Kegan Paul, 1967), 122.

10. Hsu, *The Rise of Modern China*, 436.

11. Quoted in Kuo Ting-yee, "Self-Strengthening: The Pursuit of Western Technology," in *The Cambridge History of China*, volume 10: *Late Ch'ing, 1800–1911, Part I*, 516.

12. Resat Kasaba, *The Ottoman Empire and the World Economy: The Nineteenth Century* (Albany: State University of New York Press, 1988), 47.

13. Ehud Toledano, *The Ottoman Slave Trade and Its Suppression, 1840–1890* (Princeton: Princeton University Press, 1983), 279.

14. Roger Owen, *The Middle East and the World Economy, 1800–1914* (London: Tauris, 1993), 101–4.

15. Robert Tignor, *Modernization and British Colonial Rule in Egypt, 1882–1914* (Princeton: Princeton University Press, 1966), 74–75; William Cleveland, *A History of the Modern Middle East* (Boulder: Westview Press, 1994), 95.

16. John Galbraith, "British and American Railway Promoters in Late Nineteenth Century Persia," *Albion* 21 (1989): 249–52.

17. P. J. Cain and A. G. Hopkins, *British Imperialism: Innovation and Expansion, 1688–1914* (London: Longman, 1993), 403.

18. Thomas Skidmore and Peter Smith, *Modern Latin America*, 3rd. ed. (New York: Oxford University Press, 1992), 44; Alan Knight, "Britain and Latin America,"

in *The Oxford History of the British Empire*, volume 3: *The Nineteenth Century*, ed. Andrew Porter (Oxford: Oxford University Press, 2004), 127; Cain and Hopkins, *British Imperialism*, 283.

19. Knight, "Britain and Latin America," 133.

20. Hugh Tinker, "The British Diaspora," in *The Diaspora of the British, Collected SOAS Seminar Papers*, no. 3. (London: Institute of Commonwealth Studies, 1982), 4.

CHAPTER SIX

~

Empire and Globalization

The British Empire accelerated the historical processes of globalization by breaking down geographic, political, and economic barriers throughout the world. But there was no single integrated imperial system. This "second" empire consisted of multiple and overlapping webs of governance and influence that joined diverse regions and peoples on every continent (save Antarctica) in new or expanded global networks of commerce, investment, migration, and exchange. The rulers of the British Empire did not always have full control of these processes, which meant that empire building often had unpredictable consequences.

Given the decentralized nature of the empire, as well as Britain's preference for indirect rule and informal influence, the most common point of reference for, say, a Maasai pastoralist, an Egyptian peasant, an Indian sepoy, a South Asian migrant laborer in the West Indies, and a Chinese comprador were the cultural and economic demands of British imperialism. Subject peoples of the empire often suffered considerable hardship when empire builders tried to restructure their societies to serve specific economic ends. However, the previous chapters have shown that British rule and influence was viable only when it convinced a sufficient segment of local communities to participate in the imperial enterprise. Although an influential assortment of British merchants, soldiers, administrators, missionaries, and settlers benefited from the evolution of the empire into a global institution, their control of this vast, multiethnic conglomeration of territories was never total or absolute.

Older histories of the British Empire emphasize the one-way transfer of British populations and political and cultural norms to the colonies. In reality, however, Britain's improvised institutions of rule and influence created an interconnecting network that dispersed subject populations and cultures to every corner of the empire, including Britain itself. By uniting disparate regions of the world under overlapping but largely decentralized administrative systems, the empire diffused a diverse array of peoples, cultures, flora, and fauna around the globe. The same could be said for the French Empire and, to a much lesser extent, the empires acquired by the Germans, Belgians, Italians, Japanese, and Americans during the new imperial era. But the British Empire, both formal and informal, was unmatched in its scope and global influence.

The legacy of this imperial demographic, cultural, and biological cross-pollination was decidedly mixed. British rule facilitated the exchange of new ideas and useful products, but, like all forms of globalization, it also had negative consequences. The most obvious were the deadly epidemics in formerly isolated populations resulting from exposure to new infectious diseases. Britain's technological and military superiority also often sparked profound crises of political legitimacy and confidence among non-Western populations, particularly when they entailed the introduction of new religious beliefs, collective identities, and gender roles. This was much more, however, than the story of the efforts of British administrators to impose Western values on colonial subjects. Language, religion, law, and education are ambiguous institutions that can never be fully possessed or controlled by any single government, ruling class, or cultural elite. Subject peoples frequently used Britain's own institutions and cultural values to resist or temper the impact of British rule and influence. They also used these foreign institutions to defend key social norms and practices that still had practical and emotional value.

Furthermore, British empire builders played an active but largely unthinking role in reinforcing and disseminating the cultures of their subjects. Indirect rule required the assimilation of non-Western institutions, and the co-option and standardization of these institutions introduced subject cultural elements into other colonies and even the British metropole. To be sure, Protestant Christianity, the English language, British law, and Western notions of gender and domesticity were dominant throughout the empire, but imperial administrators had to understand and embrace the customs of their subjects in order to govern them. Similarly, evangelism required close contact with local communities, and missionaries often lived, dressed, and spoke as the people they sought to convert.

Overseas Britons were often profoundly influenced by this intimacy, and many continued to indulge in non-Western languages, dress, cuisine, and sometimes even religious practices after returning to Britain. These cross-cultural exchanges were further abetted by the small handful of subject peoples who took advantage of their status as British subjects and protected persons to travel throughout the empire and work and study in Britain itself. As a result, metropolitan Britons became increasingly aware that they were part of a vast multiethnic empire over the course of the nineteenth century. Proponents of the new imperialism furthered this awareness by teaching positive imperial narratives in British schools and by celebrating Britain's imperial glories in the music halls and in popular fiction.

Yet imperial subjects also had a profound influence on the form and character of the empire that was largely out of view of the British public. Colonial administrators had to govern as Indian, African, and Asian rulers to establish their legitimacy and avoid provoking widespread unrest. They often transplanted these administrative systems and other useful cultural institutions from one territory to another. This was particularly true in regard to Ireland and India, which exerted the greatest influence on the British Empire by virtue of their status as the oldest, largest, and most economically important of Britain's possessions. Ireland was a model for overseas empire building, and Irish soldiers, missionaries, administrators, and settlers were influential agents of British imperial expansion. British bureaucrats perfected the system of indirect rule in India and exported it to most of their African colonies. Similarly, Indian merchants, soldiers, policemen, and laborers could be found in virtually every corner of the empire by the turn of the twentieth century. To a lesser degree, British imperialism also diffused African, West Indian, and East Asian peoples and cultures in a similar manner. The expansion of Britain's formal empire and informal influence thus produced a hybrid culture that was British in appearance but not entirely British in substance. The legacy of this imperial culture lives on in the English-speaking former colonies that continue to use British models as the basis of their political, educational, and legal systems, as well as in the increasingly multicultural nature of metropolitan Britain itself.

Mobility, Communication, and Settlement

The second British Empire was born of a revolution in travel in the nineteenth century that made it much easier to move goods and people around the globe. Similar improvements in communication made it easier for these travelers, merchants, and settlers to stay in touch with their home countries and each other. The development of railways and steam-powered ocean-going iron ships cut transit times remarkably. In the 1820s, it took four to five weeks to travel from London to North America and as many as five months to reach India and Australia. By the 1860s, the new ships were making the trip to North America in roughly two weeks, while the opening of the Suez Canal cut the journey to Australia and Hong Kong to about two months.[1]

Similarly, a network of undersea telegraph lines allowed officials in London to communicate rapidly with the far corners of the empire. Settlers and colonial subjects traveling in the empire also found it much easier to stay connected to their home territories or the British metropole. On the other hand, improved global communications also allowed subversive ideas to spread more easily. Much to the consternation of imperial administrators and policemen, telegraph lines, railways, and steamships spread news of the European continental revolutions of 1848 and the 1857 Indian Mutiny rapidly around the empire.

Britain's global influence at this time was due in large part to its lead in developing these advanced transportation and communication links. By the turn of the twentieth century, British companies owned 60 percent of the global telegraph network and one-third of all oceangoing cargo ships.[2] Preeminent shipping lines gave travelers embarking from Britain access to much of the world. The Cunard Line dominated the trans-Atlantic routes, the Castle Line was the main means of reaching South Africa, and most people traveled to India and the Mediterranean on the Peninsular and Oriental Line.

This mobility changed how Britons interacted with the wider empire. Missionaries found it easier to travel home on furlough, wives of administrators were more likely to join their husbands on foreign postings, and, most significant, large numbers of people could settle in the more hospitable parts of the empire. This outward flow of people was part of a larger wave of migration that saw roughly 50 million people, 13.5 million of whom were Britons, leave Europe in the second half of the nineteenth century.[3] As the British population quadrupled between 1801 and 1901, the enclosure of communal land in the countryside, the decline of older handicraft industries, low wages, and urban unemployment created a powerful incentive to take the risk of moving overseas. Most British migrants settled in the United States or the dominions of Canada, Australia, and New Zealand. In the case of Ireland, dissatisfaction with English rule, population pressure, and the potato famine of the 1840s drove as many as three million Irishmen abroad by the end of the century.[4] Overall, this wave of nineteenth-century emigration rivaled the African slave trade in its sheer numbers.

The British government did not subsidize or organize migration. Most emigrants left Britain voluntarily, but the government also forcibly deported large numbers of convicts to Australia. India attracted only a handful of merchants and planters, and less than 5 percent of all settlers went to eastern and southern Africa. In the 1820s, the British government hoped immigration to South Africa would balance the Afrikaners, and more than half a century later it allowed the East Africa Protectorate (Kenya) to recruit aristocratic settlers from Britain to provide paying customers for the Uganda railway. But since Britons emigrated without official government aid, they were free to go where they pleased. Most opted for North America, Australia, or New Zealand, which had neither an unhealthy tropical climate nor an entrenched non-Western population.

British emigrants rarely went to territories under the control of a foreign power (with the exception of the United States), and advances in communication and travel allowed them to maintain stronger ties to home than earlier generations of settlers. These personal ties paid economic dividends. From 1873 to 1913, expatriate Britons sent over £130 million back to metropolitan Britain in the form of informal cash payments and the Imperial Postal Order Service. By 1913, these remittances amounted to roughly 8 percent of Britain's gross domestic product.[5]

In the relatively rare cases where Britons did settle outside the empire, they usually were committed to preserving their cultural identity. As noted in chapter 5, the British community in Argentina maintained its own churches, newspapers, and clubs, and sent its children to be educated in Britain. There are only a handful of cases in which British emigrants, who were usually Scottish, Welsh, or Irish, accepted assimilation into a non-English-speaking majority. In the early nineteenth century, a group of Irish immigrants merged with the Afrikaner community of the Cape Colony, and in Argentina a small settlement of Scottish Catholics adopted the culture of the Spanish-speaking majority. Yet both the Argentines and the Afrikaners were of European descent, and there are no recorded instances of significant numbers of British settlers being absorbed into a non-Western society.

The impact of British emigration on non-Western peoples was largely determined by the size of their overall population, the complexity of their political institutions, their ability to resist British colonists by force of arms, and the extent of their biological resistance to contagious disease. The peoples of Africa and Asia were fortunate to live in tropical regions that were unsuitable for large-scale European settlement, and most had the social and political capacity to survive the imperial century. On the other hand, the original inhabitants of North America and Australia were largely wiped out by the disease, warfare, and economic disruption resulting from their encounter with European empire building. This process of extermination began in the sixteenth and seventeenth centuries and reached its grim conclusion over the course of the nineteenth century.

Most Aborigines were still using stone tools and subsisting by foraging when they encountered the British explorer James Cook in 1770. With no common language and no political organization larger than a clan of inter-related family groups, they could not prevent Britain from turning their land into a penal colony. In North America, Huron residents of Ontario and the Nookta of Vancouver Island lived in more complex agricultural societies, but these First Nations communities also lacked the political and military capacity to turn back the tide of European settlement. The same was true for the foragers and pastoralists of southern Africa. The geographic isolation of these peoples meant that they had little biological resistance to the old-world diseases that came with Western contact. As a result, vast numbers of people died of measles, smallpox, typhus, and typhoid.

There was no official policy to infect imperial subjects with lethal patho-gens, and Western doctors did not fully understand how infectious diseases actually spread until the mid-nineteenth century. Nonetheless, empire builders unapologetically exploited the widespread epidemics caused by their global expansion. Moreover, their appropriation of extensive tracts of land for cities and settler farms further weakened indigenous societies by depriving them of the ability to feed themselves. As a result, the Aboriginal population of Australia dropped from approximately three hundred thousand people in the late eighteenth century to just eighty thousand by the 1880s; the four thousand Aborigines living on the southern island of Tasmania were wiped out entirely during the same period.[6] Colonial administrators justified this implicit genocide by using the ideology of "natural law" and Social Darwin-ism to explain the disappearance of "backward" peoples.

For the most part, officials and settlers tended to treat the remnants of these devastated societies as pests that had to be either removed to reserva-tions or assimilated forcibly into the dominant colonial culture. The survi-vors of the destruction of Aboriginal society tended to migrate to the slums of Australia's growing cities, where some suffered from the urban vices of prostitution and alcoholism. The settlers' confiscation of hunting and grazing land in British North America caused many vulnerable groups like the Beo-thuk of Newfoundland to die out entirely. In a practice that Prime Minister Justin Trudeau in 2017 deemed a "dark and shameful chapter in our country's history," the Canadian government of the late nineteenth century endeav-ored to Westernize the children of the survivors through compulsory Chris-tian evangelism and vocational training in Indian Residential Schools. Many of these students suffered considerably after being forcibly separated from their families, and the promises of assimilation were largely hollow because Westernized Amerindians rarely had provincial voting rights. Humanitarians in both Britain and the colonies tried to temper the most destructive aspects of British emigration in Australia and North America, but most settlers rationalized their behavior by telling themselves that indigenous peoples were doomed to extinction.

The Maori of New Zealand, however, exposed the fallacy of these arguments. Although they were also vulnerable to old-world diseases, they were substantially better equipped to cope with the full onslaught of European settlers during the imperial century. Even as missionaries made destabilizing inroads into Maori society, Maori farmers turned a handsome profit by trading with the Australian colonies. Moreover, the willingness of British merchants to supply firearms to cooperative chiefs altered the balance of power in New Zealand substantially. By the 1830s, many Maori had willingly embraced a monetized economy in addition to adopting Western clothing and customs.

Yet the Maori could not escape the political crisis and social dislocation that came with increased British settlement in the 1840s. Some communities made the best of the situation by selling the same tract of land to several different buyers, but their attempts to limit the sale of land to foreigners drove them to war with the settlers within two decades. The combination of increased intercommunal warfare among the Maori themselves resulting from the introduction of firearms, the fighting with the British, and old-world contagious diseases halved the Maori population, which was approximately two hundred thousand before the era of colonization, over the course of the nineteenth century.[7] Nevertheless, the Maori still controlled large sections of the North Island in the 1870s, and their greater ability to adapt to the onslaught of Western culture and settlement allowed them to escape the fate of the indigenous societies of Australia, North America, and southern Africa.

By comparison, India and most of the Asian and African colonies acquired by Britain under the new imperialism held little appeal for British settlers. In contrast to the missionaries, the small enclaves of British officials and merchants in these territories largely lived in isolation from the non-Western majority. To avoid the necessity of "going native," a derogatory term for Britons who surrendered their culture, they developed elaborate customs and traditions to distinguish themselves from their subjects.

In India, the small permanent population of expatriate Britons identified themselves with India, but they lived apart from ordinary Indians. In Calcutta, wealthy merchants lived in pillared Greek-style mansions that provided a comforting measure of security and familiarity. When the Indian climate grew too hot, the "British Indians" retired to hill stations in the foothills of the Himalayas where the cool climate, village greens, and distinctive architecture were similar to that of an English country village. These colonial social institutions often evoked the culture of landed aristocrats, a class that was on the decline in late nineteenth-century Britain. Metropolitan distinctions of class and ethnicity tended to become less pronounced in these colonial contexts. While many Catholic Irishmen detested the English gentry at home, they also built prestigious careers as engineers, doctors, civil servants, and missionaries in India and the wider empire.[8] In virtually every imperial territory, social clubs, Masonic lodges, racetracks, and golf courses helped create the image that all overseas Britons of the right class and occupation, whether Scotch, Irish, Welsh, or English, were gentlemen and thus superior to, and separate from, the subject majority.

New urban centers further reinforced the social distance between the rulers and the ruled. In most colonies, expatriate Britons established their residences in segregated neighborhoods demarcated by walls, major roads and railway lines, urban parks, and golf courses. In Asia and Africa, unique residences known as bungalows were wrapped by cooling porches to promote the free flow of air in humid tropical regions. Only the most trusted servants could move beyond these porches into intimate domestic spaces within the home. With their high walls, stout gates, and extensive lawns, these fortified residences guarded overseas British families from the threat of physical attack and medical contamination.

Culture and Empire

Taken as a whole, these imperial institutions distinguished imperial Britons from their subjects, thereby providing the legitimacy and moral certainty that underpinned their political authority. Given the importance of segregation to governance and order, colonial officials were extremely distrustful of any practice or institution that might erode the boundaries of imperial subjecthood. Social interaction, particularly sexual relations, blurred the essential distinction between the colonizer and the colonized. Central to this project was the introduction of new notions of gender into subject societies that made European women the repositories of British honor and culture and non-Western women either oppressed victims in need of rescue or promiscuous primitives. Subject men were either effeminate weaklings incapable of protecting their women and honor or sexual predators who had to be kept apart from vulnerable British women and children.

This distinction took time to develop. In western Canada, British fur trappers married into elite First Nation families, and most of these men recognized their sons and daughters as their legitimate offspring. In the West Indies, Mary Seacole, the daughter of a Scottish soldier and a Jamaican free woman of color, earned fame in the wider empire as a proficient but informally trained "doctress" who treated the victims of cholera in Central America and wounded British soldiers in the Crimean War.[9] Company officials in eighteenth-century India behaved as Indian rulers and interacted freely with the local population. Since the British East India Company's European staff was almost exclusively male, it was not unusual for British arrivals to find an Indian mistress. In the language of the times these women were "sleeping dictionaries" because they supposedly helped their lovers master local languages. Sita Ram, who had almost fifty years' service in the army of the Bengal Presidency, recalled that most Indian soldiers approved of this practice. "Most of our officers had Hindustanee women living with them, and these had great influence in the regiment. . . . The sepoys themselves were sometimes instrumental in inducing the officers to take into their service some of their female relations."[10] The BEIC even offered a five-rupee "christening present" for every "half-caste" child on the assumption that the boys would become soldiers in the Company's armed forces and the girls would find husbands among the BEIC staff. As a result, there were over ten thousand people of mixed British and Indian parentage at the end of the eighteenth century.[11]

Sometimes confusingly called Anglo-Indians, Eurasians, or half-castes, this community played a useful intermediary role during the era of Company rule. But their ambiguous status undermined imperial social distance as the BEIC lost its economic role. In the 1790s, Governor-General Richard Wellesley strongly discouraged Company employees from taking Indian mistresses and discharged all Eurasian soldiers. Backed by missionaries who considered sexual relations with Indians immoral, Company officials now deemed the half-caste community incompatible with indirect rule. Arguing that such people embodied the combined vices of the British and Indian "races," Company administrators dismissed Eurasians as unsuitable political partners because ordinary Indians allegedly despised them. Similarly, the stigmatization of Amerindians as barbarous primitives in the mid-nineteenth century led many Canadian families to hide their "native" roots.

Improved global transportation and the opening of the Suez Canal in 1869 further widened the social distance between Britons and subject peoples. British women began to make annual visits to India in search of husbands among the administrative and officer classes. This "fishing fleet," as it was commonly known, reinforced upper-class social etiquette in the British community and conclusively ended the Raj's continued informal tolerance of Indian mistresses and their children. Expatriate women helped reinforce these new boundaries by setting an example of what it meant to be a proper wife through their organization of the household, mastery of Indian servants, and sponsorship of tea parties and other sorts of "respectable" activities. As in Britain, gender segregation became the norm, and most colonial clubs either banned women entirely or banished them to separate spaces known as henhouses.[12]

The increasing numbers of British women in India provided an excuse to insist on stricter social segregation. Based on the false reports of mass rapes during the Indian Mutiny, popular stereotypes under the Raj depicted Indian men as too sensual and lascivious to be trusted in the company of British women and children. Those who established consensual sexual relationships with British women risked being charged with rape. Conversely, many British men, particularly soldiers, still expected to have sexual access to Indian women. Mindful of the emerging imperial racial order, British military officers and administrators solved this problem by creating a system of organized and regimented prostitution where brothel workers and their clients were segregated by race and class. The Indian women who worked in these brothels were subject to mandatory medical inspections to ensure that they did not pass on venereal diseases to their clients.[13] Educated Indians recognized that the new sexual social taboos reinforced their subordinate status, and several Indian princes created headaches for their imperial minders by marrying lower-class European women. Although British administrators could not legally prevent these unions, the Raj often barred certain princes from visiting Britain on the suspicion that they were looking for a British wife.

In British Africa, the ban on sexual contact with non-Europeans in India did not immediately apply. In the later decades of the nineteenth century, it was not unusual for administrators or army officers to find an African mistress when assigned to a remote rural post. Although the colonial governments officially discouraged this practice, its defenders argued that "native concubines" provided necessary sexual release for junior officials who could not afford to marry. African mistresses were a common fixture in many administrative headquarters and military bases until 1908, when a public clash in the East Africa Protectorate (Kenya) between a district commissioner and an African policeman over an African woman embarrassed senior officials in London. The Colonial Office therefore issued a circular banning interracial sexual relations, declaring that "it is not possible for any member of the administration to countenance such practices without lowering himself in the eyes of the natives," and it threatened transgressors with "disgrace and official ruin" for ignoring the ban.[14] Although these official sanctions and informal social taboos prevented members of the colonial administration from publicly acknowledging their mistresses, in practice many men continued to pursue covert sexual liaisons with non-Western women.

Moreover, it was neither possible nor desirable to erect entirely impermeable social barriers between Britons and colonial subjects, for indirect rule required allies among the local population. In most territories, British merchants, missionaries, and administrators encouraged the creation of a comprador class by using Western culture to exploit economic and social divisions in subject societies. Just as Latin and the social and material culture of Rome were the cornerstones of the Roman Empire, British institutions were a glue linking the disparate peoples and territories of the British Empire. By fixing the values and traditions of the English gentry as symbols of authority and political legitimacy, imperial administrators made the adoption of British cultural norms the key to political and social advancement in colonial society. Consequently, educated West Indians, Africans, and Asians often appropriated and modified the dress, manners, and traditions of English gentlemen to challenge racial segregation and claim the full rights of imperial citizenship. On the other hand, in embracing new belief systems they risked becoming alienated from their own cultures, which in turn weakened the social and political cohesion needed to resist imperial expansion.

Evangelical Protestantism in particular was largely responsible for shaping and socializing this new class of Westernized elites. While they often spoke out against slavery and the worst abuses of colonial rule, clergymen like the Wesleyan missionary William Shrewsbury saw imperial conquest as the first step to Christian conversion.[15] In addition to providing a legitimizing ideology for the new imperialism, the evangelical movement helped undermine the self-confidence of subject peoples by introducing new codes of morality and social behavior. Anglican and Methodist missionaries in New Zealand, for example, sought more than Maori converts. They also pursued a program of cultural transformation that banned tattooing and other indigenous customs as sinful and promoted literacy and the discipline of the clock.[16]

Most missions did not seek to create African and Asian Englishmen. As an 1873 London Missionary Society directive admonished: "Remember that the people are foreigners. Let them continue as such. . . . Build upon [what] is sound and good; and Christianize. . . . Do not seek to make the people Englishmen. Seek to develop and mold a pure, refined and Christian character."[17] In Kenya, the Church Missionary Society did not endeavor to immediately replace African religions, rather they depicted their Christian message as compatible with local practices of belief. In this sense African religions were like Judaism, an earlier faith encompassing elements of truth that paved the way for Christianity.[18] In keeping with the philosophy of indirect rule and the supposed lessons of the Indian Mutiny, the missionaries' ultimate aim was to establish independent and financially self-supporting "native churches" that would become junior partners in evangelism.

In addition to seeking to spread Western cultural values, the missions also played an important role in creating viable colonial administrative systems. Through their near monopoly on education and medicine, missionaries linked Christianity with economic and social advancement. Mission teachers and doctors in particular offered converts access to the technological achievements of the industrial West. Although indirect rule required colonial administrators to recruit non-Christian "traditional" elites to be chiefs and headmen, educated mission converts monopolized prestigious and high-paying intermediary roles in most British territories. These commercial agents, translators, and clerks were mostly Christians who received considerable political and economic rewards as compensation for the severe social alienation resulting from their participation in the colonial regime.

The ability of a particular society to resist the new imperialism was at least partially a reflection of the degree to which it limited the influence of the Christian missions. The Ethiopian emperor Tewodros understood this perfectly. Writing to the Anglican Bishop of Jerusalem in the 1860s, he made it clear that he would welcome Western technology but not Protestant missionaries. "Now, by the power of God, I have made [Ethiopia] one and so do not let any priests come against me who will dispute the Faith. . . . Amongst the craftsmen, however, let there come . . . one who can plough by means of a combustion engine."[19] Just as the Ethiopian Orthodox Church, which is one of the world's oldest Christian denominations, checked the influence of the Protestant missions, so too did Islam, Hinduism, and Chinese Confucianism. The strength of these belief systems limited the ability of empire builders to find allies among the general population. Thus, the decision of colonial subjects to either reject or embrace the cultural values of evangelical Christianity was based on a series of interrelated factors, including ethnic homogeneity, social cohesiveness, technological accomplishment, and the strength of their own religious values. Although ruling elites in Buganda (Uganda), Basutoland (Lesotho), and Bechuanaland (Botswana) embraced Christianity, missionaries tended to have the greatest success converting ethnic or religious minorities, commercially ambitious merchants, ex-slaves, and other disadvantaged social classes.

In India, missionaries did not have much influence until the British East India Company relaxed its restriction on Christian evangelism in the early nineteenth century. Although upwardly mobile Hindu and Muslim intellectuals welcomed the opportunities offered by Western education, few embraced Christianity. The missions had the greatest success converting *dalits* ("untouchables") and other members of the lower Hindu castes. Seeking access to Western education, famine relief, enhanced social status, and political patronage, entire families and villages converted en masse. As a result, there were approximately 7 million Indian Christians by the close of the imperial century, which was a relatively insignificant fraction of the total Indian population of 294 million people.[20]

The few South Asian Muslims and high-caste Hindus to accept Christianity usually did so as students in mission schools. They inevitably faced intense social and economic pressure from their peers and families to renounce their new faith, and some required police protection to defend them from physical assaults by outraged former co-religionists. For the most part, though, Christian conversion was confined largely to India's marginalized populations. Under the system of indirect rule, Islam and Hinduism remained viable sources of status and political influence for Indian elites. Although the British conquest discredited Mughal and Maratha political institutions, the immensely influential religions that underpinned these states were sufficiently well established to resist the pressures of evangelical Christianity.

The missionary criticism of Indian beliefs also helped strengthen Hinduism by sparking a Hindu revival organized by groups like Ram Mohan Roy's Brahmo Samaj and Dayananda Sarasvati's Arya Samaj. This revitalized Hinduism further limited the spread of Christianity. Far from being threatened by the missions, many educated Indians regarded the evangelicals with amused detachment. T. N. Mukharji and his traveling companions, who were part of a governmental delegation to the 1886 Colonial and Indian Exhibition in London, brushed aside the impassioned preaching of an American missionary with the observation that it "was more necessary for a bad Christian to be good than for a good Hindu to be a Christian" because "the Christian religion teaches men to love their neighbours, [while] the Hindu religion teaches men to love every living thing as their own selves."[21] Lutfullah, a Company translator who accompanied an Indian princely delegation to London in the 1850s, found St. Paul's Cathedral too ornate and paganistic: "What I disliked most was the multitude of statues and images. . . . I know they are not worshipped, . . . but a temple dedicated to sacred purposes . . . ought to be plain."[22] Even Christian converts like Samuel Satthianadhan accepted that the majority of his countrymen were indifferent to the evangelical message: "It is the opinion of many an educated Hindu that no sensible intelligent Englishman, who is not a missionary, believes in Christianity."[23] At the popular level, however, the missionary project could appear more threatening, and Hindu mobs rioted in Madras in 1843 to protest the Church of Scotland Mission's activities in the city.

In comparison, most African societies found it harder to limit the divisive impact of the Western missions, particularly when conversion to Christianity offered former slaves, women, and other disadvantaged groups significant social advancement. African religions were every bit as vital and dynamic as Hinduism and Islam, but they lacked the scope, hierarchical organization, and written scriptures to compete with evangelical Christianity. On the coasts of West and East Africa, Muslim empire builders, merchants, and clerics had already been winning converts for several centuries, but their defeat at the hands of Europeans at the end of the nineteenth century limited their political influence. Additionally, the military disasters, epidemics, and famines that accompanied the partition of the continent caused many non-Muslims to question the validity of their religious convictions.

Most African societies retained a belief in a supreme deity, but for many individuals imperial conquest shook their faith in the pantheon of spirits and lesser deities that regulated the rhythms of daily life. As the old order appeared to collapse around them, Christianity offered a means to adapt to colonial rule and provided access to wealth, education, and medical care. On the Gold Coast, for example, conversion brought useful commercial contacts with fellow Christians and Western merchants. In Kenya, junior Kikuyu sons who lacked the livestock necessary to marry and establish themselves similarly saw the economic opportunities offered by the missions as an alternate path to full adulthood. Alternatively, in southern Africa, elites like Khama in Bechuanaland and Moshoeshoe in Basutoland used mission support to check Afrikaner expansion, consolidate political power, and secure British recognition as "kings." Throughout British Africa, Christian conversion gave women a means of escaping arranged marriages and the authority of domineering fathers and husbands, particularly once colonial governments enacted Western-style laws regulating marriage and divorce. Mission schools also admitted a small number of girls to become proper Christian wives for male converts.

Africans, nevertheless, did not entirely abandon their cultural values when they converted to Christianity, nor did conversion entail blind acceptance of imperial authority. Tiyo Soga, the son of a Xhosa royal counselor who was the first African to be ordained in the United Presbyterian Church of Scotland, actively contested settler assertions that his people were a "dying race" destined to be swept away to make room for the European settlement of southern Africa. "The fact that the dark races of this vast continent, amid intestine wars and revolutions, and notwithstanding external spoliation, have remained 'unextinct,' have retained their individuality, has baffled historians, and challenges [proponents] of the doom of the Kaffir race [to provide] a satisfactory explanation."[24] As was the case with Western education in India, British customs and culture could be as effective a means of organizing resistance to foreign rule as they were instruments of imperial social control. African converts reformulated Christian dogma to suit their own worldview, and in many societies they associated their supreme deity with the God of the Bible. To this end, some founded independent African churches to break the monopoly of the Western missions on education and evangelism. Some of these independents received aid from African-American missionaries.[25] Along with the doctrine of Ethiopianism, which established an explicitly African conception of Christianity, these churches were a direct challenge to the ideological bases of the new imperialism.

The contested nature of Christianity in the empire illustrates the contradictions in Britain's cultural influence on its colonies. Even as imperial Britons tried to segregate themselves physically and culturally from subject communities, they tried to use Western culture to expand their social influence. As noted in previous chapters, imperial regimes sought to strengthen their control over India and South Africa by imposing the English language on Indians and Afrikaners. Yet Britons in India jealously resisted attempts by Indians to adapt the English language to local circumstances by ridiculing the "babu English" used by members of India's educated classes. Originally a term of respect in Bengali, babu became a slur during the imperial century. In Rudyard Kipling's famous *Kim*, the character Hurree Chunder Mookerjee, whom Kipling describes as a "hulking obese," has a master's degree from the University of Calcutta and aspires to become a member of the learned Royal Society. While Hurree ends up as something of an improbable hero at the end of the novel, Kipling makes him a figure of fun by having him mangle common English expressions liking "pulling my legs" and peppering his accented broken English with words and phrases like "verree good," "by Jove," "affeeliate," "opeenion," and "jolly beastly." Most tellingly, Hurree declares "All we Babus talk English to show off."[26] Educated Indians resented these slurs, and the poet and journalist Behramji Malabari, who traveled extensively in Britain, asked: "I should like to know how many Englishmen speak Bengali half so well as Bengalis speak English."[27] Ridiculing nonstandard dialects undercut official efforts to promote British culture in the empire, but the extensive use of English today by Britain's former imperial subjects demonstrates that colonized peoples still found the language useful.

The contradictory but potent influence of imperial popular culture was also evident in the widespread embrace of British styles of dress and recreation throughout the empire. In most territories, missionaries and administrators dressed as gentlemen. This made Western clothes into symbols of affluence, education, and social status. Mission converts, clerks, translators, and compradors therefore adopted the same style of dress and played tennis, croquet, and other sorts of respectable games to back up their demand for social equality. In the Caribbean, West Indians took up cricket for just these reasons. In time, by defeating "white" teams of planters, who had made cricket a marker of racial and social exclusivity, through more aggressive bowling and other tactics they eventually altered how the game was played worldwide.

More marginal and uneducated colonial peoples who aspired to British respectability also used Western-style clothing to subvert the imperial order. In the early decades of the twentieth century, a form of popular dance known as Beni spread throughout East Africa. Beni consisted of competing troupes of dancers who satirized European popular culture and military brass bands by affecting elaborate and often outrageous Western styles of dress. African soldiers in Nyasaland sang "*Amekwiba sokosi ya Bwana Major*" (he has stolen the major's socks) during their celebrations, which led some nervous officials to worry that Beni might undermine military discipline and destabilize colonial society.[28] Their fears that dancing societies might inspire Africans to turn to burglary to acquire European clothing were ridiculous and never materialized, and Beni was more a matter of entertainment than politics. On the other hand, putting on Western-style clothing, particularly uniforms and other standardized forms of dress, provided a means to claim, or at least undermine, some of the imperial regime's authority.

Whose Empire?

The global use of English and prevalence of British cultural norms, which are an obvious legacy of the imperial century, mask the influence of subject peoples on both the culture of the British Empire and the contemporary nation-states that are its legacy. By adapting British institutions to suit local circumstances, subject populations fundamentally altered the cultural cornerstones of British rule. Conversely, the very nature of indirect rule and informal influence had a profound cultural influence on overseas Britons who had to co-opt the cultural practices of their non-Western subjects in order to govern them. The new imperialism therefore did more than simply transfer British culture to the far corners of the globe in a straightforward fashion. The resulting second British Empire's interlocking and overlapping imperial networks of exchange and migration created a hybrid multiethnic imperial culture whose lasting influence has been just as significant as the more easily recognized legacies of formal British rule.

While the global wave of European migration and settlement resulting from advances in transportation is well documented, British empire building also opened the way for non-Westerners to move about the world. In the late nineteenth century, the colonial governments in Canada, Australia, and Natal took steps to limit large-scale Asian labor migration and settlement, but individual diplomats, merchants, scholars, students, and wanderers rarely faced any restrictions on imperial travel if they had the means to purchase long-distance railway and steamship tickets. Generally speaking, formal passports were not in widespread use before the First World War. West Africans began sending their children to school in Europe centuries before the imperial conquest of Africa, and in the mid-nineteenth century, West Indians like Mary Seacole were free to travel from Jamaica to Panama, Britain, and the Crimea. Merchant seamen settled where they wished by jumping ship, and students, petitioners, and potentates from around the empire were regular visitors to London. Some stayed a few days, some remained for years, others never returned home at all.

These networks meant that the British Empire was not as British as it first appeared. As Britain's oldest, largest, and most valuable overseas possession, India exerted a profound influence on the greater empire. The British East India Company laid down the fundamental principles of indirect rule, and the Raj provided most of the army officers and administrators who conquered and governed territories acquired during the new imperial era. These men often applied Indian solutions to problems in Africa and other parts of Asia. Most of the consuls who ran the Chinese treaty ports were posted from India, and the police force of Shanghai's international settlement was largely composed of Sikhs. Similarly, many senior British civil servants in South Africa, including Lord Macartney and Sir John Craddock, began their careers in India. In 1869, the chief commissioner for India's central provinces went back to Britain to assist in adapting the Bengal Tenancy Act to Ireland.[29]

The Indianization of the empire accelerated in the era of the new imperialism when men like Frederick Lugard adapted indirect rule to Africa. Lugard, who began his career as an officer in the Indian army, played a central role in three different private chartered company armies that conquered British Central, East, and West Africa, and he eventually became the governor of Nigeria. Similarly, rank-and-file Indian sepoys fought for Britain in China, Persia (1856), Egypt (1882), Burma (1885), Nyasaland (1893), and Uganda (1896). As the military experts of the empire, British officers like Lugard and Indian noncommissioned officers on loan from the Indian army popularized

Indian military traditions in British Africa and Asia. This was particularly the case in the belief that only "martial races" should be recruited as soldiers. These stereotypes tended to fix ethnic identity throughout the empire, thereby contributing to the codification of tribalism in Africa.

Indian institutions also influenced economic and urban policy in every corner of the empire. The rupee became the standard currency for British colonial territories throughout Asia and East Africa. In the latter case, the East Africa Protectorate also adopted Indian civil and penal codes, and most of the new urban centers in the region included a central business district modeled on an Indian bazaar. Indian laborers built the railway from Mombasa to Uganda, whose one-meter gauge matched the standard of Indian railways. In terms of culture, Lachlan Macquarie, the governor of New South Wales in the early nineteenth century and a career Indian army officer, introduced the Indian bungalow's verandah to Australian architecture. In China, many of the buildings in the treaty ports followed Anglo-Indian styles by featuring squared columns and sweeping verandahs.

The British Empire thus took on more of an Indian appearance as the imperial century progressed. This was particularly the case once individual Indians began to travel the empire as diplomats, scholars, merchants, clerks, soldiers, and indentured laborers. British India was an empire in its own right, and Indian merchants followed its imperial networks to found trading communities throughout Southeast Asia. In East Africa, where the Swahili city states' commercial contacts with India long predated the British conquest, Bombay-based merchants were well placed to take advantage of new imperial networks that ran through Zanzibar. As British subjects they enjoyed the protection of the British Consul on the island, and by the 1860s they controlled nearly 80 percent of the sultanate's foreign trade.[30]

While the aristocratic Britons lobbied strenuously to bar South Asian emigration to the East African Protectorate, colonial administrators, many of whom had begun their careers in the Raj, initially favored such settlement on the grounds that Indians were supposedly more civilized and industrious than Africans. This was obviously not the case, but Indian capitalists like Allindina Vishram and Alibhai Mulla Jeevanjee played pioneering roles in developing the Ugandan and Kenyan infrastructure and export economies.

It is arguable, however, that simple South Asian workers contributed even more to the Indianization of the second British Empire. As British influence expanded around the globe, large numbers of Indian indentured laborers emigrated, often under duress, to other British colonies. Over the course of the century, approximately five million South Asians went to work on Ceylonese tea estates, Malayan rubber plantations, Burmese rice farms, the Uganda railway, and sugar plantations in Fiji, Mauritius, Natal, and the West Indies.[31] Similarly, large numbers of indentured Chinese servants, who usually left through British-controlled treaty ports, did agricultural work in Malaya and Australia and labored in South African mines. Taken as a whole, Chinese and Indian emigration in the British Empire during the nineteenth century must be counted along with the African slave trade and the European settlement of North America as one of the great population shifts of world history.

The British government's formal abolition of slavery throughout the empire in 1834 helped set this process in motion. As the middle classes in Europe and North America developed an appetite for candy, baked goods, and sweetened tea, West Indian sugar growers faced a chronic shortage of disciplined and affordable labor in the postemancipation era. After their attempts to force former slaves to continue working as apprentices failed, and efforts to recruit free workers in West Africa were understandably unsuccessful given the centuries of European slave trading, sugar planters looked to India for relief. The West Indian governments sympathized with this problem and subsidized the recruitment of workers in India and in the Chinese treaty ports.

These laborers entered into binding labor contracts for a variety of reasons. Unscrupulous recruiters duped many South Asians by concealing the true terms of indentured service, which usually required a person to work for a fixed period at relatively low pay with few legal protections. In 1858, former sepoys who were involved in the Indian Mutiny escaped prosecution by signing on with a labor recruiter, and many civilians joined the outward migration to escape landlessness, poverty, rising rents and taxes, famine, and the decline of handicraft industries that made life difficult under the Raj. In doing so, many suffered terribly on the densely packed ships that carried them to the far corners of the empire. At midcentury, mortality rates reached almost 20 percent on the longer voyages to the West Indies.

Most commonly, contracts required South Asians to work overseas for five years in return for a fixed wage and a return ticket home upon completion of their term. Indentured servants worked for low wages, but their primary value lay in their contractual obligation not to change employers in search of better pay and working conditions. Without any legal means of contesting unfair labor practices, the indentured workers' lot was particularly hard. Plantation owners often beat employees who demanded better terms, and they could count on sympathetic colonial courts to prosecute those who broke their contracts by running away. The Raj tried to ensure that its subjects received fair treatment while overseas and temporarily suspended recruiting operations altogether when conditions grew bad enough to become politically embarrassing in India. But they did not have the influence in London to thwart the influential sugar growers. It took targeted criticism from Indian nationalists during the First World War to finally put an end to foreign labor recruiting.

The legacy of these dramatic population shifts was profound. Although most indentured servants expected only a brief sojourn abroad, many took up permanent residence in Africa, Fiji, and the Caribbean because they lacked either the funds or the inclination to return home. Only a quarter of the approximately three hundred forty thousand Indians who emigrated to the Indian Ocean island of Mauritius between 1842 and 1900 ever went back to India. Other repatriation rates ranged from as high as 90 percent in Burma to as low as 20 percent in Trinidad, where the colonial government sought a permanent solution to its labor shortage by offering free land to indentured servants.[32]

Most colonial governments, however, were not as accommodating because they worried that Indians would clash with indigenous populations or compete with European settlers. They therefore used high taxes and trade licensing fees to discourage indentured servants from becoming permanent residents. Responding to settler pressure, the governor of the East Africa Protectorate refused to grant Indian workers land along the Uganda railway on the grounds that the colony was "a white man's country." Similarly, South African officials feared that former South Asian laborers who moved into commerce would take business away from European merchants and imposed an annual tax of £3 on every Indian resident to pressure them into leaving the territory.

This discrimination did not prevent former indentured laborers from founding communities of South Asian descent throughout the empire. These expatriate enclaves became self-sustaining rather quickly because imperial administrators, who worried Indian workers would fight over women, insisted that approximately one-third of all labor migrants had to be female. As a result, Indians replaced former African slaves as the dominant population group on Reunion, Mauritius, and, to a lesser degree, on Trinidad. On the Pacific island of Fiji, they constituted approximately 30 percent of the total population. In South Africa, Indians outnumbered Europeans in Natal by the end of the nineteenth century.

In addition to facilitating migration, expanded imperial networks also created a counterweight to the Protestant global evangelical project by providing greater opportunities for British subjects to convert to Islam. Much to the annoyance of the missions, Indian soldiers helped make the new African colonial armies into largely Muslim institutions where recruits were much more likely to convert to Islam than to Christianity. This was due in part to the biases of ex-Indian army officers who remained distrustful of Christian converts. Similarly, the empire's expanded network of roads and railways opened the way for Muslim merchants, who often acted as informal Islamic evangelists, to reach new parts of the continent.

In the Punjab, a religious reformer named Mirza Ghulam Ahmad founded a new Islamic movement known as the Ahmadiyya that used missionary Protestantism as an evangelical model. Under Ahmad's son and successor, the Ahmadis built a worldwide network of missions that spread throughout the British Empire and the United States. In 1914, they even established a central mission in London.[33] The criminal lawyer Abdullah (born Henry William) Quilliam was not part of this movement, but after converting to Islam in 1887 he established a prominent mosque in Liverpool and became a representative of the Ottoman sultan and Persian shah in Britain.[34]

In the metropole, the main beneficiaries of the new empire building were a small largely London-based group of financiers, industrialists, merchants, bureaucrats, and social elites, a group A. G. Hopkins and P. J. Cain labeled "gentlemanly capitalists."[35] Although a vocal coalition of middle-class reformers and humanitarians never stepped back from their criticism of formal empire, many politicians came to embrace its possibilities over the course of the nineteenth century. As population growth, rapid industrialization, and the threat of radical socialism sparked fears of popular unrest, Prime Minister Benjamin Disraeli and his Tory successors sought to promote social stability by celebrating Britain's imperial genius. In depicting the empire as a symbol of heroism and national superiority, they played down ethnic and class differences in British society, in addition to courting lower-class voters in national elections. Most British Liberals were also committed to imperial causes, particularly in instances where non-Western rulers violated their standard of human rights. For the most part, they only differed with Conservatives on how the empire should be governed.

During the final decades of the nineteenth century, imperial issues ranging from the search for David Livingstone to the purchase of the Suez Canal shares to the Anglo–South African War captured the public's popular imagination. London music halls nurtured this imperial enthusiasm by offering nationalistic performances celebrating the glory and unity of the empire. One song about the confrontation with Russia over the great game in Central Asia famously introduced "jingoism" into the English language as an expression for excessive popular nationalism: "We don't want to fight, but by jingo if we do, we've got the shops, we've got the men, we've got the money too." The newly literate middle and lower classes avidly consumed magazines and newspapers that presented an equally romanticized view of imperial issues. Correspondents turned Britain's countless small colonial wars into great heroic adventures, depicting the fall of Khartoum and the death of Gordon as a morality play about a devout Christian's lone struggle against great hordes of slave-trading heathen.

Similarly, Rudyard Kipling, Rider Haggard, John Buchan, and other popular imperial writers captured the reading public's attention with fictionalized accounts of British adventurers in exotic African and Asian settings. Like Kipling's *Kim*, Haggard's *King Solomon's Mines* and Buchan's *Prester John* belittled non-Westerners and romanticized imperial expansion. History textbooks took up these themes by emphasizing the morality and courage of the empire's founders. Imperial exhibitions similarly helped lower-class Britons envision their new colonies through displays of stuffed tropical animals and models of "native villages" in artificial jungles. The middle classes were equally swept up in imperial enthusiasm and emulated aristocratic colonial elites by decorating their homes with stuffed animal heads and similar imperial totems.[36]

In contrast to what Britons read about the empire and saw in the imperial exhibitions, daily life in the new industrial cities seemed drab and stifling. Having read stirring stories about imperial heroes and exotic subjects, schoolboys rushed to join the Boy Scouts. This was a new youth movement that its founder General Robert Baden Powell, who became famous for his defense of Mafeking in the South African War, claimed was based on Zulu age grades.[37] Adults were also inspired to copy people that, according to imperial propaganda, were inferior. In attending a "fancy ball," the translator Lutfullah was surprised to encounter a "gentleman in Persian dress" he took to be a countryman. "Not only his dress, but his manners, too, appearing to us those of a Mughal." But when addressed in Persian "the man smiled and spoke in English, which betrayed him to be an Englishman wearing a false beard."[38] As tea, sugar, cocoa, and other agricultural products of the empire became staple foods, Britons also developed their own versions of their subjects' cuisines. Curry, which was actually an invention of British India, became a staple food in the mid-nineteenth century as local grocers stocked a wide array of tinned spice mixes.

The English language also came to reflect these cross-cultural exchanges. In 1928, the *Oxford English Dictionary* listed approximately nine hundred English words that had Indian origins.[39] Some of the more common examples still in use today include shampoo, khaki, pajamas, polo, buggy, pundit, jungle, loot (from *lootie*, a band of plundering thieves), and thug (from *thagi*, a religious sect that supposedly preyed on travelers). Many English terms for clothing and textiles also have Indian origins: calico, chintz, dungaree, bandanna, seersucker, and cashmere. British administrators had to learn Indian words to understand Indian society, and these new concepts inevitably found their way into everyday English usage when they returned home. This is how British gentlemen came to play badminton, a game popular with British officers in India. Originally called *poona*, the English name came from "Badminton House," which was the country estate of the Duke of Beaufort.

Over time, some Britons became uncomfortable with the consequences of imperial globalization. Politicians and intellectuals first began worrying about the contaminating influence of empire building when newly wealthy and openly Indianized British East India Company employees began to retire to the metropole. Critics charged that Asiatic despotism and perversions introduced by these "nabobs," an Anglicized corruption of the South Asian word for governor or viceroy (nawab), threatened to corrupt Britain's political and cultural institutions. These concerns led to Edmund Burke's sensational prosecution of Warren Hastings, one of the wealthiest nabobs, for corruption in the 1780s.

On the other hand, ruling non-Western subjects promoted a unifying sense of British nationalism. By the end of the nineteenth century, Britons began to make much sharper racial distinctions between who could be considered Western, modern, and British and who could not. Imperial confidence led some people in the metropole to embrace select elements of subject cultures when it suited them, but worries that these cross-cultural exchanges might disrupt Britain's social and political order often produced a xenophobic, if not explicitly racist, backlash.

Asian and African visitors to Britain experienced these imperial anxieties in a variety of ways. For the ordinary merchant seamen who settled in imperial port cities like London, Cardiff, and Liverpool, these tensions usually appeared in the form of conflicts over jobs and relationships with local women. For those who came to Britain as students, scholars, and envoys, the backlash was often more subtle. Upon witnessing the exoticized depictions of non-Westerners in the 1886 Colonial and Indian Exhibition, T. N. Mukharji tellingly observed: "We are all 'natives' now. . . . We poor Indians, the aborigines of Australia and the South Sea Islands, the Negroes, the Kaffirs, the Hottentots and other races of Africa. . . . In England a French, German or Italian is a 'foreigner,' an Indian or an African is a 'native.'"[40] On the other hand, Samuel Satthianadhan wrote glowingly about how fairly and equally he was treated as a student at Oxford. In his mind, education and "the aristocracy of moral [and] intellectual excellence" brought equality and respectability regardless of "invidious distinctions of rank or race."[41]

Although he was a Hindu convert to Christianity, Satthianadhan's perspective on the British Empire was fairly representative of his social class. Regardless of their religious allegiance, elite imperial subjects were at least initially willing to embrace the concept of imperial citizenship. Having invested in the promise that the empire offered advancement to men of talent, they only began to lose faith when, to quote Mukharji, the institutionalization of pseudoscientific racism turned them en masse into irredeemable "natives." This was particularly striking on the West African coast where the famed explorer and orientalist Richard Francis Burton gave voice to the growing backlash against educated Afro-Victorians when he dismissed the Anglican minister Samuel Crowther as a "gorilla or missing link."[42] In 1890, Crowther resigned when the Church Missionary Society stripped away the last of his authority as an Anglican bishop and suspended all of the African priests he had ordained.

Empires, by their very nature, were inherently discriminatory, and frustration over the illusionary promise of imperial citizenship inspired the first organized resistance to British rule. Interestingly, most of these movements had a strong connection to metropolitan Britain, where colonial subjects enjoyed considerably more rights than in their home territories. Indian graduates of British universities played a leading role in founding the relatively moderate Indian National Congress, which initially advocated for Indian "home rule" within the empire on the Irish model. Mohandas Gandhi studied law in London before settling in South Africa, where he organized nonviolent resistance to the discriminatory Asian Registration Bill. Similarly, in 1901 a Trinidadian law student named Henry Sylvester Williams founded the Pan-African Association in London. As he told a crowd in Port-of-Prince one year later, the aim of his group was to "secure to Africans and their descendents throughout the world their civil and political rights," in addition to winning the passage of laws leading to the amelioration of "the condition of our oppressed brethren in the Continents of Africa, America, and other parts of the world."[43]

These projects were largely reformist, but by the turn of the twentieth century some Indian students in Britain had become much more radical. They developed strong alliances with Irish nationalists and aggressively celebrated the fiftieth anniversary of the Indian Mutiny on the streets of London. In 1909, an engineering student named Madan Lal Dhingra assassinated a senior member of the Indian Civil Service who had been monitoring the activities of Indian students in Britain. Showing no remorse for his actions in a final statement issued before his execution for murder, Dhingra declared: "A nation held down by foreign bayonet is in a perpetual state of war. . . . Poor in wealth and intellect, a son [of India] like myself has nothing else to offer to the Mother but his own blood. . . . The only lesson required in India at present is to learn how to die, and the only way to teach it is by dying ourselves."[44]

On the other hand, the relative freedom offered by life in Britain also gave imperial subjects an opportunity to participate in conventional metropolitan politics, a right that the colonial regimes denied them at home. In the 1890s, a pair of Indian expatriates actually won seats in the House of Commons. Dadabhai Naoroji became the representative for Central Finsbury in 1892, and three years later Sir M. M. Bhownagree captured the seat for Green North-East. Naoroji rode to victory on the public backlash against Lord Salisbury's statement that British voters would never elect a black man, and Bhownagree ran on an entirely uncontroversial platform calling for greater economic centralization in the empire.[45] Henry Sylvester Williams also considered running for Parliament to better represent African interests, but he settled for winning a seat on the council of London's St. Marylebone borough. The willingness of at least some metropolitan Britons, particularly working-class Britons, to be represented by non-Europeans reflects the complexities of the various imperial cultures that emerged from the closer interaction of British citizens and British subjects at the end of the imperial century.

Environment and Empire

In addition to facilitating the movement of peoples and cultures, British imperial networks also dispersed, both intentionally and accidentally, plants, animals, and microbes around the globe. In doing so, empire building accelerated historic processes of globalization that intensified in the sixteenth century as a result of the maritime revolution and Columbian voyages. British scientists and settlers transferred useful plants and animals throughout the empire to achieve specific economic ends. Conversely, they also brought about unforeseen environmental and epidemiological changes by reconfiguring political boundaries and linking previously isolated regions of the world into more tightly integrated overlapping economic systems. As we have seen, the unplanned introduction of old-world diseases to Australia, North America, and parts of southern Africa proved fatal to indigenous populations.

British botanists played a primary role in these processes of biological diffusion. By identifying and propagating economically useful plants, they sought to make the empire more profitable. Kew Gardens, originally a London royal residence, became Britain's main botanical clearinghouse and research center by the mid-nineteenth century. Researchers at Kew oversaw a network of subsidiary botanical gardens throughout the empire that introduced tea, cinnamon, and tobacco to India, transferred rubber trees from Brazil to Ceylon, and laid the groundwork for a nascent timber industry in Central Africa.[46] After collecting over a million new specimens by the turn of the twentieth century, imperial botanists shifted their efforts to developing the commercial applications of known plants. Working in tandem with the Imperial Institute's Scientific and Technical Research Department, their goal was to find ways to help the new imperial territories, which often lacked sufficiently valuable natural resources and willing subject workers, contribute to the overall prosperity of the empire and cover the costs of their own administration.[47]

British settlers also contributed to these biological exchanges by adapting domesticated metropolitan plants and animals to the colonies. This is how British breeds of cattle and sheep became ubiquitous in the dominions and Argentina by the turn of the twentieth century as the development of refrigerated container ships allowed ranchers to ship chilled meat to Britain. These improved transportation networks also allowed for continued imports of metropolitan breeding stock. Not unlike the settlers' determination to avoid "going native" via assimilation into subject societies, livestock breeders aimed to ensure that the domesticated animals in the colonies did not diverge too far from the tastes of the metropolitan consumer by cross-breeding with local ones.[48]

These imperial biological exchanges also served a strategic function. In the 1850s, British botanists traveled secretly to South America to collect samples of the cinchona tree, the naturally occurring source of quinine. Since daily doses of quinine were the only effective protection against malaria, imperial expansion in the tropics depended on a reliable and steady supply of the drug. Seeking to break the South American monopoly on this vital substance, British botanists established cinchona plantations in the Indian highlands to provide inexpensive quinine for the armed forces.

While these exchanges of biological material increased the security and profitability of the empire, they came at a high cost. The exotic plants that imperial botanists introduced into new ecosystems often pushed out native species. For example, gardeners and horticulturalists throughout the empire embraced the water hyacinth (*eichhornia*), a water plant native to tropical South America, for its beautiful flowers and economic value as a source of fiber and compost. Unfortunately, the plant was highly invasive outside of South America, and by the end of the nineteenth century it was choking off rivers and streams throughout Africa and Asia.[49]

Most significant were the epidemics precipitated by the spread of disease-causing microbes around the globe. Cholera was an endemic Indian disease that had previously been limited to the subcontinent by virtue of its extremely short incubation period, which meant that carriers usually died quickly before they could infect others. Killing primarily through rapid dehydration brought on by uncontrollable vomiting and diarrhea, cholera was a constant fear in British-ruled India. In Frances Hodgson Burnett's classic novel *The Secret Garden*, a young English girl named Mary became an orphan when Indian domestic servants spread the disease to her parents and their dinner guests. "There was panic on every side, and dying people in all the bungalows. . . . Everyone was too panic-stricken to think of a little girl no one was fond of. When people had the cholera it seemed that they remembered nothing but themselves."[50]

Once improved global transportation and the opening of the Suez Canal reduced travel times to and from India in the second half of the nineteenth century, cholera became a global problem. The result was a series of devastating pandemics that killed millions of people throughout Africa, the Middle East, Europe, and the Americas by spreading along Britain's network of imperial communications and the pilgrimage routes to Mecca.[51] In the West Indies, sick passengers on troopships and passenger liners stopping to take on coal at Port Royal and Kingston introduced the disease to Jamaica where, along with outbreaks of smallpox and influenza, roughly forty out of every one thousand people died of these diseases in the 1850s. It took a brave woman like Mary Seacole to care for cholera sufferers because the patients' bodily fluids were highly infectious. Not yet understanding that cholera is spread by untreated water and poor sanitation, the Jamaican authorities resorted to having a Royal Navy ship fire its guns over urban centers in the hope that the shells would disrupt disease-causing winds.[52]

Improved transportation also sparked global outbreaks of the bubonic plague, a highly infectious rat-borne disease that is usually associated with the Middle Ages. But in the era of the new imperialism, a plague outbreak in Hong Kong in 1894 spread to southern Africa six years later. In India, where the disease was virtually unknown before the 1890s, it appeared in virtually every province within a few short years. Over half a million people died in the Punjab alone, causing a 3 percent drop in the region's total population.[53]

In Africa, the thirty years between partition and the First World War were almost certainly the deadliest decades in the history of the continent. Although malaria and other tropical fevers were endemic to much of coastal Africa, virulent epidemics in these areas were relatively rare because of their close ties to Europe and Asia. In West Africa, the Asante developed a simple inoculation against smallpox that involved infecting a patient with a mild form of the disease through a series of skin punctures. In the interior of the continent, however, most societies were relatively unexposed to old-world diseases because they traded indirectly with the wider world.

Empire building and improved transportation upset this epidemiological balance by exposing once isolated societies to new infectious diseases. While imperial propagandists often pointed to Western medicine as one of the benefits of British rule, imperial policy was indirectly responsible for a deadly trypanosomiasis (sleeping sickness) outbreak in Uganda at the turn of the twentieth century that led to roughly a quarter of a million deaths. While they did not fully understand the biological causes of the disease, most people in Uganda recognized the necessity of avoiding the wet scrublands where the tsetse fly flourished. By establishing game reserves, clearing forests, and introducing widespread irrigation, conservationists, settlers, and colonial officials created new breeding environments for mosquitoes and tsetse flies, which were the main vectors for malaria and sleeping sickness.[54] Moreover, the very presence of Europeans and South Asians introduced smallpox, typhoid, cholera, and measles into African hinterlands. The result was widespread epidemics throughout eastern and southern Africa that coincided with the conquest and partition of the continent.

Many pastoral societies were further weakened by Britain's unintentional introduction of equally virulent infectious cattle diseases to the continent. In 1853, British entrepreneurs imported a number of Friesian bulls into South Africa that carried lung sickness. The disease spread quickly to African herds, thereby making the peoples of Natal and the eastern Cape less able to confront the Afrikaners and British settlers. This incident was only a precursor to the much more devastating bovine pneumonia epidemic that ravaged Africa in the 1890s. Known as rinderpest, this highly contagious disease caused severe fever, violent diarrhea, and mouth blisters before the animal died of dehydration and starvation in just six to twelve days. Like cholera, rinderpest was endemic in South Asia, and British forces in the Sudan or possibly the Italian army in Ethiopia were most likely responsible for bringing infected oxen from India to Africa. The disease was so contagious that it spread as fast as twenty miles per day by infecting wild game and domestic herds of cattle, which explains how it reached the Cape Colony in southern Africa by 1897. Sheep and goats remained unaffected, but African pastoralists and European ranchers lost up to 90 percent of their herds. In South Africa alone, the epidemic destroyed over one-third of all the cattle in the Transvaal and Orange Free State.[55]

Although these bovine epidemics created considerable problems for European settlers, they were absolutely catastrophic for African pastoral and semipastoral peoples. Since livestock was a measure of wealth in many eastern and southern African societies, rinderpest not only left most cattle herders dangerously vulnerable to famine, it also wiped out their savings. In this sense rinderpest could be compared to a modern computer virus that wipes out electronic banking records. The resulting upheaval weakened African institutions of political authority as people blamed their rulers for failing to prevent or mitigate the disaster, thereby contributing to the social divisions that made formal imperial rule possible. Such tensions were almost certainly behind the millenarian Xhosa cattle-killing tragedy covered in chapter 4. Moreover, rinderpest accelerated the transformation of Africans into wage laborers by forcing them to look for paid employment to purchase food and restock their herds.

British imperial proponents were not entirely aware of these ecological and epidemiological consequences of empire building. Although European doctors developed a much greater understanding of the causes of infectious disease over the course of the century, most overseas Britons considered epidemics and famine a natural part of life in the tropics. In eighteenth-century India, the British East India Company lost up to 75 percent of its new employees during their first year of service, and coastal West Africa had a reputation as the "white man's grave." Even in the nineteenth century, British troops in India suffered mortality rates of almost 7 percent per year, over four times the death rate of their comrades stationed in Britain.[56] As the empire expanded, Britons developed a powerful fear of the tropics that was based both on medical realities like the horrors of cholera and on pure superstition. Lacking the means to solve these problems, they instead sought to isolate themselves from subject populations, which they considered the ultimate source of most diseases.

In the absence of reliable medical information on the causes of infectious disease, midcentury doctors attributed these high mortality rates to "actinic radiation" and a variety of fanciful pseudoscientific causes. Influenced by U.S. neurologists, British tropical medical experts concluded that dark-skinned peoples had a natural defense against the photochemical effects of the ultraviolet band of the spectrum. Conversely, intense sunlight in Africa and Asia supposedly damaged the nerve tissue of Caucasians, thereby causing insomnia, memory loss, lethargy, and insanity. Tropical doctors used terms like "tropical amnesia" and "Punjab head" to explain the fatigue, diarrhea, headaches, ulcers, sexual problems, alcoholism, and suicides they diagnosed in Western patients. They also developed a series of outlandish preventative devices to guard against tropical diseases. Some of the more noteworthy quacks recommended a flannel "cholera belt" to ward off unhealthy chills in the evening and a solar topi to protect the head and neck from unhealthy sunlight.[57] Many of these "imperial ailments" were due to organic causes, but others were most likely brought on by the stress and insecurity that came from being a privileged minority in an alien colonial society.

By the end of the imperial century, public health in the British Empire was based as much on the principle of physical and social segregation between Westerners and subject peoples as it was on curing infectious disease. Greenbelts consisting of carefully manicured parks and golf courses to insulate European families from the contaminating influence of Africans and Asians surrounded most foreign settlements in colonial cities. Urban planners in Sierra Leone even calculated the nightly flight radius of a mosquito so they could locate Freetown's European suburbs a "safe" distance from African neighborhoods. Needless to say, these privileged neighborhoods were also the only areas equipped with running water and sewers. The lack of similar basic sanitation infrastructure in the African quarters of the cities led to outbreaks of contagious disease, thereby seeming to validate imperial assumptions about the inherent unhealthiness of subject populations.

Imperial urban planners and administrators did not have the resources to extend comprehensive medical care and basic sanitary services to non-Western neighborhoods. Yet colonial governments were ever mindful that widespread disease and famine could lead to economic disruption, social turmoil, and even political unrest. They therefore responded to the threat of contagious disease by subjecting key segments of the colonial population to forced segregation and mandatory medical treatment.[58] Infected domestic servants and prostitutes threatened European clients, and the British Empire needed healthy colonial soldiers and laborers for its security and economic vitality. Organized, regulated, and medically inspected brothels thus became a defensible public health measure in India, Hong Kong, and the Straights Settlements.[59]

British medical officials were more concerned with utility and efficiency than with respecting the interests or sensibilities of non-Western patients. As protected persons rather than citizens, Africans and Asians had little say in the formulation of colonial public health policy. In India, the Epidemic Disease Act of 1888 empowered the government to detain and treat suspected carriers of the plague without regard to their status, faith, or gender. Devout Hindus complained that the quarantine measures violated caste laws, and people of all faiths considered the forced inspection of women a form of sexual molestation. Public health officials also used the act to restrict long-distance travel, and they destroyed any Indian residence or business found to be harboring the infected rats that spread the plague. Similarly, British officials in southern Africa tried to contain rinderpest outbreaks through the wholesale slaughter of African-owned cattle.

These draconian measures achieved some success in limiting the spread of infectious disease, but they also intensified opposition to the most inequitable aspects of imperial rule. With some justification, subject peoples suspected that colonial public health measures were also intended to assist in reordering non-Western economies and societies to serve British interests. The London Missionary Society saw rinderpest as an opportunity to teach Africans the virtues of paid employment, and the South African Chamber of Mines exploited the resulting labor surplus to increase working hours while cutting African wages by 30 percent. In India, British officials used the plague as an excuse to undermine the authority of elected Indian city councils on the grounds that they had not taken the necessary steps to contain the epidemic.

Sometimes these public health measures were so invasive that they brought about the very unrest they were designed to contain. In Basutoland (Lesotho), widespread rumors accused Europeans of intentionally spreading the rinderpest, and the unpopular measures used to control the cattle epidemic led to an armed uprising that laid the groundwork for African political opposition to British rule. Similarly, the Indian National Congress made the Raj's public health policies into a political issue, while ordinary people spread rumors that Britain invented the plague to create work for European doctors, steal Indian property, and conceal news of an alleged anti-British uprising in the countryside. In 1897, dissatisfaction with the Epidemic Disease Act grew so intense that the plague commissioner for the city of Pune was assassinated by outraged Indians who would no longer tolerate the government's unprecedented intervention in their daily lives.

Notes

1. Yrjo Kaukiainen, "Shrinking the World: Improvements in the Speed of Information Transmission, c1820–1870," *European Review of Economic History* 5 (2001): 8–22.

2. A. N. Porter, ed., *Atlas of British Overseas Expansion* (New York: Simon & Schuster, 1991), 144, 148.

3. Gary Magee and Andrew Thompson, *Empire and Globalisation: Networks of People, Goods and Capital in the British World, 1850–1914* (Cambridge: Cambridge University Press, 2010), xi–xii.

4. R. F. Foster, *Modern Ireland, 1600–1972* (London: Penguin Books, 1988), 345.

5. Magee and Thompson, *Empire and Globalisation*, 98–99.

6. Robert Hughes, *The Fatal Shore: The Epic of Australia's Founding* (New York: Vintage Books, 1988), 10, 423.

7. Brian Fagan, *Clash of Cultures*, 2nd ed. (Walnut Creek, CA: AltaMira Press, 1998), 277.

8. Barry Crosbie, *Irish Imperial Networks: Migration, Social Communication and Exchange in Nineteenth-Century India* (Cambridge: Cambridge University Press, 2012), 257–61.

9. Mary Seacole, *Wonderful Adventures of Mrs. Seacole in Many Lands* (Oxford: Oxford University Press, 1988).

10. D. C. Phillott, ed., *From Sepoy to Subadar: Being the Life and Adventures of a Native Officer of the Bengal Army Written and Related by Himself*, translated by Lieutenant-Colonel Norgate (Calcutta: Baptist Mission Press, 1911), 15.

11. C. A. Bayly, *Indian Society and the Making of the British Empire* (New York: Cambridge University Press, 1990), 70.

12. Mrinalini Sinha, "Britishness, Clubbability, and the Colonial Public Sphere," in *Bodies in Contact: Rethinking Colonial Encounters in World History*, ed. Tony Ballantyne and Antoinette Burton (Durham, NC: Duke University Press, 2005), 184–88.

13. Philippa Levine, "'A Multitude of Unchaste Women': Prostitution in the British Empire," *Journal of Women's History* 15 (2004): 160–62.

14. Ronald Hyam, "Concubinage and the Colonial Service: The Crewe Circular, 1909," *Journal of Imperial and Commonwealth History* 14 (1986): 172–73.

15. David Lambert and Alan Lester, "Missionary Politics and the Captive Audience: William Shrewsbury in the Caribbean and the Cape Colony," in *Colonial Lives Across the British Empire: Imperial Careering in the Long Nineteenth Century*, ed. David Lambert and Alan Lester (Cambridge: Cambridge University Press, 2006), 107.

16. Tony Ballentyne, *Entanglements of Empire: Missionaries, Maori, and the Question of the Body* (Durham, NC: Duke University Press, 2014), 2, 21.

17. Quoted in Andrew Porter, *Religion Versus Empire? British Protestant Missionaries and Overseas Expansion, 1700–1914* (Manchester: Manchester University Press, 2004), 238.

18. Derek Peterson, *Creative Writing: Translation, Bookkeeping, and the Work of Imagination in Colonial Kenya* (Portsmouth, NH: Heinemann, 2004), 43–44, 49.

19. "Tewodros II to Samuel Gobat" in *Letters from Ethiopian Rulers*, ed. R. K. P. Pankhurst (London: Oxford University Press, 1985), 137.

20. Kenneth Ballhatchet, *Race, Sex and Class under the Raj* (New York: St. Martin's Press, 1980), 294; Percival Spear, *A History of India*, volume 2 (New York: Penguin Books, 1981), 164.

21. T. N. Mukharji, *A Visit to Europe* (Calcutta: W. Newman & Co., 1889), 16–17.

22. Lutfullah, *Autobiography of Lutfullah, a Mohamedan Gentleman: And His Transactions with His Fellow-creatures: Interspersed with Remarks on the Habits, Customs, and Character of the People with Whom He Had to Deal*, ed. Edward Eastwick (London: Smith, Elder and Co, 1857), 407–8.

23. S. Satthianadhan, *Four Years in an English University* (Madras: Lawrence Asylum Press, 1890), 107.

24. Tiyo Soga, "What Is the Destiny of the Kaffir Race?" in *From the South African Past: Narratives, Documents and Debates*, ed. John Williams (Boston: Houghton Mifflin, 1997), 153.

25. National Baptist Convention of the United States, Foreign Mission Board, *In Our Stead* (Philadelphia: Foreign Mission Board, c. 1913).

26. Rudyard Kipling, *Kim* (Garden City, NY: Doubleday Page and Company, 1912), 225. Hurree Chunder Mookerjee also appears in the poem "What Happened," in which Kipling pokes fun at politically active Indians.

27. Behramji Malabari, *The Indian Eye on English Life or Rambles of a Pilgrim Reformer*, 3rd ed. (Bombay: Apollo Printing, 1895), 13.

28. Assistant Resident Lilongwe to Nyasaland Chief Secretary, 10 March 1921, Malawi National Archives, S2/1/21/12.

29. Thomas Metcalf, *Imperial Connections: India in the Indian Ocean Arena, 1860–1920* (Berkeley: University of California Press, 2008), 19–26, 30, 43–45.

30. Jeremy Prestholdt, *Domesticating the World: African Consumerism and the Genealogies of Globalization* (Berkeley: University of California Press, 2008), 78–82.

31. David Northrup, *Indentured Labor in the Age of Imperialism* (Cambridge: Cambridge University Press, 1995), 65.

32. M. D. North-Coombes, "From Slavery to Indenture: Forced Labour in the Political Economy of Mauritius, 1834–1867," in *Indentured Labour in the British Empire 1834–1920*, ed. Kay Saunders (London: Croom Helm, 1984), 92; Northrup, *Indentured Labor in the Age of Imperialism*, 130–34.

33. John Hanson, *The Ahmadiyya in the Gold Coast: Muslim Cosmopolitans in the British Empire* (Bloomington: Indiana University Press, 2017), 118, 123–25.

34. W. H. Quilliam, *The Faith of Islam: An Explanatory Sketch of the Principal Fundamental Tenets of the Moslem Religion* (Liverpool: Willmer Brothers & Company, 1892).

35. P. J. Cain and A. G. Hopkins, *British Imperialism: Innovation and Expansion, 1688–1914* (London: Longman, 1993), 17, 28.

36. John MacKenzie, *The Empire of Nature: Hunting, Conservation and British Imperialism* (Manchester: Manchester University Press, 1988), 29, 31.

37. Timothy Parsons, "Een-Gonyama Gonyama! Zulu Origins of the Boy Scout Movement and the Africanisation of Imperial Britain," *Parliamentary History* 27 (2008).

38. Lutfullah, *Autobiography of Lutfullah*, 409–10.

39. G. Subba Rao, *Indian Words in English: A Study in Indo-British Cultural and Linguistic Relations* (Oxford: Clarendon Press, 1969), 2.

40. Mukharji, *A Visit to Europe*, 132.

41. Satthianadhan, *Four Years in an English University*, 22–23.

42. Richard Francis Burton, *Wanderings in West Africa from Liverpool to Fernando Po*, volume 1 (London: Tinsley Brothers, 1863), 207.

43. Quoted in Susan Martin, Caroline Daley, Elizabeth Dimock, Cheryl Cassidy, and Cecily Devereux, eds., *Women and Empire 1750–1939*, volume 3: *Africa* (New York: Routledge, 2009), 81–82.

44. Quoted in Wilfrid Scawen Blunt, *My Diaries: Being a Personal Narrative of Events 1888–1914, Part Two* (New York: Alfred A. Knopf, 1921), 443.

45. Anonymous, *The First Indian Member of the Imperial Parliament* (Madras: Addison & Company, 1892), 115.

46. Daniel Headrick, *The Tentacles of Progress: Technology Transfer in the Age of Imperialism, 1850–1940* (New York: Oxford University Press, 1988), 212–23.

47. Michael Worboys, "The Imperial Institute: The State and the Development of the Natural Resources of the Colonial Empire, 1887–1923," in *Imperialism and the Natural World*, ed. John MacKenzie (Manchester: Manchester University Press, 1990), 170–73.

48. Rebecca J. H. Woods, *The Herds Shot Round the World: Native Breeds and the British Empire, 1800–1900* (Chapel Hill: University of North Carolina Press, 2017), 4–6, 11.

49. Jeremiah Mutio Kitunda, *A History of the Water Hyacinth in Africa: The Flower of Life and Death from 1800 to the Present* (Lanham, MD: Lexington Books, 2018), xiv–vi.

50. Frances Hodgson Burnett, *The Secret Garden* (New York: Frederick A. Stokes Company, 1911), 5–9.

51. Richard Evans, "Epidemics and Revolutions: Cholera in Nineteenth-Century Europe," in *Epidemics and Ideas*, ed. Terence Ranger and Paul Slack (Cambridge: Cambridge University Press, 1992), 150–54.

52. C. H. Senior, "Asiatic Cholera in Jamaica, 1850–1855, Part I," *Jamaica Journal* 25 (1994): 24–31.

53. David Arnold, "Touching the Body: Perspectives on the Indian Plague," in *Selected Subaltern Studies*, ed. Ranajit Guha and G. C. Spivak (New York: Oxford University Press, 1988), 394.

54. Maryinez Lyons, "African Trypanosomiasis (African Sleeping Sickness)," in *The Cambridge World History of Human Disease*, ed. Kenneth Kiple (Cambridge: Cambridge University Press, 1993), 556–58.

55. Pule Phoofolo, "Epidemics and Revolutions: The Rinderpest Epidemic in Late Nineteenth-Century Southern Africa," *Past and Present* 138 (1993): 124–26.

56. Karl de Schweinitz, *The Rise and Fall of British India: Imperialism as Inequality* (London: Methuen, 1983), 111; Thomas Metcalf, *Ideologies of the Raj* (Cambridge: Cambridge University Press, 1994), 181.

57. Dane Kennedy, "The Perils of the Midday Sun: Climatic Anxieties in the Colonial Tropics," in *Imperialism and the Natural World*, 121–23.

58. Alison Bashford, "Medicine, Gender, and Empire," in *Gender and Empire*, ed. Philippa Levine (New York: Oxford University Press, 2004), 117.

59. Philippa Levine, *Prostitution, Race, and Politics: Policing Venereal Disease in the British Empire* (New York: Routledge, 2003), 15.

CHAPTER SEVEN

~

Historiography

One of the great challenges in writing world history in general, and empire history in particular, is striking the right balance between global and local perspectives. Imperial rule was a transformative globalizing process, but subject peoples also had their own histories separate from that of the British Empire. Focusing too much on these local narratives risks underestimating their larger influence on world and imperial history, but too much attention on the imperial thread in the histories of Africa, Asia, and Latin America makes the British Empire appear more powerful than it actually was.

The second British Empire belonged to a specific historical era, which means that British rule was but one episode in the separate but interwoven histories of particular peoples and places. For those who endeavor to write about the British Empire from the perspective of both local and world history, the challenge is to properly situate Britons and their empire in these local histories. Overall, the literature on the British Empire is dauntingly vast given that it touches on virtually every corner of the globe. At best any historiographical treatment of the empire, even one confined to the nineteenth century, can never be more than representative of a much wider and diverse body of scholarship.

There are a considerable number of studies that seek to provide a narrative history of the British Empire in its totality. Bernard Porter's *The Lion's Share: A Short History of British Imperialism, 1850–1970* is a representative but somewhat dated example. For a more recent example of empire history written from the perspective of British imperial institutions see John Darwin's *The*

Empire Project: The Rise and Fall of the British World-System, 1830–1970. The most useful narrative imperial history focused specifically on the nineteenth century is still undoubtedly *Britain's Imperial Century, 1815–1914: A Study of Empire and Expansion* by Ronald Hyam. *Africa and the Victorians* by Ronald Robinson and John Gallagher remains one of the most influential works explaining Britain's participation in the new imperialism, one that can productively read in conjunction with the theory of "gentlemanly capitalism" advanced by P. J. Cain and A. G. Hopkins in *British Imperialism: Innovation and Expansion, 1688–1914*.[1] Those seeking a comprehensive treatment of the British Commonwealth and the dominions are still best served by reading Nicholas Mansergh's *The Commonwealth Experience*. Finally, A. N. Porter's *Atlas of British Overseas Expansion* is a highly useful reference work for the British Empire.

One of the most important and influential treatments of the British Empire to come out after the publication of the first edition of *The British Imperial Century* is the multivolume *Oxford History of the British Empire*. Seeking to move beyond earlier conventional studies of how the empire was governed, the editors and authors in the series aimed to document the diverse systems of British rule while, in the words of the series editor Wm. Roger Louis, explaining the "meaning of British imperialism for the ruled as well as the rulers."[2] The four primary volumes in the series are based on the seventeenth, eighteenth, nineteenth, and twentieth centuries, and there is a fifth historiography volume. In response to critics who argued that these volumes were still too conventional, the Oxford editors brought out fifteen companion volumes focused on particular geographic areas and related imperial topics. Obviously, the third volume of the series edited by Andrew Porter will be of most use to readers specifically interested in the nineteenth century. There are also chapters relevant to the nineteenth century in the companion volumes relating to Ireland, India, Canada, Australia, gender, missions, settlers, migration, and the "black experience and the empire."[3]

To a large degree, the *Oxford History of the British Empire*'s focus on imperial processes of interaction, adaptation, and exchange overlaps with the "new imperial history" school's conceptualization of the British Empire as interconnected webs of commerce, knowledge, migration, and military power.[4] More of a philosophical approach to the study of empire than a formal historical field, the new imperial history's emphasis on the body, gender, and race had its roots in South Asian subaltern studies and Africanist social history. For illustrative examples by two of its noteworthy practitioners see Tony Ballantyne's *Entanglements of Empire: Missionaries, Maori, and the Question of the Body* and Antionette Burton's *The Trouble with Empire: Challenges* to *Modern British Imperialism*. As well, *Prostitution, Race, and Politics: Policing Venereal Disease in the British Empire* by Philippa Levine is a masterfully comprehensive comparison of gender and imperial policy relating to sex and prostitution in Hong Kong, the Straits Settlements, India, and Australia's Queensland colony. Mrinalini Sinha's slightly older *Colonial Masculinity: The 'Manly Englishman' and the 'Effeminate Bengali' in the Late Nineteenth Century* is a highly influential work that served as an inspiration for the new imperial historians' work on gender.

One of the most interesting projects arising out of this greater emphasis on subject perspectives is the Mutiny at the Margins series, a projected seven-volume collection of essays revisiting the various ways South Asians and Britons from all walks of life experienced the Indian Mutiny of 1857. Volume 1: *Mutiny at the Margins: New Perspectives on the Indian Uprising of 1857, Anticipations and Experiences in the Locality*, edited by Crispin Bates, provides a good example of the series's holistic treatment of the mutiny and various aspects of British rule in India. Similarly, Barry Crosbie's *Irish Imperial Networks: Migration, Social Communication and Exchange in Nineteenth-Century India* is a new and original look at the role of Irishmen in India and the larger empire.

Connectivity and cross-cultural interactions are two additionally significant themes arising from the reconsideration of empire in the last two decades. Read together, Thomas Metcalf's masterfully encyclopedic *Imperial Connections: India in the Indian Ocean Arena, 1860–1920* and Jeremy Prestholdt's *Domesticating the World: African Consumerism and the Genealogies of Globalization* make a strong case that the empire was as Indian as it was British. For further examples of the insights yielded by the closer examination of imperial networks see *Empire and Globalisation: Networks of People, Goods and Capital in the British World, 1850–1914* by Gary Magee and Andrew Thompson, and David Lambert and Alan Lester's *Colonial Lives Across the British Empire: Imperial Careering in the Long Nineteenth Century*. Perhaps the most intriguing study of how subject peoples moved throughout the empire in ways unanticipated by British empire builders is John Hanson's *The Ahmadiyya in the Gold Coast: Muslim Cosmopolitans in the British Empire*, which tells the story of how Ahmadi Muslims built a network of missions stretching from South Asia to London to the Gold Coast.

In the two decades since the publication of the first edition of *The British Imperial Century* virtually every aspect of the British Empire has been productively studied from this heightened focus on networks and subject perspectives. H. Lyman Stebbins's *British Imperialism in Qajar Iran: Consuls, Agents and Influence in the Middle East* is a nuanced and sophisticated reconsideration of British imperial interest in Central Asia. Those interested in religion and empire should consult Andrew Porter's *Religion Versus Empire? British Protestant Missionaries and Overseas Expansion, 1700–1914* for a provocative challenge to assumptions that the evangelical and imperial projects went hand in hand. Dane Kennedy's *The Last Blank Spaces: Exploring Africa and Australia* similarly revises classic narratives of exploration by showing that nineteenth-century explorers were heavily dependent on Africans and Aborigines for knowledge and logistical support. Two titles that productively blend John MacKenzie's groundbreaking work on empire and the environment with the new imperial history's focus on networks and exchanges are *The Herds Shot Round the World: Native Breeds and the British Empire, 1800–1900* by Rebecca J. H. Woods and Jeremiah Kitunda's *A History of the Water Hyacinth in Africa: The Flower of Life and Death from 1800 to the Present.*

Finally, no survey of the historical treatment of the British Empire over the last two decades would be complete without a consideration of what Dane Kennedy has deftly labeled the "imperial history wars." In contrast to the new imperial historians' depiction of the British Empire as decentralized, improvised, and often disordered, Niall Ferguson's *Empire: How Britain Made the Modern World* hearkens back to older, more laudatory and conventional imperial histories by crediting British empire builders with spreading free trade, liberal capitalism, parliamentary democracy, Protestant Christianity, the English language, and team sports on a global scale. In his *In Praise of Empires: Globalization and Order,* Deepak Lal similarly credits the British Empire with being an "international Leviathan" that imposed global security and stability. Published in 2004, one year after the American and British invasion of Iraq, both books appeared to make an argument for the reimposition of Western rule on disordered parts of the world.

To some extent the neoimperial enthusiasts were not so much writing about actual empires but making policy arguments about how the historical "lessons" of empire building, particularly in regard to the efficacy and legitimacy of hard power, apply to the present day. Consequently, they have only been in partial conversation with the new imperial historians. Nonetheless, scholarly disagreements over the nature and legacy of the British Empire have occasionally been tense in the last two decades. Dane Kennedy's *The Imperial History Wars: Debating the British Empire* is a judicious and even-handed assessment of the scope and implications of the debate. One of Kennedy's most telling observations is that historians based in Britain and the United States often have very different perspectives when they write about the British Empire. Where scholars in America often focus on the racial aspects of empire building, many British historians understandably are more concerned with understanding how the empire has shaped Britain's past, present, and potential futures. Much of the acrimony surrounding the imperial history wars also turns on questions of whether non-British historians are qualified to interpret the British Empire, and some scholars have staked out their claims to this territory more aggressively than others.[5]

Notes

1. For a concise but comprehensive survey of the various other explanations of the new imperialism, see Harrison M. Wright, ed., The "New Imperialism": Analysis of Late Nineteenth-Century Expansion (Lexington, MA: D.C. Heath & Co, 1976).

2. Wm. Roger Louis, foreword to The Oxford History of the British Empire, volume 3: The Nineteenth Century, ed. Andrew Porter (Oxford: Oxford University Press, 2004), vi.

3. Philippa Levine, ed., Gender and Empire (Oxford: Oxford University Press, 2004); Kevin Kenny, ed., Ireland and the British Empire (Oxford: Oxford University Press, 2004); Philip Morgan and Sean Hawkins, eds., Black Experience and the Empire (Oxford: Oxford University Press, 2004); Norman Etherington, ed., Missions and Empire (Oxford: Oxford University Press, 2005); William Beinart and Lotte Hughes, eds., Environment and Empire (Oxford: Oxford University Press, 2007); Phillip Bucker, ed., Canada and the British Empire (Oxford: Oxford University Press, 2008); Deryck Schreuder and Stuart Ward, eds., Australia's Empire (Oxford: Oxford University Press, 2008); Robert Bickers, ed., Settlers and Expatriates: Britons Overseas (Oxford: Oxford University Press, 2010); Marjory Harper and Stephen Constantine, eds., Migration and Empire (Oxford: Oxford University Press, 2010); Douglas Peers and Nandini Gooptu, eds., India and the British Empire (Oxford: Oxford University Press, 2012).

4. Andrew Porter, introduction to The Oxford History of the British Empire, volume 3: The Nineteenth Century, 4; Tony Ballantyne and Antoinette Burton, "Introduction: Bodies, Empires, and World Histories," in Bodies in Contact: Rethinking Colonial Encounters in World History, ed. Tony Ballantyne and Antoinette Burton (Durham, NC: Duke University Press, 2005), 3.

5. Stephen Howe, "Introduction: New Imperial Histories," in The New Imperial Histories Reader, ed. Stephen Howe (London: Routledge, 2010), 4, 16.

Recommended Reading

Ballantyne, Tony. Entanglements of Empire: Missionaries, Maori, and the Question of the Body. Durham, NC: Duke University Press, 2014.

Ballantyne, Tony, and Antoinette Burton, eds. Bodies in Contact: Rethinking Colonial Encounters in World History. Durham, NC: Duke University Press, 2005.

Bates, Crispin, ed. *Mutiny at the Margins: New Perspectives on the Indian Uprising of 1857*, volume 1: *Anticipations and Experiences in the Locality*. New Delhi: Sage Publications, 2013.

Bayly, C. A. *Imperial Meridian: The British Empire and the World, 1780–1830*. London: Longman, 1989.

Bayly, C. A. *Indian Society and the Making of the British Empire*. New York: Cambridge University Press, 1990.

Bender, Jill. *The 1857 Indian Uprising and the British Empire*. Cambridge: Cambridge University Press, 2016.

Boahen, A. A. *African Perspectives on Colonialism*. Baltimore: Johns Hopkins Press, 1987.

Burton, Antoinette. *The Trouble with Empire: Challenges to Modern British Imperialism*. New York: Oxford University Press, 2015.

Cain, P. J., and A. G. Hopkins. *British Imperialism: Innovation and Expansion, 1688–1914*. London: Longman, 1993.

Cannadine, David. *Ornamentalism: How the British Saw Their Empire*. New York: Oxford University Press, 2001.

Carter, Marina, and Crispin Bates, eds. *Mutiny at the Margins: New Perspectives on the Indian Uprising of 1857*, volume 3: *Global Perspectives*. New Delhi: Sage Publications, 2013.

Charlesworth, Neil. *British Rule and the Indian Economy, 1800–1914*. London: Macmillan Press, 1982.

Crosbie, Barry. *Irish Imperial Networks: Migration, Social Communication and Exchange in Nineteenth-Century India*. Cambridge: Cambridge University Press, 2012.

Darwin, John. *The Empire Project: The Rise and Fall of the British World-System, 1830–1970*. Cambridge: Cambridge University Press, 2009.

Davis, Lance, and Robert Huttenback. *Mammon and the Pursuit of Empire: The Political Economy of British Imperialism, 1860–1912*. Cambridge: Cambridge University Press, 1986.

Dean, Britten. "British Informal Empire: The Case of China." *Journal of Commonwealth and Comparative Politics* 14 (1976).

Eldridge, C. C., ed. *British Imperialism in the Nineteenth Century*. New York: St Martin's Press, 1984.

Ferguson, Niall. *Empire: How Britain Made the Modern World*. London: Penguin Books, 2003.

Fryer, Peter. *Staying Power: Black People in Britain since 1504*. Atlantic Highlands, NJ: Humanities Press, 1984.

Galbraith, John. "British and American Railway Promoters in Late Nineteenth Century Persia." *Albion* 21 (1989).

Galbraith, John, and Afaf Lufti Al-Sayyid-Marsot. "The British Occupation of Egypt: Another View." *International Journal of Middle East Studies* 9 (1978).

Goldblatt, David. *The Ball Is Round: A Global History of Soccer*. New York: Riverhead Books, 2014.

Greenlee, James G., and Charles M. Johnston. *Good Citizens: British Missionaries and Imperial States, 1870–1914*. Montreal and Kingston: McGill and Queen's University Press, 1999.

Grove, Richard. *Green Imperialism: Colonial Expansion, Tropical Island Edens, and the Origins of Environmentalism, 1600–1860*. Cambridge: Cambridge University Press, 1995.

Guha, Ranajit, and C. C. Spivak, eds. *Selected Subaltern Studies*. New York: Oxford University Press, 1988.

Hanson, John. *The Ahmadiyya in the Gold Coast: Muslim Cosmopolitans in the British Empire*. Bloomington: Indiana University Press, 2017.

Headrick, Daniel. *The Tentacles of Progress: Technology Transfer in the Age of Imperialism, 1850–1940*. New York: Oxford University Press, 1988.

Hopkins, A. G. "The Victorians and Africa: A Reconsideration of the Occupation of Egypt, 1882." *Journal of African History* 27 (1986).

Hyam, Ronald. *Britain's Imperial Century, 1815–1914: A Study of Empire and Expansion*. New York: Barnes & Noble Books, 1976.

Jones, Charles. "Mercantile Nationalism, Technological Change and the Evolution of Argentine Dependence." In *The Diaspora of the British*, Collected SOAS Seminar Papers, No. 31. London: Institute of Commonwealth Studies, 1982.

Karsten, Peter. "Irish Soldiers in the British Army, 1792–1922: Suborned or Subordinate?" *Journal of Social History* 17 (1983).

Kennedy, Dane. *The Imperial History Wars: Debating the British Empire*. London: Bloomsbury, 2018.

Kennedy, Dane. *The Last Blank Spaces: Exploring Africa and Australia*. Cambridge, MA: Harvard University Press, 2013.

Kitunda, Jeremiah Mutio. *A History of the Water Hyacinth in Africa: The Flower of Life and Death from 1800 to the Present*. Lanham, MD: Lexington Books, 2018.

Lal, Deepak. *In Praise of Empires: Globalization and Order*. New York: Palgrave MacMillan, 2004.

Lambert, David, and Alan Lester, eds. *Colonial Lives Across the British Empire: Imperial Careering in the Long Nineteenth Century*. Cambridge: Cambridge University Press, 2006.

Lawrence, Benjamin, Emily Lynn Osborn, and Richard Roberts, eds. *Intermediaries, Interpreters, and Clerks*. Madison: University of Wisconsin Press, 2006.

Levine, Philippa, ed. *Gender and Empire*. New York: Oxford University Press, 2004.

Levine, Philippa. *Prostitution, Race, and Politics: Policing Venereal Disease in the British Empire*. New York: Routledge, 2003.

MacDonald, Robert H. *Sons of the Empire: The Frontier Movement and the Boy Scout Movement, 1890–1918*. Toronto: University of Toronto Press, 1993.

MacKenzie, John. *The Empire of Nature: Hunting, Conservation and British Imperialism*. Manchester: Manchester University Press, 1988.

MacKenzie, John, ed. *Imperialism and the Natural World*. Manchester: Manchester University Press, 1990.

Magee, Gary, and Andrew Thompson. *Empire and Globalisation: Networks of People, Goods and Capital in the British World, 1850–1914*. Cambridge: Cambridge University Press, 2010.

Mangan, J. A., ed. *The Imperial Curriculum: Racial Images and Education in the British Colonial Experience*. New York: Routledge, 1993.

Mansergh, Nicholas. *The Commonwealth Experience*. New York: Frederick Praeger, 1969.

Martin, Susan, Caroline Daley, Elizabeth Dimock, Cheryl Cassidy, and Cecily Devereux, eds. *Women and Empire 1750–1939*, volume 3: *Africa*. New York: Routledge, 2009.

McD. Beckles, Hilary. *The Development of West Indies Cricket: The Age of Nationalism*. London: Pluto Press, 1998.

Metcalf, Thomas. *Imperial Connections: India in the Indian Ocean Arena, 1860–1920*. Berkeley: University of California Press, 2008.

Miller, Rory. *Britain and Latin America in the Nineteenth and Twentieth Centuries*. London: Longman, 1993.

Morgan, Cecilia. *Building Better Britains? Settler Societies Within the British Empire 1783–1920*. Toronto: University of Toronto Press, 2017.

Northrup, David. *Africa's Discovery of Europe, 1450–1850*. New York: Oxford University Press, 2002.

Northrup, David. *Indentured Labor in the Age of Imperialism*. Cambridge: Cambridge University Press, 1995.

Porter, A. N., ed. *Atlas of British Overseas Expansion*. New York: Simon & Schuster, 1991.

Porter, Andrew. *Religion Versus Empire? British Protestant Missionaries and Overseas Expansion, 1700–1914*. Manchester: Manchester University Press, 2004.

Porter, Bernard. *The Lion's Share: A Short History of British Imperialism, 1850–1970*. New York: Longman, 1975.

Prestholdt, Jeremy. *Domesticating the World: African Consumerism and the Genealogies of Globalization*. Berkeley: University of California Press, 2008.

Robinson, Ronald, and John Gallagher. *Africa and the Victorians*. New York: St. Martin's Press, 1961.

Sinha, Mrinalini. *Colonial Masculinity: The 'Manly Englishman' and the 'Effeminate Bengali' in the Late Nineteenth Century*. Manchester: Manchester University Press, 1995.

Stebbins, H. Lyman. *British Imperialism in Qajar Iran: Consuls, Agents and Influence in the Middle East*. London: I.B. Tauris, 2016.

Stokes, Eric. *The Peasant Armed: The Indian Revolt of 1857*. Oxford: Clarendon Press, 1986.

Taylor, Miles, ed. *The Victorian Empire and Britain's Maritime World, 1837–1901*. New York: Palgrave Macmillan, 2013.

Walker, Cherryl, ed. *Women and Gender in Southern Africa to 1945*. Cape Town: David Philip, 1990.

Wallace, Elizabeth. *The British Caribbean: From the Decline of Colonialism to the End of Federation*. Toronto: University of Buffalo Press, 1977.

Walls, Andrew. *The Missionary Movement in Christian History: Studies in the Transmission of Faith*. Maryknoll, NY: Orbis Books, 1996.

White, Landeg. *Magomero: Portrait of an African Village*. Cambridge: Cambridge University Press, 1987.

Woods, Rebecca J. H. *The Herds Shot Round the World: Native Breeds and the British Empire, 1800–1900*. Chapel Hill: University of North Carolina Press, 2017.

Index

~

About the Author

Timothy Parsons holds a joint appointment as professor of African history in the departments of History, and African and African American Studies at Washington University in St. Louis. As a social historian of Africa, he seeks to understand the experience of empire and the creation of new national states. His books to date have explored how ordinary people navigated the shifting realities of repression and opportunity that emerged during the colonial and postcolonial eras. His primary publications include *The African Rank-and-File: Social Implications of Colonial Service in the King's African Rifles, 1902–1964* (1999), *The 1964 Army Mutinies and the Making of Modern East Africa* (2003), *Race, Resistance and the Boy Scout Movement in British Colonial Africa* (2004), *The Rule of Empires: Those Who Built Them, Those Who Endured Them, and Why They Always Fall* (2010), *The Second British Empire in the Crucible of the Twentieth Century* (Rowman & Littlefield 2014), and *The British Imperial Century, 1815–1914: A World History Perspective, Second Edition* (Rowman & Littlefield 2019).

CRITICAL ISSUES IN WORLD AND INTERNATIONAL HISTORY

Series Editor: Morris Rossabi

Printed in the USA
CPSIA information can be obtained
at www.ICGtesting.com
LVHW090106081223
765871LV00001B/54